The Ethics
of Supervision
and Consultation

The statements and opinions published in this book are the responsibility of the author. Such opinions and statements do not represent the official policies, standards, guidelines, or ethical mandates of the American Psychological Association (APA), the APA Ethics Committee, the APA Ethics Office, or any other APA governance group or staff. Statements made in this book neither add to nor reduce requirements of the APA "Ethical Principles of Psychologists and Code of Conduct" (2002; hereinafter referred to as the APA Ethics Code or the Ethics Code), nor can they be viewed as a definitive source of the meaning of the Ethics Code standards or their application to particular situations. Each ethics committee or other relevant body must interpret and apply the Ethics Code as it believes proper given all the circumstances of each particular situation. Any information in this book involving legal and ethical issues should not be used as a substitute for obtaining personal legal and/or ethical advice and consultation prior to making decisions regarding individual circumstances.

The Ethics of Supervision and Consultation

PRACTICAL GUIDANCE FOR
MENTAL HEALTH PROFESSIONALS

Janet T. Thomas

AMERICAN PSYCHOLOGICAL ASSOCIATION
WASHINGTON, DC

Published by
American Psychological Association
750 First Street, NE
Washington, DC 20002
www.apa.org

To order
APA Order Department
P.O. Box 92984
Washington, DC 20090-2984
Tel: (800) 374-2721; Direct: (202) 336-5510
Fax: (202) 336-5502; TDD/TTY: (202) 336-6123
Online: www.apa.org/books/
E-mail: order@apa.org

In the U.K., Europe, Africa, and the Middle East, copies may be ordered from
American Psychological Association
3 Henrietta Street
Covent Garden, London
WC2E 8LU England

Typeset in Goudy by Circle Graphics, Inc., Columbia, MD

Printer: Edwards Brothers, Inc., Ann Arbor, MI
Cover Designer: Berg Design, Albany, NY

The opinions and statements published are the responsibility of the authors, and such opinions and statements do not necessarily represent the policies of the American Psychological Association.

Library of Congress Cataloging-in-Publication Data

Thomas, Janet T.
  The ethics of supervision and consultation : practical guidance for mental health professionals / Janet T. Thomas. — 1st ed.
     p. ; cm.
  Includes bibliographical references and index.
  ISBN-13: 978-1-4338-0723-7
  ISBN-10: 1-4338-0723-8
  1. Mental health personnel—Supervision of—Moral and ethical aspects. I. American Psychological Association. II. Title.
  [DNLM: 1. Ethics, Professional. 2. Mental Health Services—ethics. 3. Administrative Personnel—ethics. 4. Interpersonal Relations. 5. Mental Health Services—organization & administration. 6. Personnel Management—methods. WM 62 T458e 2010]
  RC440.8.T56 2010
  362.196'890068—dc22

                                    2009029708

British Library Cataloguing-in-Publication Data

A CIP record is available from the British Library.

Printed in the United States of America
First Edition

CONTENTS

PREFACE

It was the late 1970s. Infused with the energy of the women's movement and eager to practice my newly acquired listening skills, I enthusiastically began my undergraduate psychology internship at a women's health clinic. One of my duties was to accompany physicians into exam rooms and to provide support to patients whose diagnoses were likely to be distressing. My first such assignment involved a patient who was informed that she had a "venereal disease," as it was called at the time (i.e., a sexually transmitted infection). On hearing the news, she began to cry and said something about how her fiancé must have cheated on her. Just as the physician was about to leave us to discuss the import of this new information, I burst into tears and told her how sorry I was about this tragic event in her life. The now wide-eyed patient stopped crying almost immediately and handed me the Kleenex. The physician, also startled, made some reassuring comment to the patient, excused himself, and escorted me across the hall to his office, where I was to wait while he returned to the exam room.

I sat there alone, feeling deflated and embarrassed. I tried to pull myself together as I contemplated alternative careers. When the physician finally returned, I apologized profusely and preemptively offered my resignation.

After hearing me out, he told me that he believed I was in exactly the right field. He expressed confidence that I could fortify my boundaries and, with further training, learn to use my skills effectively. I was subsequently invited to observe and later assist staff members as they talked with patients. Eventually, I was able to achieve my goal of delaying crying episodes until after the patient had gone and, ultimately, to offer helpful assistance.

This experience marked one of my first lessons in the importance of a clear boundary between helper and helpee. The patient in this story quickly ascertained that I was unable to distinguish between her problem and mine and that I was therefore not capable of helping. I saw firsthand that unbridled empathy and overidentification with the patient were not useful and in fact could be detrimental to the helping process.

Beyond insights about the importance of clinical boundaries, I learned something about supervision. This physician–supervisor took immediate steps to reestablish a safe and therapeutic environment for the patient. He ensured that I was in a place where I could regain my composure in private while he attended to the patient's needs. And finally, he helped to reconceptualize the experience in a way that allowed me to learn and grow from it.

Although unable to absorb all of this at the time, I believe that the supervisor's decisive actions were as instructive as any course I had in counseling skills, ethics, or supervision. His calm reassurance, confident clarity, quick reconfiguration of my training plan, and primary commitment to the welfare of the patient illustrate many of the concepts and values that I have tried to convey in this book.

In the years since, I have been fortunate to have had many opportunities to obtain my own supervision in practicums, internships, and employment settings. Now in independent practice, I participate in regular and frequent consultation, both individually and in two specialized groups.

My background in ethics has developed through years of study and related work. But the most valuable lessons were learned through my experiences as a psychotherapist and client, teacher and student, supervisor and supervisee, and consultant and consultee. Through it all, I have concluded that no amount of professional experience or education makes us immune to errors.

Practicing ethically requires ongoing effort and commitment. Standards of practice, ethics codes, and laws relevant to mental health practice are evolving rapidly. Reading professional literature, participating in continuing education, and engaging in meaningful interactions with colleagues all are necessary to stay abreast of changes. Further, our objectivity and effectiveness are vulnerable to personal stressors and clinical challenges introduced by clients. When compromised, they are only as good as the safety net we construct around ourselves in our work. Supervision and consultation are cornerstones of this safety net.

The genesis of this book, then, is complex and multifaceted, but its roots are in the humbling failures and gratifying successes that form the foundation of my work. It is my hope that prospective and current supervisors and consultants reading the book will learn to recognize the myriad ethical challenges and pitfalls inherent in this work, prevent or avoid them where possible, acknowledge mistakes when they occur, and make repairs when necessary. And finally, I wish us all the ability to strive to accomplish these goals with patience and compassion for our supervisees, consultees, and for ourselves.

ACKNOWLEDGMENTS

The task of writing a book has been far greater than I imagined and more than I could have accomplished without the support and generosity of colleagues, friends, and family.

I am grateful to the students and colleagues to whom I've had the privilege of providing supervision and consultation. They have taught me most of what I know about these topics. Library staff members, especially Jesse Leraas, at Argosy University, Saint Paul, Minnesota, have been generous and tenacious as they helped me to locate the resources I needed. The staffs of the many professional associations whose ethics codes and specialty guidelines appear in this book have been helpful to me in understanding and applying each of these documents. These individuals include Lee Greenwood at the American Association for Marriage and Family Therapy; Linda Crede, Pete Cullen, and Brenda Martin at the American Association for Pastoral Counselors; Larry Freeman and Paul Fornell at the American Counseling Association; Harriet Glosoff and David Kleist at the Association for Counselor Education and Supervision; Allison Moraske at the American Psychiatric Association; Stephen Behnke at the American Psychological Association (APA); Barbara VanHorne at the Association of State and Provincial Psychology Boards; Ann Marie Plante at the Canadian Psychological Association; Shirley Beckett Mikell at the National Association for Alcohol and Drug Abuse Counselors; and Miriam Coleman and Dawan Jones at the National Association for Social Workers. I also have benefited greatly from the guidance of the staff at APA Books, including Debbie Felder, Genevieve Gill, Harriet Kaplan, Peter Pavilionis, Edward Porter, Susan Reynolds, and Ron Teeter.

Ellen Green of E. B. Green Editorial in Saint Paul, Minnesota, has used her exceptional editorial skills to help me refine my writing and has guided me through this process from beginning to end. I cannot imagine how I would have completed the work without her patience, dedication, and expertise.

Janet Schank is the one colleague who read every word of the early drafts of this book. I am grateful for her personal and professional support and her insightful and candid feedback. Many other colleagues lent their expertise by reviewing and critiquing chapters: Jean Birbilis, Jane Brodie, Jeffrey Brown, Charlene Follett, Steven Gilbert, John Gonsiorek, Mary Hayes, Jane Koster, Nickey Larson, Cynthia Meyer, Jack Schaffer, the late Scott Terhune, and Natalie (Pat) Torrey. Other colleagues with particular expertise in supervision provided consultation and encouragement at various stages of the process: Jane Campbell, Allen Hess, Daniel Jacobs, Cal Stoltenberg, William Robiner, and Steven Walfish.

I am also thankful to so many colleagues and friends whose support and practical assistance have sustained me as I wrote, especially Laurene Barsi, Mindy Benowitz, Karrol Butler, Margaret Charmoli, Linda Flies Carole, Anne Fletcher, Rosario Grau, Ken Green, Carolyn Halliday, Carol Houston, Kelle Kjer, Ruth Markowitz, Patty Majewski, Barbara Maki, Mary Ann McLeod, Shepherd Myers, Joan O'Connell, Pat Ryan, Barbara Sanderson, Chris Servaty, Connie Swenson, Michael Wilke, and M. Sue Wilson.

My family members, Eric Thomas, Scott Thomas, and Karis Thomas, have all, in their own ways, contributed to this effort. My husband, Ron Commins, and son, Daniel Thomas-Commins, have made innumerable sacrifices, enabling me to carve out the time needed to write. I feel blessed each day by their love and encouragement.

Finally, I am grateful to my father, Frederick Thomas, who, despite his many health challenges, has continued his unfailing encouragement of my academic and professional endeavors—something that has made all the difference in my life.

The Ethics
of Supervision
and Consultation

1

THE ETHICAL PRACTICE OF
SUPERVISION AND CONSULTATION

When mental health professionals reflect on the milestones of their careers, images of supervisors past invariably come to mind. For better or worse, supervisors play a significant role in the professional development of their supervisees. The professional ethics that they teach, and more so that they model, make an indelible impression. Lessons learned, particularly during the early formative years, will reverberate in the years to come. The responsibility of a clinical supervisor cannot be overstated. For these reasons, clinical supervision has long been considered an essential and fundamental component of the training and sometimes of the rehabilitation of psychologists and other mental health professionals. Welch (2003) characterized supervision as "the scaffolding from which all clinical work is taught" (p. 1).

Consultation is often mentioned as a postsupervision method for developing and maintaining competence in particular areas of practice (Knapp & VandeCreek, 2006), improving clinical effectiveness, and mitigating the risk of clinical and ethical errors (G. Corey, Corey, & Callanan, 2007; Haas & Malouf, 2005; Nagy, 2005; Schank & Skovholt, 2006; Welfel, 2006). Further, professional ethics codes and guidelines commonly recommend that members consult with colleagues when they are faced with ethical dilemmas

(American Association for Marriage and Family Therapy [AAMFT], 2001, 2007; American Association of Pastoral Counselors [AAPC], 1994, 2009; American Counseling Association [ACA], 2005; American Psychiatric Association [ApA], 2009; American Psychological Association [APA], 2002; Association for Counselor Education and Supervision [ACES], 1993; Association of State and Provincial Psychology Boards [ASPPB], 2003, 2005; Canadian Psychological Association [CPA], 2000; National Association of Alcohol and Drug Abuse Counselors [NAADAC], 2008; National Association of Social Workers [NASW], 2005, 2008).

A significant component of the development of all psychologists and mental health professionals is learning and internalizing the ethics of their professions. Without exception, a framework of ethical principles undergirds every aspect of psychological services. Handelsman, Gottlieb, and Knapp (2005) described *ethical acculturation* as "a developmental process during which students can use several types of adaptation strategies" (p. 59) as they develop their professional identities. In addition to students learning ethics codes, observing role models, and studying risk management strategies, Handelsman et al. (2005) noted the importance of their learning the profession's "discrete culture with its own traditions, values, and methods of implementing its ethical principles" (p. 59). Clinical supervision and consultation are two primary vehicles for facilitating this critical process.

Objectives of this chapter include the following:

- defining supervision and consultation,
- describing the intersection of supervision and consultation with professional ethics,
- presenting a rationale for integrating ethics into the education of supervisors and consultants,
- offering an overview of the ethical issues most relevant to supervisors and consultants, and
- describing the contents of this volume as a whole.

SUPERVISION DEFINED

Definitions of *supervision* in the literature vary in terms of their inclusiveness. Some include only one-to-one relationships (Hart, 1982; Loganbill, Hardy, & Delworth, 1982). Reid (1999) defined supervision as "an ongoing relationship with a colleague, often an academic or professional superior, which carries either a mandate or a strong suggestion that the supervisor's recommendations will be followed in some way" (p. 8). His definition emphasized the supervisor's ultimate responsibility for supervisees and their clients.

Bernard and Goodyear (2009) offered a more comprehensive definition:

> Supervision is an intervention provided by a more senior member of a profession to a more junior member or members of that same profession. The relationship is evaluative and hierarchical, extends over time, and has the simultaneous purposes of enhancing the professional functioning of the more junior person(s), monitoring the quality of professional services offered to the clients that she, he, or they see, and serving as a gatekeeper for those who are to enter the particular profession. (p. 7)

Bernard and Goodyear's (2009) addition of the gatekeeping responsibility is noteworthy. Sometimes personal circumstances, academic deficits, acute mental health problems, or characterological difficulties present significant obstacles to learning and/or professional functioning (Ladany, Friedlander, & Nelson, 2005). When such indicators of deficient competence become apparent, supervisors incur an ethical and professional responsibility to recognize, assess, and intervene (Kaslow et al., 2007). If remedial efforts are deemed unsuccessful, or, as Elman and Forrest have stated, "when character or moral issues impede capacity for progress toward competence" (W. B. Johnson et al., 2008), supervisors and others who share responsibility for the individual's professional development must be willing to recommend dismissal from a training program or termination from a position or be willing to withhold endorsement for professional credentials. McCutcheon (2008) pointed out that given APA's policy recommending that psychologists be eligible for licensure immediately after graduation, internship supervisors and training directors have increased responsibility for ensuring supervisees' readiness for independent practice. In short, gatekeeping is a critical, albeit challenging, aspect of a supervisor's responsibilities (W. B. Johnson et al., 2008).

Supervisees often are students, postdoctoral trainees, or employees, whereas those charged with overseeing their work are "more senior members" (Bernard & Goodyear, 2009) of the profession. An exception to this arrangement occurs when trained professionals must obtain supervision from colleagues with particular expertise, who may or may not be senior, to obtain additional licenses or certifications. Another exception occurs when the supervision is required as part of a rehabilitation plan following disciplinary action by a licensing board, professional ethics committee, or employer. The supervisor in these circumstances must not only be skilled in the supervisee's areas of practice but also have expertise in ethics and in providing mandated rehabilitative supervision.

To account for these additional types of supervision, an even more comprehensive definition must be considered. Falender and Shafranske (2004) defined supervision as

> a distinct professional activity in which education and training aimed at developing science-informed practice are facilitated through a collaborative interpersonal process. It involves observation, evaluation, feedback, the facilitation of supervisee self-assessment, and the acquisition of knowledge and skills by instruction, modeling, and mutual problem solving. In addition, by building on the recognition of the strengths and talents of the supervisee, supervision encourages self-efficacy. Supervision . . . is conducted in a competent manner in which ethical standards, legal prescriptions, and professional practices are used to promote and protect the welfare of the client, the profession, and society. (p. 3)

Falender and Shafranske's (2004) definition includes supervision of professionals as well as students, and its focus on legal, ethical, and professional issues adds to its relevance here.

Legal liability (M. T. Johnson, 1995; Saccuzzo, 2002) is an important characteristic of supervision, permeating all three areas of supervisory responsibility (i.e., client welfare, supervisee's professional development, and gatekeeping). Knapp and VandeCreek (2006) stated that "the supervisee is legally an agent of the supervising psychologist" (p. 151).

Supervision occurs in various settings; private, academic, and employment settings are examples. An outside entity, such as an academic program, credentialing body, or licensing board, may determine length and frequency of meetings, duration, and format of the supervision. Outside requirements as well as the needs of the supervisee and the preferences of the supervisor influence decisions about specific content and focus of supervisory meetings.

CONSULTATION DEFINED

Clinical consultation in this context refers to a service provided by a senior mental health professional or by any individual who possesses the particular expertise needed by a consultee, regardless of the parties' relative status or profession. Consultation is generally, though not always, voluntary. Definitions of clinical consultation, like supervision, have varied in scope (Caplan, 1970; Reid, 1999). Reid (1999) clarified that consultation is "a brief, advisory event that does not generate any mandate to act as the consultant may suggest" (p. 9). Knapp and VandeCreek (2006) described consultation as "an arrangement between legal equals in which the consultant provides the service, such as an opinion on a particular case, but the professional receiving the consultation has the right to accept or reject the opinion of the consultant" (p. 151).

Generally, consultation is tailored to meet the specific needs of the individual recipients. The range of services that may be offered under the rubric of clinical consultation is broad and might include, for example, an assessment of conceptual or skill deficiencies, provision of focused or remedial education, or recommendations for systemic change. Remedial consultation might take the form of individualized "classes." Problems related to boundaries, confidentiality, report writing, record keeping, or assessment, for example, may be addressed through consultation with an expert in those areas. The consultant might develop a syllabus or learning contract identifying goals and expectations. Relevant readings and review of educational DVDs may be assigned. The frequency and format of meetings may be determined by mutual agreement on the basis of consultee preferences and consultant recommendations.

Consultation may also be designed to help colleagues who elect or are required by their employers to develop, expand, or update their skills in a particular area of practice. For example, an individual wishing to further develop skills in psychological assessment might hire a consultant with the needed expertise. The consultant may agree to demonstrate test administrations; observe or listen to the consultee's recorded test administrations; and critique the consultee's scoring, interpretations, and assessment reports.

Unlike supervisors, consultants do not assume clinical and legal responsibility for the actions of their consultees. Although, like any professional, consultants may be held legally liable for their actions relative to consultees, the vicarious liability that supervisors incur does not typically apply to consultants.

Most of the relevant professional literature focuses exclusively on supervision rather than consultation. Psychotherapy-based and developmental models consider only supervision, for example. Authors of supervision texts generally have not addressed clinical consultation as a distinct topic (Borders & Brown, 2005; Falender & Shafranske, 2004; Haynes, Corey, & Moulton, 2003; Ladany et al., 2005; Neufeldt, 2007). They have sometimes discussed consultation in the context of supervision, as a point of contrast or as one function of supervision (Bernard & Goodyear, 2009; Knapp & VandeCreek, 2006). Additionally, the preponderance of related ethical standards and practice guidelines addresses supervision. Therefore, this book maintains supervision as its primary focus. Consultation is addressed in that context as appropriate.

THE INTERSECTION OF SUPERVISION AND CONSULTATION WITH ETHICS

Increasing recognition of the importance of professional ethics is reflected in required graduate course work and continuing education in many mental health professions. Graduate texts and professional books have addressed the topic of supervision; even more have dealt with professional ethics. Contemporary ethics texts typically include a chapter on supervision (G. Corey et al., 2007; Cottone & Tarvydas, 2003; Knapp & VandeCreek, 2006; Koocher & Keith-Spiegel, 1998; Pope & Vasquez, 1998; Welfel, 2006). Other ethics books have addressed supervision in the context of specific ethical issues such as competence, confidentiality, boundaries, multiple relationships, exploitation, informed consent, and liability (Bersoff, 2003; C. B. Fisher, 2003; Herlihy & Corey, 2006; Knapp & VandeCreek, 2003; Nagy, 2005; Schank & Skovholt, 2006).

Authors writing about supervision generally discuss ethics in a chapter or a section of a chapter (Bernard & Goodyear, 2009; Borders & Brown, 2005; Bradley & Ladany, 2001; J. M. Campbell, 2000; Driver & Martin, 2005; Falender & Shafranske, 2004; Fall & Sutton, 2004; Haynes et al., 2003; Hess, 2008; Kaiser, 1997; Ladany et al., 2005; Neufeldt, 2007; Powell, 2004; Stoltenberg & McNeill, 2009; Stoltenberg, McNeill, & Delworth, 1998; Watkins, 1997a). Others have presented clinical cases containing ethical issues but have not necessarily framed them as such (Holloway & Carroll, 1999; D. Jacobs, David, & Meyer, 1995). Falvey (2002) is one author who has integrated the topics of ethics, law, and supervision, emphasizing risk management for supervisors. In addition to discussing ethical requirements for supervisors, Falvey reviewed 13 legal cases involving supervisors. Clearly, there is a need for a more comprehensive integration of these topics.

WHY INTEGRATE ETHICS INTO SUPERVISION AND CONSULTATION CURRICULA?

Certainly, ethics may be addressed as one topic in the context of a supervision course. Yet, virtually no aspect of supervision or consultation is without ethical underpinnings. As supervision is recognized as a specialized area of practice requiring particular expertise, (Bernard & Goodyear, 2004, 2009; Falender & Shafranske, 2004; Falvey, 2002), the need for the seamless integration of ethical dimensions into related training and education is increasingly apparent (Kurpias, Gibson, Lewis, & Corbet, 1991).

More precisely, graduate students and other mental health professionals need specific training in the ethical aspects of supervision for several reasons. First, in recognition of the professionalization of supervision, internship sites are more likely to require students to provide supervision as part of their training. Doctoral student interns, for example, may be required to supervise masters or doctoral practicum students. These novice supervisors are typically inexperienced psychotherapists. Yet they are responsible, with the support of their own supervisors, for monitoring the clinical and ethical behavior of students who are generally engaged in their first experience as clinicians. These practicum students rely on their novice supervisors to recognize ethical issues and to provide appropriate guidance.

Following graduation and licensure, new professionals may, on the basis of their degrees, be assigned to supervise other professionals, students, and paraprofessionals. In fact, careers in the mental health professions likely require the provision of supervision at some point (Bernard & Goodyear, 2004; Norcross, Prochaska, & Farber, 1993; Osipow & Fitzgerald, 1986).

A second reason for incorporating ethics into the preparation of clinical supervisors is their legal liability (Falvey, 2002; Hopkins & Anderson, 1990; M. T. Johnson, 1995; W. B. Johnson et al., 2008; Saccuzzo, 2002). Not only are supervisors legally responsible for their own professional behavior with clients and supervisees (direct liability) but they also are charged with ensuring "adherence to the ethical codes, standards of conduct, legal statues, and licensing regulations of each discipline represented in the supervision dyad or group" (Falvey, 2002, p. xiv). In other words, supervisors may be held vicariously liable for the negligent acts of their supervisees (Caudill, 1996). Beyond the risk of lawsuits, supervisors may have complaints against their licenses (Recupero & Rainey, 2007). Harris (2003) identified psychologist–supervisors as being at high risk of experiencing licensing board complaints.

The third and probably most important reason for thoroughly addressing the ethical aspects of supervision in graduate training is that supervisees, and especially novice professionals, are impressionable. Barring some egregious behavior on the part of supervisors, novice psychotherapists lacking alternative experiences are likely to assume that their supervisors are competent and that their behavior accurately reflects standards of practice. Although most often this is an accurate assumption, when ethical errors occur, the repercussions can be significant and far-reaching. Role modeling sound ethical practice in the context of teaching and supervision is probably more influential in fostering ethical practitioners than even the most conscientious attention to the ethical issues arising in academic courses and the cases presented in supervision.

Additionally, many ethical issues in treatment have analogues in supervision. Poor management of these challenges by supervisors may result in replication of that behavior in the supervisee's clinical work. Building on the seminal work of Ekstein and Wallerstein (1958), many authors have discussed the "parallel process" occurring in the dynamics of the supervisory and therapeutic dyads (Doehrman, 1976; Frawley-O'Dea & Sarnat, 2001; Yorke, 2005). Thus, problems in either relationship may be replicated in the other. Therefore, when a supervisor demonstrates poor boundaries, for example, the likelihood of the supervisee mismanaging boundaries in his or her therapeutic relationships increases.

In summary, supervisors' responsibilities for supervisees and supervisees' clients and as gatekeepers for their professions are significant. The need for specific and thorough ethics training cannot be overstated.

GUIDELINES FOR USE OF THIS BOOK

Almost any ethical challenge arising in psychotherapy or assessment has an analogue in supervision and consultation. Yet the ability to apply ethical standards in these contexts requires additional and distinct expertise. Graduate students and trainees preparing to become supervisors and consultants as well as novice and experienced professionals serving in these roles will benefit from learning to anticipate, prevent, minimize, and respond effectively to the myriad ethical challenges they will encounter in this work. Case examples are included throughout the book.[1]

Chapter 2: Ethical and Practice Standards

This book begins by providing the reader with an overview and comparison of the ethics codes (AAMFT, 2001; 2007; AAPC, 1994; ACA, 2005; APA, 2002; ASPPB, 2005; CPA, 2000; NAADAC, 2008; NASW, 2008) and practice guidelines (AAPC, 1997, 2009; ACES, 1993; ASPPB, 2003; Center for Credentialing & Education [CCE], 2008; CPA, 2009; NASW, 2005) of various disciplines. Because supervision sometimes occurs across disciplines, supervisors have the added responsibility of knowing and understanding codes and guidelines applying not only to themselves but also to supervisees in allied professions.

Twenty-five specific ethical issues are delineated and defined in Appendix A, and each is discussed in one or more chapters. In Appendixes B through E, readers are directed to particular sections of ethics codes and guidelines that address these ethical issues. Each document reviewed has its strengths and advantages, and together they offer supervisors and consultants a thorough introduction to contemporary thinking about relevant ethical issues.

Chapter 3: Ethical Issues in Psychotherapy-Based Models of Supervision

On the foundation provided in Chapter 2, psychotherapy-based models of supervision are described and analyzed in terms of the ethical challenges

---

[1]Although cases are based on actual events, they have been modified, combined, and otherwise fictionalized to carefully protect the identities of all involved parties.

most likely to occur when the supervision or the psychotherapy being supervised is grounded in a particular theoretical approach. In Chapter 3, five theoretical models of supervision are described: client/supervisee-centered, behavioral, cognitive–behavioral, systemic, and psychodynamic supervision. Case examples illustrate some of the ethical challenges encountered by both supervisors and supervisees using these approaches. Applicable ethical principles and standards are identified. Supervisors are provided with guidance for prevention, identification, assessment, and remediation of ethical problems.

Chapter 4: Ethical Challenges at Various Stages of Professional Development

Numerous authors have proposed developmental models of supervision that emphasize the importance of considering the supervisee's stage or level of professional development. Developmental models may be considered metatheoretical in that supervisors representing various theoretical orientations can hone their interventions by considering the developmental needs of their supervisees. In Chapter 4, these developmental models of supervision are described and critiqued. The Integrated Developmental Model (Stoltenberg et al., 1998), including its latest revision, the Integrative Developmental Model (Stoltenberg & McNeill, 2009), is highlighted and discussed in detail. Specifically, in this chapter ethical challenges commonly encountered by supervisees at various stages of development are identified and a case illustration for each level is included. Chapter 4 also includes a framework with which supervisors may conceptualize and respond to supervisees' ethical errors and anticipate or avoid ethical problems in their own work as they develop as supervisors.

Chapter 5: Boundaries and Multiple Relationships

The education and training of prospective and practicing supervisors and consultants relying on any theoretical or developmental model must address the unique boundary challenges inherent in these relationships. Related ethical violations are relatively common. The APA Ethics Committee (2008) reported that 60% of cases opened in 2007 included multiple relationships as at least one factor. The Ethics Committee report did not specify how many of these cases involved supervision or consultation, but these data do reflect the pervasiveness and complexity of multiple relationships.

Despite overlap, boundary challenges in the contexts of supervision and consultation are substantially distinct from those characterizing clinical services. Differences between supervisory and collegial, social, and other types of relationships may not be readily apparent to new supervisors. In Chapter 5, these nuances are examined in light of relevant ethics codes and specialty guidelines. A discussion of social power and influence provides a backdrop for exploration of the nature of professional boundaries, the roles of supervisors and consultants, and ethical violations in the context of various practice settings. Personal characteristics of members of the supervisory triad (i.e., supervisor, supervisee, and client) are considered in terms of their implications for power dynamics; gender, sexual orientation, race, ethnicity, religion, and physical ability are examples. Special topics examined include sexual relationships with prospective, current, and former supervisees; collegial and social relationships; rural and small community issues; and subtle and transient role shifts. Existing ethical decision-making models are reviewed, and a model for supervisors and consultants is presented.

Chapter 6: Informed Consent

As discussed previously, supervisors assume full professional responsibility for supervisees, and unless otherwise specified, they must commit to overseeing all aspects of the work. Responsibilities of consultants are more variable and are designed collaboratively to meet the particular needs of the consultee. Supervisors and consultants both must establish procedures for obtaining the informed consent of participants. To do so, they must provide supervisees and consultees with information about any aspect of the supervision or consultation that reasonably might be expected to influence their ability to make sound decisions about participation.

Chapter 6 outlines the requirements of various ethical standards and recommendations of specialty guidelines regarding informed consent to supervision and consultation. Suggestions for developing contracts are included. Written contracts may be the most efficacious method for ensuring that expectations are clearly established (J. M. Campbell, 2000; Cobia & Boes, 2000; Fall & Sutton, 2004; Falvey, 2002; Luepker, 2003; McCarthy et al., 1995; Osborn & Davis, 1996; Sutter, McPherson, & Geeseman, 2002). Therefore, readers are given an annotated menu of 15 matters that might be addressed in such a written contract. The limits of privacy, evaluation, grievance procedures, and criteria for success are some examples.

Chapter 7: Group Supervision and Consultation

Supervision and consultation groups meet some of the same goals and objectives as their individual counterparts in terms of augmenting training, enhancing clinical effectiveness, and mitigating ethical errors. Thoughtful and careful planning enhances these benefits and simultaneously minimizes risks. Chapter 7 outlines the differences between supervision and consultation groups in terms of their functions, benefits, and limitations, and it provides strategies for forming and maintaining consultation groups. Included is a list of factors to consider in initiating a supervision or consultation group. This chapter also addresses confidentiality rights of clients and group participants as well as potentially avoidable problems that can sabotage a group's success.

Chapter 8: Mandated Supervision

Perhaps the most advanced type of supervision is that of professionals at any stage of development—including those with many years of experience—who have been found in violation of the law or of ethical or practice standards and are required to participate in supervision as part of their rehabilitation. Those who agree to provide supervision mandated by licensing boards, professional ethics committees, or employers must understand the ethical challenges that arise in any supervision as well as the unique goals and significant responsibilities inherent in this work. In Chapter 8 these responsibilities are described, and the associated clinical and ethical challenges encountered by both supervisors and supervisees in this circumstance are highlighted. In this chapter the effective management of the transference and countertransference themes that commonly emerge in mandated supervision is discussed.

The role of the licensing board or other referring entity is considered along with the importance of presupervision assessment and ongoing evaluation to ensure the viability of the supervision. Specific methods and strategies useful in mandated supervision are described.

Chapter 9: Documentation and Record Keeping

The documentation of clinical work is standard practice in most mental health professions (Wiger, 2005; R. L. Worthington, Tan, & Poulin, 2002). Recognition of the need for documentation in supervision has emerged with clarification of the extent of supervisors' responsibilities for supervisees and their clients (Falvey, Caldwell, & Cohen, 2002; Luepker, 2003). Further, many professional ethics codes and supervision guidelines require or recommend the documentation of supervision (AAMFT, 2001; 2007; ACA, 2005; ACES, 1993; APA, 2002; CCE, 2008; CPA, 2000, 2009; NASW, 2005, 2008). Consultation, also considered an aspect of a psychologist's "professional and scientific work" (APA, 2002, p. 8), must be documented as well.

In Chapter 9 the purposes and objectives of record keeping are described, and the importance of documentation of supervision and consultation by both the recipient and the provider of these services is considered. The content and format of these records vary according to setting and purpose. Alternative types of documentation are presented. Supervisors are responsible for ensuring that supervisees comply with ethics codes, rules, laws, and institutional and agency policies. A record of their efforts to execute these responsibilities serves as verification of their supervisory directives, assessments of supervisee performance, decisions, and recommendations. Forms for recording supervision or consultation (Appendix G) and for evaluating completeness (Appendix H) and quality (Appendix I) are included as appendixes.

Case examples are included throughout the book. Although cases are based on actual events, they have been modified, combined, and otherwise fictionalized to carefully protect the identities of all involved parties.

CONCLUSION

Topics discussed in this volume are among the most important ethical issues facing clinical supervisors and consultants. As such, their inclusion in the initial training and continuing education of supervisors and consultants is critical. Standards of practice are evolving rapidly. To develop and maintain their knowledge and skills in this area, prospective and practicing supervisors and consultants must continually inform themselves and incorporate their learning into their work with supervisees and consultees.

2

ETHICAL PRACTICE STANDARDS FOR SUPERVISION AND CONSULTATION

Any examination of the ethical challenges inherent in supervision and consultation requires a foundation reflective of the state of the art. The direction provided by professional associations in the form of ethical standards and practice guidelines offers supervisors and consultants such a primary resource.

Most professional associations have developed codes of ethics for their members (American Association for Marriage and Family Therapy [AAMFT], 2001; American Association of Pastoral Counselors [AAPC], 1994; American Counseling Association [ACA], 2005; American Psychiatric Association [ApA], 2009; American Psychological Association [APA], 2002; Association of State and Provincial Psychology Boards [ASPPB], 2005; Canadian Psychological Association [CPA], 2000; National Association of Alcohol and Drug Abuse Counselors [NAADAC], 2008; National Association of Social Workers [NASW], 2005, 2008), and some have credentialing bodies (AAMFT, 2007; Center for Credentialing & Education [CCE], 2008). In addition to these ethics codes, various books describing their application have been published (AAMFT, 2001b; C. B. Fisher, 2003; Nagy, 2005). Some organizations have published specialty guidelines or codes of ethics specifically for supervisors (AAPC, 2009; ACES, 1993; ASPPB, 2003; CPA, 2009).

Formal consideration of the ethics of consultation and supervision is in its infancy. The standards of practice are evolving, and ethics codes and guidelines require continual revision to provide appropriate guidance. To date, some professional mental health associations have thoroughly addressed ethical issues for supervisors, and others have done so only generally or not at all. Although separate codes for clinical consultation are not available, documents pertaining to supervision sometimes refer to consultation. The codes guide and inform clinical consultants and supervisors whether or not they are members of the particular organization or profession. Further, reviewing the various issues raised in each affords readers an opportunity to consider and prepare for or avoid potential challenges that may not otherwise have been anticipated. This chapter provides a foundation for those that follow. It sets the stage for more in-depth consideration of the ethical issues most pertinent to supervisors and consultants.

The following are examples of ethical dilemmas and questions faced by supervisors for which the codes and guidelines described may be helpful.

- I am supervising a doctoral intern in providing outpatient psychotherapy. He has previous training in hypnosis, an area in which I have no background. He has a new client for whom he believes hypnosis would be helpful. Should I allow this?
- I recently received an e-mail from a former supervisee notifying me that she just received her license to practice. I would like to take her out for dinner to celebrate. What should I consider before extending this invitation?
- My private practice has been a bit slow recently, and so I was pleased to receive a request for prelicensure supervision from a new doctoral-level psychologist in my community. However, she is struggling financially and so proposed that she develop and maintain a website for me in exchange for supervision. I certainly have room in my caseload, and I have wanted to have a website, so this seems ideal. Is there anything that would prohibit the arrangement?
- I am 2 months into supervising a master's practicum student, and it appears that he has serious mental health problems. I am concerned about my liability for his work and would like to discontinue the supervision. How can I get out of this ethically?
- I have agreed to provide monthly consultation to the staff of a mental health agency. What, if any, official records am I required to maintain about this work?
- I have found that self-understanding is a fundamental component of being able to provide effective psychotherapy. To that end,

I require students in my supervision groups to participate in experiential exercises designed to help them explore their personal histories. I've had a couple of student complaints and so am wondering how to proceed.

- A colleague who works at a local hospital recently called me to ask about one of my former supervisees who applied for a position in her department. He didn't list me as a reference. Can I share my assessment of his capabilities?
- My supervisee spoke favorably about some of her own psychotherapist's behavior with her. I was shocked at what seemed to me to be inappropriate boundaries, and I am worried about the role models she is being exposed to and apparently admires. I know this guy and am considering reporting him to the licensing board. But I am sure my supervisee would be furious with me, and I'm afraid that would destroy our relationship. Should I report him? Am I required to do so? What about her preferences?

Each of these questions is complex. Each involves competency, multiple relationships, liability, informed consent, record keeping, and confidentiality. Supervisors and consultants encountering them will find direction through examination of relevant ethics codes and specialty guidelines. Although this chapter does not directly resolve these dilemmas, supervisors and consultants are given a map with which they can navigate such challenges.

The objectives of this chapter, then, are to provide consultants and supervisors with

- an overview of related ethics codes and specialty guidelines,
- an introduction to some of the ethical challenges they are likely to encounter, and
- a quick reference for help with ethical dilemmas.

To this end, several general ethics codes (APA, 2002; ASPPB, 2005; CPA, 2000) and specialty (i.e., supervision) guidelines or codes of ethics (AAPC, 2009; ASPPB, 2003; CCE, 2008; CPA, 2009) are described in terms of their format, scope, and applications for consultants and supervisors. Appendix B provides an overview of relevant sections of psychology ethics codes in terms of their coverage of 25 ethical issues defined in Appendix A. Finally, the general strengths and limitations of each document for consultants and supervisors are discussed. Relevant sections of other professional ethics codes and guidelines are reviewed more briefly (see Appendixes C, D, and E, this volume).

Some existing ethics codes and guidelines for consultants and supervisors are more general, whereas others are specific and detailed. Each approach has advantages and disadvantages. A general code or set of guidelines offers greater flexibility in using professional judgment to consider the unique aspects of particular individuals and situations. However, it also may be considered too vague to be helpful. Further, expectations for compliance and specific application may be unclear and the determinations of violation, more subjective.

PSYCHOLOGY PROFESSIONAL ASSOCIATIONS: ETHICS CODES

The APA and the CPA are organizations consisting of and representing psychologists. The ASPPB represents the boards that regulate psychologists in the United States and Canada. Each of these associations has developed a code of ethics, described in the sections that follow.

American Psychological Association

Membership in the APA requires a commitment to comply with its *Ethical Principles of Psychologists and Code of Conduct* (APA, 2002; hereinafter referred to as the APA Ethics Code; available at http://www.apa.org/ethics/code2002.html). This document includes an introduction, a preamble, five general principles, and 10 categories of ethical standards. The introduction clarifies that the APA Ethics Code applies to "psychologists' activities that are part of their scientific, educational, or professional roles as psychologists" (p. 2). The preamble underscores the applicability of both the principles and ethical standards by identifying consultant and supervisor among the roles performed by psychologists. The general principles are considered aspirational: They are intended "to guide and inspire psychologists toward the very highest ethical ideals of the profession" (APA, 2002, p. 2).

Conversely, the ethical standards establish the minimum criteria for acceptable practice that form the basis for determining violations. Many standards are "written broadly, in order to apply to psychologists in varied roles" (APA, 2002, p. 2). When they apply only to a particular area of psychological practice or to consumers of certain services, this is clearly stated (e.g., Standard 6.05, Barter with Clients/Patients, and Standard 7.06, Assessing Student and Supervisee Performance).

The accessible format and broad applicability of the APA Ethics Code represent significant advantages to consultants and supervisors. Even when consultation and supervision are not specifically mentioned, there are often implications for those areas of practice.

The APA Ethics Code addresses nearly all of the 25 ethical issues considered here (see Appendix B, this volume). It includes, for example, a section on education and training with a specific standard pertaining to the assessment of supervisee performance (7.06) and another prohibiting sexual relationships between psychologists and supervisees (7.07). The APA Ethics Code also provides detailed guidance on several issues either not addressed or referred to only generally in other codes. The section on informed consent, for example, mentions education and training programs (7.02), requirements for student disclosure of personal information (7.04), and student and supervisee performance assessment (7.06). Similarly, the Ethics Code establishes a requirement for the competence of both supervisors (2.01, 2.03) and supervisees (2.05).

A potential disadvantage of the APA Ethics Code is that it does not consider some of the issues involving the mechanics of consultation and supervision. Examples include crisis procedures, due process for supervisees, endorsement of supervisees for professional credentials, and methods for supervision and consultation.

Association of State and Provincial Psychology Boards

The primary object of the ASPPB is to assist licensing boards in discharging their responsibilities. To this end, the ASPPB has developed training materials and model publications related to the credentialing and regulation of psychologists.

The *ASPPB Code of Conduct* (available at http://www.ok.gov/OSBEP/documents/ASPPB_Code_of_Conduct_2005[1].pdf) is designed to be "non-optional . . . coercive, not advisory or aspirational. . . . any violation is basis for formal disciplinary action, including loss of licensure" (ASPPB, 2005, p. 3). But it is only binding on licensees and applicants for licensure if their particular regulatory board elects to adopt the code as rule or statute in that jurisdiction.

The *ASPPB Code of Conduct* includes four sections: a foreword, an introduction, definitions, and rules of conduct. The rules of conduct section addresses 12 ethical issues, many of which have application in consultation and supervision. The term *supervisee* is specifically defined as "any person who functions under the extended authority of the psychologist to provide, or while in training to provide, psychological services" (ASPPB, 2005, p. 4). The rules of conduct section includes five subsections specifically addressing supervision (see Appendix B, this volume). These sections offer supervisors specific direction with regard to establishing and maintaining their own competence (III. A1, 2), delegation of responsibilities to supervisees (III. A10, III. K2), and the public presentation of supervisees' credentials (III. K1). The content and maintenance of supervision records (III. A7) and client privacy in the context of supervision (III. F 1, 9) are also addressed. Finally, the rules of conduct require supervisors to avoid behaviors that are "seductive, demeaning, or harassing or exploit a supervisee in any way—sexually, financially or otherwise" (ASPPB, 2005, p. 8).

The *ASPPB Code of Conduct* does not address many other ethical issues related to supervision: evaluation, endorsement, reporting obligations, supervisory methods, crisis procedures, diversity, fees, supervisee privacy, and informed consent of supervisees and clients regarding supervision are examples. Multiple relationships are mentioned, but the focus is primarily on client welfare, and the relevance for supervisors is not highlighted (III. B1).

Perhaps the existence of the ASPPB's *Supervision Guidelines* (ASPPB, 2003) has contributed to the decision not to directly address related issues in the code. Guidelines, however, are not as binding as codes, and although they can be helpful to supervisors, they are not a substitute.

The *ASPPB Code of Conduct* mentions consultation with colleagues as a strategy for developing competency in a service or technique and for maintaining competence (III. A2). These sections apply to those who are seeking rather than those who are providing consultation. Because consultation could be conceptualized as a "professional service" (defined as "all actions of the psychologist in the context of a professional relationship with a client"; ASPPB, 2005, p. 4), codes with implications for professional services may apply.

Canadian Psychological Association

The *Canadian Code of Ethics for Psychologists* (CPA, 2000; hereinafter referred to as the Canadian Code; available at http://www.cpa.ca/cpasite/userfiles/Documents/Canadian%20Code%20of%20Ethics%20for%20Psycho.pdf) includes an introduction, preamble, and four principles. The introduction specifically mentions supervision and consultation, clarifying the applicability of this code. The preamble includes information about the structure of the code and definitions. Each principle is followed by a "values statement" and the standards that amplify it.

Unique to the Canadian Code is a 10-step ethical decision-making process designed to guide psychologists practicing in any area, including consultation and supervision. The 10 specific steps require psychologists to identify groups affected, relevant ethical issues, the potential impact of personal bias and self-interest, and alternative courses of action along with the risks and benefits of each. Then, with due consideration of principles, values, and standards, psychologists are directed to choose and implement a course of action, evaluate results, make corrections, and take action to prevent future occurrences. The CPA also has published a companion manual (2001) to further assist psychologists in applying the Canadian Code. This manual includes 13 references to supervision.

Discussions of several general ethical issues apply to both consultation and supervision (CPA, 2000). Sections focusing on diversity, competence, informed consent, and multiple relationships are examples (see Appendix B, this volume). Supervision is specifically mentioned in sections pertaining to supervisees' privacy (I.40), avoiding harm (II.2), refusing to train people likely to cause harm (II.4), and informing clients about trainees' status (III.22). Further, Section II.28 prohibits supervisors from engaging in "sexual intimacy with students or trainees with whom the psychologist has an evaluative or other relationship of direct authority" (CPA, 2000, p. 18).

Although not defined, references to consultation appear throughout the Canadian Code. The context refers to both providing and seeking input from colleagues. The distinction between consultation and supervision in the Canadian Code hinges on authority. Consultation occurs between peers or between senior and junior professionals, whereas supervision is provided by an individual with responsibility for the supervisee's work.

A primary strength of the Canadian Code is its section titled Ethical Decision-Making Process (CPA, 2000, p. 2). This process offers a practical tool that is particularly useful to consultants and supervisors facing ethical dilemmas for which existing codes do not offer definitive direction. The advantage that comes with such flexibility, however, carries with it the disadvantage of ambiguity apparent in several sections. Psychologists are directed, for example, to "respect the right of . . . clients, employees, supervisees, students, trainees, and others to safeguard their own dignity" (CPA, 2000, I.8, p. 9). Precisely what constitutes ethical behavior according to this standard is difficult to determine.

COUNSELING PROFESSIONAL ASSOCIATIONS: ETHICS CODES

The AAPC, the ACA, and the NAADAC represent counselors with various specializations. Like the psychology organizations described previously, each of these counseling associations has an ethics code.

American Association of Pastoral Counselors

The AAPC *Code of Ethics* (available at http://www.aapc.org/content/ethics) begins with seven foundational premises (AAPC, 1994, pp. 1–2) that underlie the principles that follow. The preamble to Principle V, Supervisee, Student and Employee Relationships, offers protections for the welfare of these individuals. This principle prohibits exploitation, sexual behavior, and dual relationships with supervisees. Supervisors are further charged with ensuring that supervisees practice within the boundaries of their competency. Client privacy is also protected in the context of supervision.

A limitation of the AAPC *Code of Ethics* is its narrow focus. Although the issues mentioned previously are considered, others are omitted. Supervisory methods, endorsement, due process, and informed consent are not addressed. Also, the AAPC *Code of Ethics* specifically addresses ethical issues facing supervisors, although those providing consultation must extrapolate.

American Counseling Association

The ACA *Code of Ethics* (available at http://www.counseling.org/ Resources/ CodeOfEthics/TP/Home/CT2.aspx) includes eight sections, each beginning with aspirational statement (ACA, 2005, p. 3). A glossary defining 18 terms is unique to this code and aids interpretation.

Various sections of the ACA *Code of Ethics* contain information applicable to supervision, but Section F, Supervision, Training, and Teaching, is most pertinent. Specific supervisory methods are described. Supervisors are required, for example, to meet regularly with supervisees, review case notes, and observe or examine work samples (F.1.a.). Additionally, the ACA *Code of Ethics* includes requirements for supervisors regarding diversity and continuing education. Although certain nonprofessional relationships with supervisees are specifically prohibited (e.g., sexual relationships), "potentially beneficial [nonprofessional] relationships" (ACA, 2005, F.3.e., p. 14) are permissible. The *Code of Ethics* also addresses informed consent to supervision (F.4.a.), clinical emergencies (F.4.c.), termination of supervision (F.4.d), and gatekeeping responsibilities (F.5.).

The ACA *Code of Ethics* addresses clinical consultation, though not as extensively as supervision. (A section titled Consultation addresses organizational consultation and so is not pertinent.) Requirements for preserving client confidentiality in consultation are included in sections pertaining to treatment teams (B.6.b.), observation, and review of transcripts or recordings (B.6.c). Counselors are further instructed to seek consultation when making decisions about dismissing supervisees from training programs and when facing with ethical dilemmas. Other sections of the ACA *Code of Ethics* describe the ethical obligations of counselors in several roles that are relevant to supervision and/or consultation. Examples include Recruiting Through Employment (C.3.d., p. 10) and Nondiscrimination (C.5., p. 10).

The ACA *Code of Ethics* offers many advantages over similar codes. The glossary, clear section titles, and in-text references to other relevant sections enhance accessibility. Its length and related redundancy (e.g., F.5.b. and F.9.b.) represent potential disadvantages.

National Association of Alcohol and Drug Abuse Counselors

The NAADAC *Code of Ethics* (2008; available at http://www.naadac. org/index.php?option=com_content&view=article&id=185&Itemid=115) is a set of standards designed for alcohol and drug abuse counselors. This code incorporates nine principles, each followed by statements explicating its application. All are written in first person, in the form of an oath.

The NAADAC *Code of Ethics* does not use the terms *supervision* and *consultation*, but several sections implicate these areas of practice. Principle 3, Client Relationship, for example, addresses the need to obtain a client's informed consent before recording or observing sessions for training purposes. Other sections written for treatment providers may be applicable to supervisors and consultants, such as those that address dual relationships, reporting obligations, and competence (see Appendix B, this volume).

OTHER MENTAL HEALTH PROFESSIONAL ASSOCIATIONS: ETHICS CODES

The AAMFT and the ApA represent mental health professionals. The NASW represents social workers in varied settings, including those who provide psychotherapy and other mental health services. Codes of ethics have been developed by each of these associations.

American Association for Marriage and Family Therapy

The AAMFT *Code of Ethics* (2001; available at http://www.aamft.org/ resources/LRM_Plan/Ethics/ethicscode2001.asp) includes eight principles, followed by subprinciples elucidating their applications. No clear distinction is made between the two regarding enforceability. The preamble describes the AAMFT *Code of Ethics* as binding on all members, approved supervisors, and applicants and as enforceable by the Ethics Committee.

Principle IV, Responsibility to Students and Supervisees, focuses largely on the risks that multiple relationships pose for impaired objectivity and exploitation. Supervisee competency (4.4) and confidentiality rights (4.7) are also covered.

Although the AAMFT *Code of Ethics* is broad in its coverage of clinical consultation and supervision, one limitation is that the language varies in precision, complicating the determination of whether a standard has been met. Some sections are relatively uncomplicated (e.g., supervisee privacy, 2.6, 4.7; protection of client privacy in supervision, 2.1), but others are more ambiguous. For example, Subprinciple 7.5 allows bartering for services when the supervisee requests the arrangement and is not exploited, a written contract is established, and "the relationship is not distorted" (AAMFT, 2001, p. 8). Although identifying the initiator and whether a contract exists is relatively straightforward, determining whether a relationship has become "distorted" is more complex and subjective.

Another area of potential confusion involves sexual relationships. Section 4.3 prohibits sexual relationships between supervisors and current supervisees. However, Section 4.6 implies that such relationships are permissible if they are (a) unavoidable and (b) the supervisor's objectivity can be maintained. So, are current sexual relationships between supervisors and supervisees prohibited or permissible (if unavoidable)? Further, when such relationships "cannot be avoided" (AAMFT, 2001, p. 6), therapists are instructed to "take appropriate precautions to maintain objectivity" (p. 6). In the event of a complaint, the burden is on the supervisor to demonstrate that there was no alternative and that appropriate precautions were taken. If the supervisor has not attempted to avoid the adverse outcome, demonstrating objectivity will be difficult. Perhaps more challenging will be proving that a situation was unavoidable.

Technical issues not addressed in the *AAMFT Code of Ethics* include supervisee evaluation, documentation, endorsement, methods, crisis procedures, due process, and interruption of supervision. However, many of these issues are addressed in the "Responsibilities and Guidelines for AAMFT Approved Supervisors and Supervisor Candidates" (included in AAMFT, 2007).

American Psychiatric Association

The American Medical Association's *Principles of Medical Ethics* (2001; available at http://www.cirp.org/library/statements/ama/) applies to physicians in all specialty areas. In 1973, the ApA published a supplemental text to assist psychiatrists, *The Principles of Medical Ethics With Annotations Especially Applicable to Psychiatry*, revised in 2009 (available at http://www.psych.org/MainMenu/PsychiatricPractice/Ethics/Resources Standards.aspx). The document includes an introduction, foreword, and preamble, followed by nine principles. Each principle is followed by statements explaining its applications for psychiatrists.

Most ApA principles apply to the provision of medical care and to the doctor–patient relationship, but some also have implications for consultation and supervision. For example, they address ethical issues such as patient privacy, physician competency, discrimination, exploitation, boundaries, and fees. A few sections apply specifically to consultation. Psychiatrists are repeatedly directed (1:3, 5, 5:2, 5:5) to maintain competency, in part through consultation with colleagues. The ApA principles further remind psychiatrists of their responsibility to monitor colleagues for impairment and to intercede when necessary to protect patient welfare (2:4). This principle could arguably be applied to supervisors' responsibility to intervene when supervisees are impaired.

The ApA principles delineate three ethical issues with specific application to supervisors. First, psychiatrist–supervisors must ensure that they "expend sufficient time to assure that proper care is given" (ApA, 2009, p. 8). Second, psychiatrists are prohibited from offering supervision in exchange for a percentage of the supervisee's fee or gross income (2:7). Finally, the ApA principles indicate that sexual contact between a supervisor and trainee or student "may be unethical" (2009, p. 6) because "any treatment of a patient being supervised may be deleteriously affected; it may damage the trust relationship between teacher and student; teachers are important professional role models for their trainees and affect their trainees' future professional behavior" (ApA, 2009, p. 7). Unlike some other ethics codes (AAPC, 1994; ACA, 2005; APA, 2002), which prohibit sexual contact with supervisees, the goal of ApA seems to be to raise the consciousness of members about the potential for problems and thereby discourage it.

The ApA principles emphasize the importance of clinical supervision and encourage psychiatrists to take that responsibility seriously for the benefit of both supervisees and the patients they serve. A limitation is the minimal attention paid to issues specific to consultation and supervision. Documentation, informed consent, and evaluation, for example, are absent.

National Association of Social Workers

The NASW *Code of Ethics* (2008; available at http://www.naswdc.org/pubs/code/code.asp) includes the preamble, purpose, ethical principles, and ethical standards, and it applies to both professional and student members. Social workers provide a wide range of services, and only some offer psychotherapy. The NASW code therefore has broader applicability. The introduction indicates that these codes are "enforceable guidelines for professional conduct, and some are aspirational" (NASW, 2008, p. 5). Thus, the task of distinguishing between minimum requirements and aspirational goals is left to "those responsible for reviewing alleged violations of ethical standards" (NASW, 2008, p. 5).

In addition to a mention in the preamble, the NASW *Code of Ethics* includes subsections entitled Consultation (2.05, which refers to obtaining rather than providing consultation) and Supervision and Consultation (3.01). This section of the NASW code emphasizes competency, fair evaluation of supervisees, culturally sensitive boundaries, and avoiding multiple relationships and exploitation. The NASW code addresses many other ethical issues relevant to supervision and consultation. Examples include client privacy, impairment, recording and observing sessions, and reporting obligations (see Appendix C, this volume).

Perhaps the most helpful sections of the NASW *Code of Ethics* for supervisors and consultants are those focusing specifically on these areas of practice. These advantages are enhanced by a readily accessible format and cogent organization. However, the seamless combination of minimum standards with aspirational goals introduces an element of confusion.

MENTAL HEALTH PROFESSIONAL ASSOCIATIONS: SPECIALTY GUIDELINES AND CODES

Several professional associations have developed practice guidelines or codes of ethics specifically for supervisors. Although similar guidelines for consultants are not available, some aspects of supervision guidelines are applicable and may be adapted for consultation. Unlike codes and ethical standards, which are generally binding and enforceable, guidelines tend to be aspirational; that is, they provide suggestions or recommendations rather than requirements. Because the guidelines exclusively address the practice of clinical supervision, they tend to offer more specific prescriptions for professional conduct.

American Association for Marriage and Family Therapy Responsibilities and Guidelines

The AAMFT published the *Approved Supervisor Designation Standards and Responsibilities Handbook* (2007), which includes "Responsibilities and Guidelines for AAMFT Approved Supervisors and Supervisor Candidates" (hereinafter referred to as Responsibilities and Guidelines). The AAMFT is both a professional association and a credentialing body, and in the latter capacity has established the Responsibilities and Guidelines as minimum standards of practice (in contrast to the aspirational nature of other guidelines) for mentors (i.e., those who supervise supervisors-in-training), approved supervisors, and supervisor candidates.

The AAMFT's Responsibilities and Guidelines specifically addresses endorsement, evaluation, supervisee confidentiality, informed consent, fees, and documentation. Supervision is not allowed when any concurrent or past relationship with a supervisee "makes difficult the establishment of a professional relationship" (AAMFT, 2007, p. 11), and supervising family members is specifically prohibited. (This requirement may conflict with the AAMFT *Code of Ethics*, 2001; see previous related section.) Peer supervision, administrative supervision, didactic programs, and consultation do not meet criteria for the required supervision.

The Responsibilities and Guidelines allows for considerable professional judgment within defined limits, an advantage to those preferring such flexibility. A possible disadvantage, however, is the format. Unlike other guidelines reviewed, Responsibilities and Guidelines is presented in a narrative rather than outline form. Lacking subheadings and topic-related sections, this format makes it difficult to locate and cite relevant text.

American Association of Pastoral Counselors Supervision Standards of Practice

The AAPC (1997), like the AAMFT, is both a professional association and a credentialing body. The AAPC offers members two documents related to supervision. The first, *Supervision Standards of Practice* (1997, available from the AAPC office, 703-385-6967), is designed for use by pastoral counseling supervisors. It includes an introduction, preface, and six standards, and is intended to be both realistic and "as close to ideal as possible" (AAPC, 1997, p. 1). Although described as *standards*, in practice they are guidelines not intended to establish a minimum standard of practice (L. M. Crede, personal communication, September 11, 2006).

This AAPC *Supervision Standards of Practice* is relatively brief—fewer than four pages—yet these guidelines offer a detailed consideration of several specific supervisory issues. For example, the *Supervision Standards of Practice* clearly states the importance of a supervisory agreement or informed consent, the competency of both supervisor and supervisee, the supervisory relationship, documentation of supervision, reporting obligations, and the supervision of supervision. Issues not addressed include endorsement, crisis procedures, fees, and due process. Another disadvantage is that the document has not been widely disseminated and is available only by request from the AAPC office (L. M. Crede, personal communication, March 1, 2005).

The second relevant AAPC document, the "Supervision Standards," is included in the *Membership Standards and Certification Committee Operational Manual* (AAPC, 2009) and describes supervision requirements for certification as a pastoral counselor, fellow, or diplomate. Supervisory formats (individual, group) are specified, as are the required number of hours and specific supervisory methods to be used. This most recent revision addresses "distance supervision"

(AAPC, 2009, p. 32) as meeting the requirement for live supervision if it is conducted in real time, that is, "telephone conversation, video-teleconference, or a live internet 'chat' technology" (AAPC, 2009, p. 32).

Although these requirements (AAPC, 2009) apply only to applicants for certification, they may be of interest to those developing similar requirements or attempting to structure a supervisory arrangement. The specific discussion of the use of modern technologies provides a helpful alternative that may be especially beneficial for members in locations where readily available supervision is lacking. Further, the combination of the two documents (AAPC, 1997, 2009) provides a cogent and concise set of suggestions likely to benefit any supervisor.

Association for Counselor Education and Supervision Ethical Guidelines for Counseling Supervisors

The ACES, a division of the ACA, represents those educating and supervising counselors and counselors-in-training. The *Ethical Guidelines for Counseling Supervisors* (ACES, 1993; available at http://www.acesonline.net/ethical_ guidelines.asp) includes three sections. Client Welfare and Rights and Supervisory Role are most relevant for clinical (as opposed to administrative) supervisors.

The ACES guidelines emphasize the training aspects of the supervisor's role. *Ethical Guidelines for Counseling Supervisors* clarifies the relative importance of supervisors' various responsibilities (1.01), citing client welfare as primary. Client confidentiality in the context of supervision (1.01, 1.03) and accurate representation of supervisees to clients are among supervisor's ethical responsibilities, as are monitoring supervisees' compliance with ethical standards and licensing requirements (2.b., 2.03, 2.04) and overseeing performance and professional development (2.c.). Further, supervisors are encouraged to serve as gatekeepers by monitoring for "personal or professional limitations . . . likely to impede future professional performance" (ACES, 1993, p. 3) and to refrain from endorsing a supervisee for any credential if the supervisor believes the supervisee is impaired (2.13). Supervisee evaluations should be formal and informal, written and oral, and "be formative during the supervisory experience and summative at the conclusion" (ACES, 1993, 2.08, pp. 2–3). Supervisory methods include crisis availability (2.05), review of actual work samples (2.06), and face-to-face sessions (2.07).

The ACES provides ethical guidelines for supervisors regarding their own professional behavior specifically in terms of competence as supervisors and relationships with supervisees. Acknowledging the inevitable overlap of some roles and advising caution, the ACES clarifies that sexual contact with supervisees is prohibited (2.10), and social contact that compromises the supervisory relationship or "that might impair the supervisor's objectivity and professional judgment" (ACES, 1993, 2.10, p. 3) should be avoided. Supervisors also are prohibited from providing psychotherapy to supervisees "as a substitute for supervision" (ACES, 1993, 2.11, p. 3). "Personal issues should be addressed in supervision only in terms of their impact of these issues on clients and on professional functioning" (ACES, 1993, p. 3). All supervisory responsibilities and related requirements must be conveyed to supervisees as part of obtaining their informed consent to participation in the supervision (2.14).

The primary strength of the ACES's *Ethical Guidelines for Counseling Supervisors* is that it provides a more detailed consideration of specific issues than similar guidelines. The guidelines also delineate and order the priorities of supervisors, ranking client welfare above that of supervisees and the profession (i.e., gatekeeping). Although this publication predates others, the ACES's *Ethical Guidelines for Counseling Supervisors* addresses more of the 25 ethical issues covered here than any other ethics code or set of guidelines reviewed. A potential disadvantage of the ACES guidelines is its focus on students. Although supervision is recommended throughout one's career, these guidelines do not specifically address the supervision of employees or other professionals.

Association of State and Provincial Psychology Boards Supervision Guidelines

The ASPPB's *Supervision Guidelines*, published in 1998 and revised in 2003, is available on request from the ASPPB office (http://www.asppb.org). Revision of the ASPPB *Supervision Guidelines* is underway as of this writing (J. B. Schaffer, personal communication, July 3, 2009). As described earlier, documents produced by the ASPPB are recommendations for licensing boards to consider in writing rules for the regulation of psychologist–supervisors. Only if adopted by a board do they become requirements. The ASPPB *Supervision Guidelines*, therefore, is written in the form of minimal standards. It is divided into a preamble and three sections, each focusing on a different type of supervisee: doctoral candidates, credentialed nondoctoral personnel, and uncredentialed personnel providing psychological services. It addresses issues pertaining to the supervision of pre- and postdoctoral prospective psychologists, academics, and non-health-service professionals. These guidelines provide a detailed description of required features of pre- and postdoctoral training settings and experiences. In predoctoral settings, for example, the guidelines require (I. A-1) adequate support staff, equipment, and office space as well as "full spectrum training and provide a foundation for a career in psychology" (ASPPB, 2003, p. 3). The focus of a postdoctoral experience must be on advanced training in specialized areas and not on the financial benefits of additional personnel.

These guidelines address informed consent issues for supervisees and their clients. They require supervisors to provide written rules, goals, and/or regulations; establish a written contract that will serve as the foundation for later evaluations (I. B-1, 2, 3); and ensure that supervisees' titles accurately communicate their status to clients and others (I. C-1). Although the term *informed consent* is not used, the objective is to ensure that supervisees and clients agree to participate with an informed understanding of relevant parameters.

Competency, like informed consent, is addressed in detail as it pertains to both supervisors and supervisees. Supervisors must have "adequate training, knowledge and skill" (ASPPB, 2003, p. 3) in all areas in which their supervisees practice, must delegate responsibilities commensurate with supervisees' skill levels (I. B-1, 2, 3), and provide an appropriate level of supervision (II. B-1).

Supervisors must ensure that supervisees are appropriately supported when their clients are in crisis. More specifically, supervisors are to "provide twenty-four (24) hour availability to both supervisees and the supervisee's clients" (ASPPB, 2003, II. C, p. 3). This section implies that supervisors have direct contact with their supervisees' clients when necessary.

The *Supervision Guidelines* addresses many other ethical issues and includes specific requirements regarding, for example, the maximum number of doctoral level candidate–supervisees that can be assigned to one supervisor (i.e., II. E-1, three predoctoral, four postdoctoral) and the number of supervision hours required for specified hours worked (III. A-1, B-2). Licensing boards are further directed to establish minimum requirements regarding supervisor credentials (V. A-1, 2, 3), evaluation forms used (V. B-1, 2), maintenance of evaluations (V. B-1, 2), endorsement (V. C-1, 3), and grievance procedures (V. C-1, 3).

Although payment for predoctoral supervision is prohibited, supervisors are permitted to charge for postdoctoral supervision (III. C-1). In addition to its intended use as a model for licensing boards, the ASPPB *Supervision Guidelines* assists individual supervisors and training directors in developing policies and procedures for supervision.

Although the specificity of *Supervision Guidelines* represents an advantage in many respects, if adopted in full by a licensing board, the guidelines would become minimum standards. The detailed requirements limit flexibility. The clear determination of the number of supervisees assigned to a given supervisor is one example. In some settings where supervisors have significant clinical or administrative responsibilities, two supervisees may be too many. In other cases in which training is a high priority, they may have minimal responsibilities beyond supervision and so could effectively manage more than three or four supervisees effectively.

Center for Credentialing & Education *The Approved Clinical Supervisor (ACS) Code of Ethics*

The *ACS Code of Ethics* (CCE, 2008) is a set of standards developed for use by mental health credentialing bodies that requires applicants to participate in clinical supervision and that establishes standards for those providing that supervision. This Code of Ethics (available from http://www.cce-global.org/extras/cce-global/pdfs/acs_codeofethics.pdf) contains 14 statements clarifying what "an Approved Clinical Supervisor shall" (CCE, 2008, p. 1) do to be in compliance with the Code of Ethics. Similar to the AAMFT (2007) and AAPC (2009) codes, the CCE (2008) document represents a minimum standard for supervisors of those wishing to be certified by this credentialing body.

The *ACS Code of Ethics* is relatively brief and straightforward. It provides succinct statements addressing supervision in terms of informed consent, competency, dual relationships, confidentiality, and documentation of supervision. Protection for supervisees is afforded by sections addressing the need for timely evaluations, exploitation, and due process. The gatekeeping function of supervisors, designed to protect the public, is also incorporated into the *ACS Code of Ethics*. For example, supervisors are required to "intervene in any situation where the supervisee is impaired and clients may be at risk" (CCE, 2008, p. 1). Supervisors are further prohibited from endorsing a supervisee should he or she be impaired and if "such impairment deems it unlikely that the supervisee can provide adequate clinical services" (CCE, 2008, p. 2).

A possible advantage of the *ACS Code of Ethics* is that it is written in a way that makes it readily applicable to supervisors in any mental health profession. Further, it could be applicable to supervision across disciplines. Section 12, for example, states that supervisors must "ensure that supervisees are aware of the current ethical standards related to the supervisees' professional practice, as well as legal standards that regulate the supervisee's professional practice" (CCE, 2008, p. 2). Whatever other ethics codes a particular supervisee may be required to follow are therefore incorporated into the supervision. The document is brief yet relatively comprehensive: 18 of the 25 ethical issues considered in Appendix E are addressed in this code. Finally, the exclusive focus on clinical supervision makes the *ACS Code of Ethics* directly relevant to supervisors.

A possible disadvantage of the *ACS Code of Ethics* involves its readability. Although brief, it has no headings to aid the reader in easily locating relevant sections. Ethical issues such as the supervisee's privacy, fees for supervision, and reporting obligations are examples of topics not addressed. Ethical issues related to clinical consultation are also absent from this code.

Canadian Psychological Association *Ethical Guidelines for Supervision in Psychology*

The CPA has developed a set of specialty guidelines titled *Ethical Guidelines for Supervision in Psychology: Teaching, Research, Practice, and Administration* (hereinafter referred to as *Guidelines for Supervision*; CPA, 2009; available at http://www.cpa.ca/cpasite/userfiles/Documents/COESup GuideRevApproved7Feb09revisedfinal.pdf).

The preamble to the *Guidelines for Supervision* states that they "do not have the force of law" (CPA, 2009, p. 1) but rather, "they provide advice on the applications or interpretations of ethical principles and values to a specialized area of psychological activity" (CPA, 2009, p. 1). These guidelines are further described as "primarily aspirational and facilitative" (CPA, 2009, p. 2).

The CPA *Guidelines for Supervision* comprise a preamble, introduction, definitions, and four basic principles: (a) respect for the dignity of persons, (b) responsible caring, (c) integrity in relationships, and (d) responsibility to society. Additionally, the publication includes a lengthy bibliography.

Supervision is conceptualized in two categories: developmental and administrative. The primary objective of the former involves facilitating skill development through "education/training/mentoring supervisees" (CPA, 2009, p. 5). The administrative function is described as "management . . . that emphasizes quality control" (CPA, 2009, p. 3). Various ethical issues and related supervisory responsibilities are addressed: competency, evaluation, multiple relationships, and gatekeeping are examples. Although most sections are worded as recommendations, sexual relationships are explicitly prohibited.

Perhaps the most noteworthy feature of the CPA *Guidelines for Supervision*—one that distinguishes it from similar publications—is its emphasis on the responsibilities of supervisees as well as supervisors, although supervisors are consistently assigned "greater responsibility" (e.g., CPA, 2009, pp. 5–7) in each case. For example, the CPA (2009) requires both parties to "share in defining the goals and role expectations" (p. 5); "be well prepared, make efficient use of time, and be receptive to mutual learning" (p. 6); and "address conflict in the supervisory relationship" (p. 7).

Each of these unique features represents a strength of the CPA *Guidelines for Supervision*. A potential disadvantage is the narrative format used in presenting the preamble, introduction, definitions, and the four principles. Similar to the AAMFT publication (2007), locating and citing particular issues is complicated by the lack of topic-related sections. Finally, consultation is not specifically addressed.

CONCLUSION: UTILITY OF EXAMINING ETHICS CODES AND GUIDELINES

Practicing and aspiring supervisors and consultants will benefit from examining the professional ethics codes and specialty guidelines discussed in this chapter as they formulate their policies and procedures. Familiarity with these standards and guidelines will assist those responsible for developing training programs, internships, practica, and course work in supervision or consultation for the benefit of both supervisees and the clients they serve. Certainly, members of a particular profession and those providing supervision for licensure or certification must have a thorough understanding of documents regulating or guiding their particular work. Because each professional association offers a unique perspective, and because of the frequency of cross-discipline supervision and consultation, it will be helpful for supervisors and consultants to have a general idea of the requirements for colleagues in allied professions.

The establishment of ethical principles, standards, and guidelines for supervision and consultation is in its infancy. Many revisions will likely be published in the years to come as these areas of practice gain recognition and become more specialized. Further, professional associations seeking to develop or revise their ethical standards or guidelines for consultants and supervisors will be most effective when they attempt to build on the pioneering work of predecessors in their own and allied professions.

3

PSYCHOTHERAPY-BASED MODELS OF SUPERVISION: ETHICAL CHALLENGES

Numerous theoretical models and approaches to supervision are described in the literature of mental health professions. Authors in the fields of psychology, counseling, marriage and family therapy, social work, addiction treatment, and others have described approaches to clinical supervision. These models have been categorized in various ways. Bernard and Goodyear (2009), for example, divided them into three categories: models grounded in psychotherapy theory, developmental models, and social role models. Falender and Shafranske (2004) similarly identified psychotherapy-based approaches and developmental approaches, but they used the term *process-based* to describe what Bernard and Goodyear (2009) referred to as *social role* models. Bradley and Gould (2001) described and critiqued three psychotherapy-based models: psychodynamic, behavioral, and cognitive models of supervision.

The goals of this chapter are to

- describe five psychotherapy-based models of supervision in terms of their basic tenets, techniques for application, advantages and strengths, and disadvantages and limitations, particularly in terms of their ethical dimensions;

- examine common ethical challenges facing supervisors and supervisees working within each of these models; and
- consider clinical cases illustrating these ethical challenges.

Thorough reviews and critiques of the many existing theoretical models of supervision are available elsewhere (Bernard & Goodyear, 2009; Falender & Shafranske, 2004; Frawley-O'Dea & Sarnat, 2001), so only a sampling is discussed in this context.

The selected models vary considerably in terms of their coverage in the professional literature. Relatively few articles and book chapters address the topics of supervisee-centered and behavioral supervision. Although cognitive–behavioral supervision has received more attention than either of the first two, numerous articles and books consider systemic and psychoanalytic supervision. Further, each of these latter models include several distinct theoretical approaches or schools of thought. As a result, they are more nuanced and complex and so require longer discussion. The relative length of coverage here indicates no recommendation of one model over another.

PSYCHOTHERAPY-BASED MODELS OF SUPERVISION

Many authors have described supervision models based on theories of psychotherapy. In this chapter, five such models are described:

1. client-centered or supervisee-centered supervision,
2. behavioral supervision,
3. cognitive–behavioral supervision,
4. systemic or family systems, and
5. psychodynamic and psychoanalytic supervision.

Theory-based approaches to supervision not reviewed in this chapter but that may be of interest include the following:

- feminist (Ault-Richie, 1988; Crespi, 1995; Hipp & Munson, 1995; Porter & Vasquez, 1997; Prouty, 2001; Prouty, Thomas, Johnson, & Long, 2001; Wheeler, Avis, Miller, & Chaney, 1986),
- Adlerian (Kopp & Robles, 1989),
- rational emotive and reality (A. Ellis, 1989; Smadi & Landreth, 1988; Woods & Ellis, 1996),
- Gestalt (Hoyt & Goulding, 1989; Resnick & Estrup, 2000; Yontef, 1997),
- narrative (Bob, 1999; Parry & Doan, 1994; Polkinghorne,1988; Singer, Baddeley, & Frantsve, 2008),

- Jungian (Kugler, 1995),
- solution focused (Juhnke, 1996; Presbury, Echterling, & McKee, 1999; Rita, 1998; F. N. Thomas, 1996; Triantafillou, 1997), and
- dialectical behavioral therapy (Fruzzetti, Waltz, & Linehan, 1997).

Many similarities between theoretical approaches to supervision have been observed (Morgan & Sprenkle, 2007). Watkins (1997b), in his commentary on psychotherapy-based approaches, concluded that such models are all "oriented around and driven by the theory of therapy that one is trying to teach" (p. 605). Although these models differ in many respects, Watkins (1997b) identified four characteristics common to most of them: "They emphasize the importance of (a) a supportive, non-critical supervisor–supervisee relationship or learning alliance; (b) teaching and instructing supervisees as needed; (c) modeling desired therapeutic behaviors or attitudes for supervisees; and (d) stimulating supervisee curiosity" (p. 605).

The following sections each provide a brief description of the five psychotherapy-based models of supervision listed previously. Although many of these concepts may be generalized for application to clinical consultation, psychotherapy-based models are designed for application to supervision only. Therefore, this section focuses on supervision exclusively.

Finally, the term *theory* is sometimes used to refer to models of psychotherapy. With regard to supervision, however, the approaches discussed are extrapolations of their corresponding theories of psychotherapy. These extrapolations lack the formality, precision, and details requisite to be considered theories (Patterson, 1986) and are referred to as *models* or *approaches* in this context.

CLIENT-CENTERED OR SUPERVISEE-CENTERED SUPERVISION

Carl Rogers is credited with the development of the client-centered model of psychotherapy (1942, 1951, 1958). He viewed supervision as being on a continuum with psychotherapy. He identified four facilitative conditions—warmth, empathy, respect, and genuineness—considered essential for supervision as well as psychotherapy (Hackney & Goodyear, 1984). Patterson (1964), building on Rogers's work, asserted that supervision is an influencing process that combines aspects of teaching and counseling, but that it is neither.

Patterson (1997) further described how a client-centered theory of psychotherapy could be adapted to "supervisee-centered supervision" (p. 137). A basic tenet of client-centered psychotherapy is trust in the client's ability and desire to grow. Similarly, supervisees are assumed to have the ability and motivation to learn. Advice and direction are minimal. Supervisors must avoid asking questions and instead use reflective comments to draw out supervisees (Patterson, 1997), allowing the supervisees to confront their deficits in their own time frame. Supervisees maintain responsibility for the supervision process, selecting the cases and taped materials to be considered and raising the questions and problems they deem relevant. Although Patterson (1983) recognized that evaluation is the responsibility of the supervisor, he recommended that supervisors "avoid an evaluative attitude during the course of the practicum, reserving it for the end of the period" (p. 23). He also noted that this final opportunity for providing evaluative feedback is often unnecessary, "since [supervisees] are aware of their level of achievement" (1983, p. 23).

Like client-centered psychotherapy, supervisee-centered supervision is nondirective. Freeman (1993a) underscored the value of this nondirective approach:

> We want counselors to recognize that responsibility for monitoring is a self-responsibility. Counselors who are at the point of internship should be providing the same standards for care that professionals provide . . . we can expect that trainees are able to be responsible for themselves ethically and, thus, to raise potential ethical problems." (p. 214)

Freeman rejected the need for developmental models: "A supervisor who is empathic will respond to the individual needs of the counseling student at that moment without requiring a set of artificial boundaries such as stages to instruct a response" (1993a, p. 214).

ETHICAL CONSIDERATIONS IN PERSON-CENTERED SUPERVISION

Patterson's (1983, 1997) person-centered model of supervision has been criticized on several points, primarily related to one of its cornerstone concepts: a nondirective approach. More specifically, Bernard (1992) and Davenport (1992) have argued that supervisees do not receive adequate direction. These critics point out that supervisors are charged with significant ethical responsibilities for both their own professional behavior and that of their supervisees. Supervisors must ensure, for example, that supervisees practice within their areas of competency, understand confidentiality standards and statutes, meet mandatory reporting obligations, obtain informed consent before providing clinical services, and establish and maintain appropriate boundaries with their clients. Davenport (1992) has argued that Patterson's approach does not afford supervisors access to enough information and control to execute these responsibilities.

Trainees, particularly those who are novices, are likely to need more monitoring and direction than Patterson's (1983) person-centered approach affords. The same is true for professionals whose supervision is required by their licensing boards as part of a disciplinary action. Such supervision generally is initiated with the primary objectives of rehabilitation of the professional and protection of the public. Effectively meeting these objectives requires greater vigilance and involvement by the supervisor. Further, supervisors' liability for the actions of supervisees requires that they (supervisors) rely on more than supervisees' self-reports to ensure that they are practicing ethically and effectively (Davenport, 1992).

The following case illustrates risks associated with a person-centered approach.

Supervisee-Centered Supervision Case: I Just Want to Help

The supervisee, Dr. Amador, recently completed her doctorate in clinical psychology and is accruing supervised hours toward licensure. As a Christian, she is committed to helping disenfranchised people who otherwise would not have access to psychological services. Her internship in a college career counseling center has left her with a desire for closer connections with more needy clients, so she is grateful to have found employment in a setting offering in-home psychotherapy. She shares her supervisor Dr. Jackson's client-centered orientation and is eager to demonstrate respect and positive regard for those whose difficulties do not always allow them to experience these qualities in others. Dr. Jackson has expressed confidence in her ability to know when she needs his input, and Dr. Amador appreciates his respect for her.

One of Dr. Amador's first clients is a rural family struggling with poverty, alcoholism, and children with academic and emotional problems. Her heart goes out to the mother, but she has more difficulty empathizing with the father, who does little to help with household chores or child care and who seems to resent Dr. Amador's presence. The four children are emotionally needy, but the mother has little time or energy for them.

Reflecting on A. H. Maslow's (1998) hierarchy of needs, Dr. Amador concludes that this family's ability to benefit from psychotherapy cannot be realized when more basic needs are unmet. To ensure that her treatment is client centered, Dr. Amador asks the mother how she can be most helpful to the family. The mother identifies a list of practical problems with which she needs assistance. Dr. Amador attempts to help by doing laundry, feeding the baby, and showing the mother how to clean the house. She encourages the mother to pursue a dental assistant training program, and because she cannot afford books, Dr. Amador lends her $150 to buy them. When the husband objects to his wife pursuing further education, Dr. Amador helps her conceal her schooling by providing psychotherapy for the children when the mother is in class.

Dr. Amador knows that her supervisor trusts her judgment, but she is not confident he shares her commitment to go the extra mile with people in need, so she tells him only that the case is going well. He is surprised when the husband, on discovering his wife's secret, schedules an appointment with the supervisor to express his outrage.

Supervisee-Centered Case Discussion

Lacking a method for tracking Dr. Amador's cases, Dr. Jackson risked being blindsided by her errors in judgment. Reliance on supervisees' ability to discern what they need to discuss in supervision is not necessarily enough to meet supervisory obligations. Particularly, but not exclusively, novice clinicians may have blind spots rendering them unable to determine exactly which elements of a case should be reviewed. Possible naiveté, along with Dr. Amador's reluctance to share this case in supervision, resulted in misapplications of client-centered theory.

If Dr. Jackson had had a method for monitoring cases or if he had provided Dr. Amador with clear guidance about the types of cases and circumstances that should trigger a case presentation, he might have avoided or at least minimized the clinical and ethical pitfalls encountered in this case. For example, Dr. Jackson might have discussed with his supervisee each decision point in the treatment in terms of its possible risks and benefits. Dr. Amador might then have reached different conclusions about how to proceed in a way that would have addressed her clients' needs within the parameters of counseling services. An exploration of complementary resources might have helped the family meet its other needs as well as benefited the developing clinician.

Allowing the supervisee to explore and perhaps diffuse her own feelings about the client and her difficult circumstances, as suggested by Rogers (Freeman, 1993b), would have afforded the supervisor access to potentially problematic endeavors as they were unfolding. It might also be argued that such a scenario is unlikely, given that graduate students typically take an ethics course and generally would be unlikely to engage in such behavior. Knowing that some multiple relationships are unethical (American Psychological Association [APA], 2002, Standard 3.05, Multiple Relationships) and understanding the applications of the standard in real-life cases, however, are not the same thing. Application of the standard is a skill developed through clinical experience coupled with careful guidance and supervision. Freeman's (1993a) assertion that interns can be expected to function as well as professionals is questionable.

BEHAVIORAL SUPERVISION

Some publications on behavioral supervision have described it in terms of learning theory (Boyd, 1978; Delany, 1972; Jakubowski-Spector, Dustin, & George, 1971; Levine & Tilker, 1974; Milne & James, 2000; Muesser & Liberman, 1995). Although supervision in the context of this model is not a primary source of experiential learning or personal growth (Bradley & Gould, 2001), developing a working alliance (Follette & Callighan, 1995) and an atmosphere of trust (Rosenbaum & Ronen, 1998) are fundamental components of behavioral supervision.

The goal of behavioral supervision is to teach supervisees the skills needed to conduct behavior therapy and to help them "to extinguish inappropriate counseling behaviors" (Bradley & Gould, 2001, p. 157). Given this goal, Bradley and Gould outlined a five-step sequence for behavioral supervisors. Supervisors are first to establish a supervisory relationship, and then conduct a skill analysis and assessment. On the basis of the outcome of these measures, supervisors execute the third step: establishing goals and objectives. The fourth step includes constructing strategies to accomplish these goals. Finally, plans for implementing them are designed. The strategies applied typically parallel those used in behavior therapy.

An apprenticeship model is characteristic of this approach. Related techniques include didactic instruction, modeling, homework (e.g., assigned readings), reinforcement of desired counseling behaviors, and role-playing (Bradley & Gould, 2001; Rosenbaum & Ronan, 1998). Throughout the process, assessment is used to identify specific deficits along with complementary strategies for ameliorating them. Self-monitoring is another technique used in both behavior therapy and supervision (Mahoney, 1991). Evaluation and follow-up, cornerstones of behavior therapy and supervision, are included to ensure that problems have been addressed.

Boyd (1978) identified four tenets or "propositions" of behavioral supervision:

1. Proficient performance is a function of learned skills and not personality fit.
2. The therapist's role consists of identifiable tasks, each requiring specific skills.
3. Skills are definable and responsible to learning theory.
4. Supervisors should employ learning theory in their procedures. (p. 89)

Boyd's (1978) propositions suggest that supervision, like psychotherapy, involves a set of skills that can be learned using basic behavioral principles.

In contrast to person-centered supervisors, behavioral supervisors maintain an active, directive role with supervisees.

ETHICAL CONSIDERATIONS IN BEHAVIORAL SUPERVISION

The primary emphasis of behavioral supervision is on helping supervisees learn techniques and develop skills in their application. Certainly behavioral supervisors, like other psychotherapy supervisors, are not oblivious to interpersonal dynamics in these relationships; as mentioned, a working alliance is considered an important component (Follette & Callaghan, 1995). Yet the primary emphasis on skill acquisition introduces the risk that supervisors may overlook important interpersonal dynamics in both the supervisory and psychotherapy relationships that may portend ethical difficulties. The following case is an example.

Behavioral Supervision Case: I Don't Do Transference!

Carl, a psychology intern at the Behavioral Health Clinic, requests help with a case involving Ann, who presents with anxiety about public speaking. The supervisor, Dr. Swanson, helps Carl to identify target behaviors, therapeutic goals, and strategies the client might use to manage her anxiety. Carl and Dr. Swanson also consider the case in light of Carl's professional development and discuss the potential opportunities for practicing his skills in behavior therapy.

As part of her treatment, Ann is assigned to chart her progress using an online form and to e-mail these records to Carl each week in advance of their sessions. In addition to completing the forms, Ann starts to include commentary regarding her feelings about the treatment. Although her remarks are initially expressions of gratitude for Carl's assistance, which he greatly appreciates, they increasingly focus on Carl himself. Feeling uncomfortable, Dr. Swanson concurs with Carl's inclination to avoid reinforcing the expression of personal feelings by focusing exclusively on the records.

Contrary to Carl's theoretical predictions, his decision not to directly address Ann's communications seems to exacerbate rather than defuse her feelings. Most recently, Ann writes,

> I don't believe anyone has ever shown so much interest in me as you have during our time together. I sense that you too recognize the special connection that is developing between us. Now that my symptoms have improved so much, thanks to you, I hope we will be able to get to know each other even better. Can't wait to see you on Tuesday.—A

Carl, who prides himself in his commitment to ethical behavior, is alarmed to receive this communication. His anxiety prompts him to wonder why he left his previous career in actuarial science. Dr. Swanson agrees with Carl's assessment that he is no longer the best person to work with Ann. Greatly relieved, Carl immediately sends a termination letter stating: "Because of your recent comments, I can no longer work with you. The following are the names of three psychologists who may be able to help you. Good luck." In his haste to wrap up this unhappy chapter in his training, Carl mails the letter without reviewing it with Dr. Swanson. Dr. Swanson, for her part, is content to know the treatment is terminated and does not ask for details.

Throughout the next few weeks, Ann leaves Carl a series of remorseful, apologetic messages, begging him to reconsider. This plaintive tone gives way to anger as the messages continue. Carl considers that he is no longer Ann's therapist, and he certainly does not want to reinforce this inappropriate behavior. Therefore, Carl does not return her calls and, in fact, begins erasing them without listening. Finally, the calling behavior is successfully extinguished.

About 2 months later, however, Dr. Swanson receives a letter from the state Board of Psychology. It includes notification that a complaint had been filed against her, as a supervisor, for her supervisee's abandonment of a client. A subpoena for treatment records is enclosed.

Behavioral Supervision Case Discussion

Undoubtedly, most behavioral supervisors would have recognized that this situation called for a more direct intervention than just "not reinforcing the behavior," and they would likely have coached the supervisee to address it. Behavioral supervisory techniques, such as role-playing, didactic instruction about establishing clear boundaries, and the assignment of relevant reading, could have been used to help Carl respond effectively and sensitively to Ann's feelings while continuing the treatment. Or, Dr. Swanson and/or Carl could have determined that his objectivity was too compromised to continue. It is also possible that in spite of Carl's attempts to clarify boundaries and diffuse Ann's feelings, she might have continued to be too distracted by them to benefit from the treatment. In either case, Dr. Swanson could have used the opportunity to teach Carl about effectively and sensitively executing an appropriate termination.

Clearly, behavioral supervisors overseeing behavior therapy can remain true to their principles while accurately identifying and effectively managing interpersonal dynamics that sometimes arise in either the treatment or the supervisory relationship. Yet, behavior theory does not specifically offer a mechanism for addressing these challenges, and behavioral supervisors must find ways to extrapolate and to creatively apply their skills to ethically manage them.

COGNITIVE–BEHAVIORAL SUPERVISION

Many of the concepts and strategies underlying behavioral supervision are evident in cognitive–behavioral therapy (CBT) supervision (Perris, 1994). Further, techniques used in CBT are also used in supervision. Examples include setting and prioritizing the agenda, structuring sessions, assigning homework, and applying standard techniques such as role-playing (Beck, Sarnat, & Barenstein, 2008).

CBT supervision also emphasizes the identification of the supervisee's pertinent thoughts and beliefs (Beck et al., 2008; Schmidt, 1979). The CBT model suggests that emotive responses are triggered by self-statements or thoughts and that negative emotions can be altered by changing these thoughts (Schmidt, 1979). Some self-statements are likely to fuel anxiety and insecurity and might impede the supervisee's effectiveness (e.g., "I'm incompetent and will hurt my client"). According to this model, other more realistic cognitions enhance learning and help supervisees develop confidence commensurate with their skills. An important part of the supervisor's role, then, is to be alert to statements that reveal erroneous assumptions and beliefs that impede learning. Supervisors can then assist supervisees in self-monitoring and correcting these beliefs using a cognitive-restructuring format (Schmidt, 1979).

Schmidt (1979) listed examples of erroneous beliefs that novice therapists commonly hold:

- "I must show the supervisor how perfect I am at therapy."
- "I must make the right decision or something terrible will happen."
- "I must love doing therapy to be a good therapist." (p. 280)

Schmidt described a clear refutation for each of these beliefs that, presumably, supervisors could share with supervisees.

Schmidt stated that the primary goal of cognitive-behavioral supervision is "to produce a clinician who can respond in a relatively anxiety-free way, who can . . . develop hypotheses about the nature of the client's problematic cognitions, emotions, and behaviors, and who can help choose and test appropriate techniques to change them" (1979, p. 278). Rosenbaum and Ronen (1998) identified two more specific goals of CBT supervision: "to help therapists adopt the philosophy of CBT as the basic approach for changing clients' cognitions, emotions, and behaviors," and "to teach therapists specific techniques" (p. 221). Liese and Beck (1997) emphasized listening to recorded sessions to circumvent the problem of supervisees not always being able to identify and report problems.

ETHICAL CONSIDERATIONS IN COGNITIVE–BEHAVIORAL THERAPY SUPERVISION

The similarities between the techniques of cognitive–behavioral treatment and supervision are significant (Beck et al., 2008). One distinction is that CBT supervisors, unlike therapists, have responsibility for two individuals; they are charged with examining the relevant cognitions of supervisees as well as helping them to identify and analyze the cognitions of their clients (Liese & Alford, 1998). The primary focus in supervision is on the cognitions related to the supervisee's work performance. Part of the goal is to demonstrate how CBT techniques are applied, and part is to decrease anxiety and other negative emotions that contribute to a negative self-concept and thereby compromise work performance. Professional self-concept is not unrelated to personal self-concept, however, and isolating it is both difficult and not always desirable. When supervisors address these work-related personal issues, they introduce the risk of blurring the boundary between supervision and psychotherapy, potentially creating confusion for supervisees about the nature of expectations appropriate to the relationship. Of course, such confusion is not inevitable, but awareness and caution are important and can enable supervisors to be vigilant about clarifying boundaries in a timely and effective manner.

A second ethical challenge for CBT supervisors is similar to that described previously regarding behavioral supervisors: problematic interpersonal dynamics that could go unnoticed in the context of supervision. As discussed, CBT and behavioral supervisors are certainly trained in the importance of establishing a working alliance or relationship (Beck et al., 2008; Follette & Callaghan, 1995). Because the supervisory relationship itself is not a *primary* focus, however, problematic dynamics may be unseen, misunderstood, or deliberately go unaddressed. The previous example illustrated the problems that can develop when interpersonal issues develop in the therapeutic relationship, a potential ethical challenge that could occur in the context of CBT supervision as well. The following case illustrates how transference and countertransference dynamics might go unaddressed in the supervision.

Cognitive–Behavioral Supervision Case: I Want to Be Like You

Dr. Parker recently began supervising practicum students through a women's center where she has worked as a psychotherapist for 15 years. She is pleased to be assigned to supervise Rosa, a 22-year-old master's student in counseling with a concentration in women's studies. As a feminist, Dr. Parker enjoys helping young women with their careers, particularly when they share her commitment to helping other women. She is interested in learning about other cultures and so is especially excited to learn that Rosa is Mexican American and bilingual.

From the start, Dr. Parker recognizes Rosa as bright, energetic, and highly skilled. Early in the supervision, she learns about Rosa's experience as a political activist working on behalf of women's rights. When Rosa comes out to her as lesbian, Dr. Parker is honored to be trusted and expresses admiration for Rosa's courage and commitment to women. Dr. Parker, a Caucasian, heterosexual, married mother of three sons, has had only minimal contact with lesbian women and is excited to have the opportunity to get to know Rosa. For her part, Rosa is happy to have a supervisor who appreciates her but is a bit taken aback by Dr. Parker's enthusiasm.

About 4 months into the supervision, Rosa presents a case involving Dee, a 33-year-old mother who is separated from her husband, whom she describes as emotionally and physically abusive. Rosa reports that the therapy is going very well. Dee had been depressed but is responding very well to strategies to modify the negative cognitions that have fueled her sadness and kept her feeling stuck. Dee follows through with all homework assignments and seems to feel empowered by her success. Unfortunately, as soon as Dee's divorce is final, she will lose her insurance benefits and will be unable to afford to continue. Rosa tells Dr. Parker that she is very concerned about the possible negative repercussions of terminating Dee's treatment at such a crucial time in her life and wants to find some way to continue.

Dee's primary hobby is charcoal drawing, and she loves to draw pictures of women from many different cultures doing various kinds of work. She shows Rosa samples of her work, and Rosa is very impressed. Rosa asks Dr. Parker what she thinks of her idea to suggest that Dee bring a drawing each month to pay for her therapy. The drawings would reflect the center's commitment to welcoming and providing multicultural services to women and could replace the yellowed, torn posters that currently cover the walls of the waiting room. More important, Rosa adds, the proposal will go a long way toward reinforcing Dee's fledgling self-concept.

Dr. Parker hesitates briefly as she starts to wonder about the possible complications of such an arrangement, but then she doesn't want to crush Rosa's enthusiasm. She also is determined to be sensitive and respectful of Rosa's cultural background and so is reluctant to be critical. Dr. Parker also considers how difficult it is for women to leave destructive relationships, and she certainly doesn't want to be seen as part of what sometimes feels like a conspiracy against women. With all that in mind, she congratulates Rosa for her creativity, innovation, and commitment to going the extra mile to help a woman in need, and she encourages her to give it a try.

Cognitive–Behavioral Supervision Case Discussion

In this case, Dr. Parker's idealization of the supervisee as a lesbian and a Mexican American created an ethical blind spot. Dr. Parker's naive desire to be sensitive and respectful was not born of true multicultural sensitivity but more likely of a desire to be liked and perceived as well informed. Although obviously well intentioned, Dr. Parker missed an opportunity to help Rosa explore the possible risks, benefits, and alternatives to her proposal, a process that would likely have served her well in her future career. What might have been recognized as Dr. Parker's countertransference, or even transference to Rosa, was not on the cognitive–behavioral radar, and her intuition about the potential for a multiple relationship was ignored. Again, such oversight is certainly not endemic to this approach (Liese & Beck, 1997). Yet, a novice supervisor, such as Dr. Parker in this example, may be more focused on learning the primary techniques of CBT supervision and consequently at risk for missing the interpersonal dynamic nuances that arise.

SYSTEMIC SUPERVISION

Supervision has long been an integral part of the training of family systems therapists (Liddle, 1991). Although training institutes had previously formalized standards for the education of supervisors (D. Jacobs, David, & Meyer, 1995), the American Association of Marriage and Family Therapy (AAMFT; formerly American Association for Marriage Counseling) was the first association of mental health or counseling professionals to establish specific qualifications for the Approved Supervisor designation in 1971 (see Todd & Storm, 1997, for a more thorough review of this history). The AAMFT is currently one of the few mental health professional associations that have specific guidelines for the education and training of supervisors (AAMFT, 2007; American Association of Pastoral Counselors [AAPC], 1994; Association of State and Provincial Psychology Boards [ASPPB], 2003; Canadian Psychological Association [CPA], 2009). These guidelines essentially establish what is required to be qualified to assume the role of clinical supervisor. Only two of these organizations, AAMFT and AAPC, explicitly approve supervisors and require that their members obtain supervision from one of these designated individuals.

It is important to note that systemic theories and models of psychotherapy and supervision are not the exclusive purview of marriage and family therapists. Psychologists, addiction counselors, social workers, and other mental health professionals who offer psychotherapy may have dual licenses or certifications and may incorporate or rely completely on these models. Yet marriage and family therapy is a profession in and of itself, and its professionals have produced much of the literature on the subject.

Note also that within systemic supervision there are different theoretical orientations that share a systemic frame but offer unique perspectives. Several authors have identified these orientations and have extrapolated from them the implications for supervision. Roberto (1997) has elucidated several such approaches that fall under the rubric of "transgenerational models" (p. 156): the natural systems theory (Bowen, 1988; Knudson-Martin, 1994), the symbolic–experiential model (Connell, Mitten, & Whitaker, 1993; Whitaker & Keith, 1981), and the contextual model (Boszormenyi-Nagy, 1976; Boszormenyi-Nagy & Krasner, 1986; Boszormenyi-Nagy & Ulrich, 1981). Morgan and Sprenkle (2007), in an effort to identify common factors in various theoretical approaches, found six distinct models within family systems: Bowenian (Getz & Protinsky, 1994), structural/strategic (Nevels & Maar, 1985), problem focused (Storm & Heath, 1991), solution focused (Wetchler, 1990), narrative (Bob, 1999), and symbolic–experiential (Connell, 1984).

Todd (1997) conceptualized supervision models differently. He provided a comparison of approaches that he termed "purposive systemic supervision models" (p. 173) because they all emphasize "purposive action on the part of the supervisor" (p. 173). More specifically, Todd (1997) suggested that the important differences between these theories of systemic psychotherapy become less significant when applied to supervision. Emphasizing their shared assumptions and implications for supervision, Todd (1997) built on the work of various authors whose theories fall on the structural–strategic continuum (Boscolo, Cecchin, Hoffman, & Penn, 1987; Cecchin, Lane, & Ray, 1993; Haley, 1976, 1980, 1987; Madanes, 1981; Minuchin, 1974; Minuchin & Fishman, 1981; Minuchin, Lee, & Simon, 1996: Pirrotta & Cecchin, 1988; Selvini-Palazzoli, Boscolo, Cecchoin, & Prata, 1980; Tomm, 1987a, 1987b, 1988). Conceptualizing the task slightly differently, McDaniel, Weber, and McKeever (1983) reviewed four schools of systemic family therapy (strategic, Bowenian, structural, and experiential) and discussed the theoretical implications of each for supervision.

Clearly, there have been many attempts to analyze the similarities and differences between various systemic approaches to psychotherapy and supervision. Systemic approaches are considered together in terms of their common elements for the purpose of examining their ethical dimensions and related implications for supervisors.

Models of family systems therapy tend to be "active, directive, and collaborative" (Liddle, Becker, & Diamond, 1997, p. 413), and the corresponding supervision reflects these characteristics. Further, these models emphasize present interactions; pragmatic, simple, goal-directed interventions; observable goals; positive reframing valued over insight; and a focus on the strengths of both clients and supervisees (Stanton, 1981; Todd, 1997). Systemic models further share their recognition of the importance of the contexts of the client-family, supervisee-therapist, and the supervisor (J. J. Montgomery, Hendricks, & Bradley, 2001; White & Russell, 1995).

Systemic supervision, like its psychotherapeutic counterpart, includes a focus on relationships between members of the client-family, between the client-family and the therapist-supervisee, and between the therapist-supervisee and the supervisor. The structures that characterize each relationship have corresponding or parallel structures in the other relationships. Such structures have been described as "isomorphic" (Haley, 1976; Liddle, Breunlin, Schwartz, & Constantine, 1984; Liddle & Saba, 1982) or as representing a "parallel process" (Holloway, 1995; Kadushin & Harkness, 2002), a concept rooted in psychodynamic theory (described subsequently). In other words, dynamics or structures present within a client-family may be replicated in their relationship with the therapist, and a similar, corresponding structure may develop in the supervisory relationship.

One of the most notable strengths of systemic approaches, in terms of their reflection of ethical standards, is their focus on context. A cornerstone of systemic theories is an appreciation for the impact and relevance of context for clients, supervisees, and supervisors. In fact, proponents of systemic models often specifically take into account institutional and cultural contexts as well as the family and psychotherapy contexts that are their primary focus (Monk, Winslade, Crocket, & Epston, 1997; Wheeler et al., 1986). This integral emphasis on context provides a natural vehicle for understanding and addressing race, ethnicity, culture, gender, sexual orientation (AAMFT, 2001; AAPC, 1994; American Counseling Association, ACA, 2005; APA, 2002; CPA, 2000, 2009; Constantine, 2001; Constantine, Fuertes, Roysircar, & Kindaichi, 2008; Estrada, 2005; Hays, 2008; Hernandez, 2008; Miville, Rosa, & Constantine, 2005; National Association of Social Workers [NASW], 2005, 2008), and other factors that characterize and influence all members of the system in significant ways (Burkhard et al., 2006; Fukuyama, 1994; Gatmon et al., 2001; Leong, 1994; Ryan & Hendricks, 1989).

The importance of considering these contextual factors in supervision has been well documented (Cashwell, Looby, & Housley, 1997; Constantine, Warren, & Miville, 2005; Cook & Helms, 1988; Jordan, 1998; Ladany, Brittan-Powell, & Pannu, 1997; Tummala-Narra, 2004). Supervisees, particularly those who identify as members of a racial and ethnic minority, benefit from such consideration both in terms of their satisfaction with the supervisory relationship (Cook & Helms, 1988; Fukuyama, 1994; D. Hilton, Russell, & Salmi, 1995) and in their (self-assessed) competence in providing multicultural counseling and psychotherapy (Ladany et al., 1997; Ladany, Inman, Constantine, & Hofheinz, 1997; Pope-Davis, Reynolds, Dings, & Nielson, 1995; Pope-Davis, Reynolds, Dings, & Ottavi, 1994)

Perhaps the most fundamental tenet of systemic approaches in general is the assumption that understanding the system in which individuals exists is a prerequisite for understanding them and for facilitating desired change. This general assumption is shared by those who advocate for a multicultural perspective in counseling, psychotherapy, and supervision (Constantine et al., 2005; Gloria, Hird, & Tao, 2008; Kadushin & Harkness, 2002) and is reflected throughout the APA "Guidelines for Providers of Psychological Services to Ethnic, Linguistic, and Culturally Diverse Populations," (APA, 1993). Similarly, supervision specialty guidelines and ethics codes promulgated by AAMFT (2007), ASPPB (2003), and the Center for Credentialing & Education (CCE; 2008) all underscore the importance of considering cultural context in supervision.

Many of the concepts and methods used by supervisors with varying orientations are rooted in systemic theories of treatment and supervision. The following discussion of systemic supervision methods is not intended to be comprehensive but rather to provide a sampling of those techniques embedded with more salient ethical dimensions and implications for supervisors. Three such methods will be considered: required supervisee self-disclosure, strategic interventions, and live supervision.

Required Supervisee Self-Disclosure: Genograms and Autobiographies

Systemic approaches include recognition that supervisees, like client-families, "are influenced by features of their internal and external context—their own histories and goals, work and family environment, legal or instructional requirements for supervision hours, and the structure of the supervision relationship itself" (Montgomery et al., 2001, p. 306). Supervisees' own family of origin dynamics and cultural backgrounds, then, will likely influence their perceptions, attitudes, biases, and interactions with clients, and learning more about them is an important part of their training (Emerson, 1995; Montgomery et al., 2001; Roberto, 1997; V. Thomas & Striegel, 1994). Ideally, supervisory interventions that involve self-examination and disclosure will result in benefits for supervisees, including improved mental health, increased effectiveness in relationships, and greater empathy for the experiences of their clients when they use these techniques (Montgomery et al., 2001).

The completion of a family genogram (Bowen, 1978, 1980) is one systemic therapy technique that has been advocated for use in supervision as a strategy for assisting supervisees in exploring their own family histories. A *genogram* is essentially a family tree typically depicting three generations and including information about family members and their relationships with one another (McGoldrick & Gerson, 1985). According to Bowen (1978), whose work formed the foundation for the technique, family relational patterns are transmitted across generations. Requiring supervisees to write family autobiographies is another strategy for compiling and analyzing such potentially relevant historical information.

There are multiple objectives for assigning genograms and autobiographies. Clear benefits can be derived from the experience of completing a task that supervisees are likely to assign to their own clients. Such benefits include the development of increased empathy for the practical and emotional challenges, greater understanding of the potential benefits, and increased credibility when explaining the assignment to clients. Having completed the assignment themselves may also increase supervisees' effectiveness in their clinical use of the technique.

Supervisors' effectiveness can also be enhanced by knowledge of supervisees' backgrounds and unique dynamics. Such information may help them recognize ways in which the dynamics of client-families might be interacting with those of their supervisees. Supervisors can also use supervisees' genograms as a teaching tool, providing a model for use with their clients. When genograms are presented in a supervision group, learning opportunities are enhanced. Group members benefit from hearing the stories of colleagues and practicing the application of systemic principles to conceptualize generational patterns, dynamics, and interaction patterns.

Strategic Interventions

Strategic interventions evolved from the work of Jay Haley (1976) and the Mental Research Institute in the 1970s (Boscolo et al., 1987). Restraining clients from engaging in behaviors that might actually be helpful and prescribing an exacerbation of problematic symptoms are two examples of strategic or paradoxical techniques designed with the goal of having the opposite impact, thereby creating the desired effect (Haley, 1976; Todd, 1981).

Although controversial, strategic techniques developed for use in treatment have been used in supervision as well (Masters, 1992; Protinsky & Preli, 1987; Sexton, Montgomery, Goff, & Nugent, 1993; Storm & Heath, 1982; Todd, 1981). As is the case in treatment, such interventions circumvent the awareness and insight of the supervisee-recipient (Bernard & Goodyear, 2009). Todd provided an example of "warning the supervisee of the dangers of changing too fast" (1997, p. 181) when in fact the client does not seem to be progressing. Insight is not considered a requirement for such techniques to be effective, and in fact, they are thought to be most effective if they occur outside of the supervisee's awareness (Protinsky & Preli, 1987; Storm & Heath, 1982).

Once the supervisee's behavior has changed in the desired direction, the supervisor can then consider whether to discuss the intervention and its goals with the supervisee, who may then glean insight about the process (Protinsky & Preli, 1987).

Sexton et al. (1993) drew a distinction between paradoxical techniques that are defiance based and those that are more cooperative. Defiance-based techniques involve recommending that a supervisee take a particular action when, in reality, the supervisor prefers that they do the opposite. Thus, the desired response essentially requires the supervisee to violate a supervisory directive, posing a dilemma for the supervisee as well as setting an undesirable precedent. Sexton et al. (1993) recommended avoiding defiance-based interventions in supervision.

Live Supervision

Live supervision, described by Montalvo in his seminal article (1973), has become a hallmark of systemic supervision, particularly associated with structural/strategic approaches (Haley, 1976; Minuchin & Fishman, 1981). Live supervision typically involves a team of psychotherapists or trainees observing treatment sessions through a one-way mirror (Madanes, 1984). This technique allows supervisors and team members (also known as *observing*, *treatment*, or *reflecting* teams; Landis & Young, 1994; Pirrotta & Cecchin, 1988; Prest, Darden, & Keller, 1990; Stycznski & Greenberg, 2008) to observe supervisees' clinical work in real time and to provide suggestions that can be immediately incorporated into their work (Colapinto, 1988; Pirrotta & Cecchin, 1988; Schwartz, Liddle, & Bruenlin, 1988). These suggestions can be delivered to the therapist by telephone with a "bug-in-the-ear" (Ward, 1960) microphone, during midsession consultation breaks, or by live walk-in visits from the supervisor and members of the treatment team (Schroll & Walton, 1991; Storm, 1997; Todd, 1997).

Proponents of live supervision describe its many advantages (Piercy, Sprenkle, & Constantine, 1986; Storm, 1997). Supervisees have opportunities to take risks and experiment with new techniques knowing they have the safety net of a supervisor. They are able to implement suggestions and evaluate their effectiveness immediately with assistance from others who witnessed the work. Other supervisees learn from firsthand observation, "without the pressure of being responsible for therapy and with the luxury of time to assess cases and consider possibilities" (Storm, 1997, p. 285). Supervisors do not have to rely on supervisees' self-reports or choices about which recordings and case material to present. They have the opportunity to demonstrate techniques, intervene directly with clients when necessary, and closely monitor supervisees. Clients may also benefit from the additional clinical wisdom that comes from having a group of trainees and professionals collaborate on their case (Piercy et al., 1986).

Others have argued against the use of live supervision, citing supervisees' lack of autonomy and resulting dependency (Elizur, 1990) and compromises to client privacy (Storm, 1997), Additionally, supervisees' credibility with clients may be undermined if it seems that they lack authority and that their suggestions may be overruled by others. Such supervision is also labor intensive and expensive, which may make it impractical in many settings.

ETHICAL CONSIDERATIONS IN SYSTEMIC SUPERVISION

These three systemic techniques—examination of personal history through required self-disclosure, application of strategic techniques, and the use of live supervision—are each considered in terms of their ethical implications.

Supervisee Self-Disclosure

First, any supervisory technique requiring self-disclosure represents a double-edged ethical sword. On one hand, when supervisees examine and share their personal histories in the context of supervision, they are provided with opportunities for both personal and professional growth (Montgomery et al., 2001), and their competency is enhanced. Supervisees can use the exercise to increase awareness of unresolved personal and family issues, any of which has the potential to become a psychological land mine that could be detonated by clients presenting with similar histories and lead to ethically compromised practice. Further, such insights will, theoretically, help supervisees to differentiate their own issues from those of their clients, thus decreasing emotional reactivity and increasing objectivity and effectiveness (Braverman, 1997; Kramer, 1985). Insight alone does not guarantee immunity from problems created by a lack of self-awareness, but it does create the possibility that the supervisee will recognize such problems when they occur and seek whatever assistance is necessary to make adjustments and corrections. Unexamined, these issues have the potential to compromise, if not impair, clinical objectivity and effectiveness.

On the other hand, requiring supervisees to engage in such personal introspection and to then share autobiographical material with supervisors and/or fellow trainees in the context of group supervision may represent an invasion into their privacy. Failure to obtain the supervisees' informed consent to participation in training with clear awareness of all requirements represents another ethical problem. Section 7.4 of the *AAMFT Code of Ethics* (2001) states, "Marriage and family therapists represent facts truthfully to clients, third-party payors, and *supervisees* [italics added] regarding services rendered" (p. 8). Similarly, other ethics codes and supervisory guidelines require or recommend that students and trainees be clearly informed about any requirements for participation in personal development activities, including those that involve personal growth and require self-disclosure, in advance of their participation in the academic program or supervision (AAMFT, 2001; ACA, 2005; ACES, 1993; APA, 2002). APA is particularly clear in Standard 7.04 (Student Disclosure of Personal Information):

> Psychologists do not require students or supervisees to disclose personal information in course- or program-related activities, either orally or in writing, regarding sexual history, history of abuse and neglect, psychological treatment, and relationships with parents, peers, and spouses or significant others except if (1) the program or training facility has clearly identified this requirement in its admissions and program materials or (2) the information is necessary to evaluate or obtain assistance for students whose personal problems could reasonably be judged to be preventing them from performing . . . in a competent manner. (2002, pp. 9–10)

Introducing such personal information into the supervision creates the potential for dual or multiple relationships between supervisors and supervisees. Supervisors are at risk for responding to supervisees as a therapist might, encouraging the therapeutic exploration, rather than just identification and examination of personal problems in terms of their relevance to clinical work (Taibbi, 1993). Supervisees' vulnerability is increased, and they may become confused about the nature of the relationship. Further, transgressing the boundary between therapy and supervision creates a poor role model for supervisees trying to learn to clarify their boundaries (e.g., personal and professional) with their clients.

Montgomery et al. (2001) recognized the potential for such problems and advised that supervisors be careful "to sidestep the dangers while capturing the benefits of using family-of-origin assignments for supervisees" (p. 310). Goodman and Carpenter-White (1996) offered specific suggestions for minimizing risks. They recommended that assignments requiring self-disclosure be voluntary, information shared not be used in evaluations, and that identifying information about supervisees' family members be disguised to minimize privacy intrusions.

Although these suggestions address some of the major problems inherent in assignments requiring self-disclosure, their application may be more difficult. If, in the process of discussing a supervisee's family history and experiences, the supervisor becomes aware of serious mental health problems that might affect supervisees' ability to function professionally, he or she will be faced with a dilemma about whether and how to use this information (Taibbi, 1993). Weighing the potential risk to clients against the welfare of supervisees, a supervisor must guard client welfare as primary (ACES, 1993). Yet, supervisees in this situation are likely to feel betrayed if they perceive that their disclosures—made in the spirit of trying to comply with supervisors' requirements or invitations—are being used against them. Particularly when these risks are not described as part of the informed consent (J. T. Thomas, 2007), the supervisor may have legal exposure for damages to the supervisee's career (Falvey, 2002; Guest & Dooley, 1999).

Strategic Techniques in Supervision

Strategic supervisory interventions have been challenged because of their manipulative dimensions operating outside of the awareness of the supervisee. Any informed consent to supervision in which such techniques will be used should minimally inform supervisees that there may be times when the supervisor will intervene in ways that are not apparent to them. It may be argued that doing this, however, would undermine or eliminate the effectiveness of the intervention.

Another ethical challenge involves maintaining the boundary between supervision and treatment. As is the case in any psychotherapy-based model, using techniques in supervision that were developed and studied primarily for use in treatment creates an ethical challenge. Finally, such techniques are quite powerful, and supervisors must have the appropriate training and supervised experience needed to demonstrate competence in using them (Protinsky, 1997).

Ethics of Live Supervision

Live supervision is one technique that may enhance supervisors' ability to discharge their ethical responsibilities. This kind of supervision can be accomplished through cotherapy or by direct observation. As discussed, observing supervisees with clients in real time allows for close monitoring of client welfare. Any supervisee behavior that puts clients at risk for harm can be readily identified and addressed by a supervisor in a timely manner. It also could be argued that the quality of supervisees' clinical work will be enhanced by the "midcourse corrections" (Liddle et al., 1997, p. 401), by the input of the more experienced supervisor, and through the collective wisdom of treatment teams. Direct observation also ensures that supervisors' understanding of what is occurring in the treatment is not diluted or filtered by supervisees' bias, naiveté, undeveloped ability to discern what should be presented, or their desire to create a favorable impression. Supervisees have the security that comes from feeling supported and knowing that they are part of a team.

Some of the advantages to live supervision, however, also have corresponding ethical disadvantages. The security for supervisees and protections for clients associated with close monitoring may come at the expense of opportunities for supervisees to develop independence, autonomy, and confidence. What represents an advantage early in supervisees' development may become a limitation as they gain experience. A supervisor who tends to be anxious or controlling, for example, may be at risk for conducting remote control treatment, depriving supervisees of opportunities to experiment, take measured risks, make mistakes, and develop their own styles. Of course, this limitation is not inevitable. Supervisors observing live sessions could elect to hold back and not intervene at times to allow supervisees such opportunities, but the risk of over control is arguably more likely with live observation.

The compromises to client privacy represent another ethical challenge associated with supervising family systems therapists using treatment teams, direct observation, and real-time interventions during treatment sessions. More traditional formats and techniques for supervision, such as creating and reviewing audio or video recordings, allow supervisee-therapists to protect their clients' identities in the context of group supervision. The supervisor may be the only individual, other than the treating therapist, to have access to identifying information about the supervisee's clients. Consultation with other students, trainees, and staff can be accomplished without disclosing clients' names. Because these individuals do not carry the same level of responsibility for clients as supervisors do, consultants do not need to have identifying information to provide input into the case. Conversely, teams of students and colleagues who observe sessions can readily identify clients and are privy to significant identifying information. Trainees still learning their ethical responsibilities may arguably be at greater risk for inadvertently breaching confidentiality.

Most professional ethics codes require that when direct observation by supervisors and/or teams is used, clients' informed consent to treatment be obtained with their full knowledge and understanding of the risks and benefits (AAMFT, 2001; AAPC, 1994; ACA, 2005; APA, 2002; CPA, 2000; National Association of Alcohol and Drug Abuse Counselors, 2008; NASW, 2005; 2008). Anticipating all of the possible repercussions is challenging for professionals, and it is doubtful that most clients will be able to truly understand what it is they are consenting to at the time. Supervisees should therefore be trained in the mechanics as well as the nuances of discussing these issues with their clients.

In summary, systemic supervision offers clinical advantages and disadvantages as well as potential benefits and ethical risks for supervisees and client families. Awareness of pitfalls allows systemic supervisors the opportunity to take steps to minimize these risks while capturing the benefits afforded by this approach.

Competence in providing systemic psychotherapy and supervision is critical (Kaslow, Celano, & Stanton, 2005), particularly when relatively high-risk techniques are used. As discussed, examination of supervisees' family of origin dynamics, use of strategic interventions with supervisees, and live supervision carry with them ethical risks, including those associated with multiple relationships, potentially compromised objectivity and effectiveness, inadequate competence resulting in the misapplication of techniques, and violations of privacy (AAMFT, 2001; AAPC, 1994; ACA, 2005; American Psychiatric Association, 2009, APA, 2002; CPA, 2000, 2009; NASW, 2005, 2008).

Systemic Supervision Case: Too Much Information

Dr. Hayes provides individual and group supervision to both masters and doctoral practicum students at the Center for Family Therapy. Her students work with individuals; couples; children; and when possible, their families.

In the fall of each academic year as the new students begin their training, Dr. Hayes requires them to complete a family genogram and to share at least parts of that with the supervision group. Historically, students have reported great benefits from having the opportunity to learn more about themselves and about a technique they will be using with clients.

One of her students, a 25-year-old Caucasian man named Tom, presents his general findings to the group, Tom discloses that there were several members of his extended family who experienced sexual abuse by other family members. He mentions to Dr. Hayes individually that he himself had lost a babysitting job after the two preschool children reported to their parents that he had touched them sexually. Tom says his parents were notified and that they firmly insisted he not repeat that behavior but were also very understanding of his "error in judgment." Tom indicates that he learned a great deal from this unfortunate experience and feels he is in a good position to help others who make the same mistake as he made 8 years earlier. He adds that working with sexually abused children will allow him to make restitution for his errors.

As they end the supervision session, Dr. Hayes commends him on his insight and openness, but as the day goes on, she begins to feel anxious, wondering whether there is a safety issue given that he is working with young children.

Systemic Supervision Case Discussion

Dr. Hayes's use of the genogram as a teaching tool solicited information that she was not prepared to manage. She is now facing a set of ethical dilemmas. Some of the questions she must consider include the following:

- What factors may have contributed to Tom's abuse of these children? Are these factors still operating or have they been ameliorated?
- Should she inquire further about the details of this incident, or would that be an invasion of Tom's privacy? Was the abuse reported to police and adjudicated?
- Does Tom pose a threat to the safety of the children with whom he will be working?
- If she does inquire further, what will she be looking for? Might she be at risk for sliding into the role of evaluator of his risk potential?
- Is making such inquiries consistent with her role as supervisor? Is she competent to conduct such a risk assessment?
- What will she do with whatever information she obtains? If the situation seems benign and she takes no further action, what is her legal liability if Tom does abuse a child?
- Do the policies governing the practicum program alert students (informed consent) that they may be required to disclose personal information?
- Should she notify the graduate program? What if Tom objects, noting that she never told him she would disclose information he shared without his authorization?

Clearly, issues related to informed consent, confidentiality, competence, and legal liability are all embedded in this ethically challenging situation. It might be argued that there are advantages to encouraging supervisees to share such information. Knowing about the personal problems of supervisees could be helpful to supervisors who are legitimately concerned with the welfare of clients. In this case, Dr. Hayes could, minimally, be particularly alert to signs of inappropriate boundaries between Tom and his child-clients. Indications of trouble could be addressed swiftly and directly, which could be helpful to Tom and could help Dr. Hayes to more effectively protect the safety of Tom's clients.

Although laudable goals, alternative means for reaching them are preferable. Directly asking on an application about violations of particular laws or ethical standards thought to be related to fitness would be clearer, but it is likely that most would not report this history in this context.

Further, before soliciting such information, those requesting it should be very clear about what they will do with it. A legal consultation would also be advisable.

If the information disclosed through completion of a genogram might also be used to evaluate fitness for duty, then supervisees should be informed in advance of completing the assignment. Supervisors should be clear that evaluation is part of their objective and thereby assume responsibility, if not liability, for acting appropriately in light of whatever information they obtain. If the information may be shared with the faculty in the student's academic program, this too should be clarified (see Chapter 6, this volume). There is also the risk that in the absence of a clear statement to the contrary, supervisees would inaccurately deduce that revealing such personal information would result in their getting therapeutic help from their supervisors with whatever problems they identify. This confusing boundary not only sets the stage for misunderstanding and potential impasses between supervisor and supervisee but also provides an undesirable role model that may have implications for supervisees' relationships with their clients.

A clear informed consent should address, in general terms, the limits to supervisee's privacy and, more specifically, should clarify the expectations regarding the genogram as well as potential uses of information disclosed. If the objectives of assigning a genogram involve building skills, developing empathy for clients, and gaining self-understanding for the purpose of professional development, then disclosure of highly personal information is not necessary. Students can be coached to compile detailed and thorough information for themselves and perhaps to explore their findings with a psychotherapist. An edited version appropriate for sharing with colleagues can be presented, and supervisees can still achieve the stated objectives. The process of making deliberate decisions about what to disclose to whom, with careful consideration of the goals of doing so and of the nature of the relationships involved, may be valuable in and of itself. Supervisees may learn something about establishing and maintaining appropriate boundaries between personal and professional relationships.

PSYCHOANALYTIC SUPERVISION

Psychoanalysis is a subspecialty for mental health professionals in various fields, including psychiatry, psychology, and social work. Specialization in psychoanalysis requires significant advanced training through an analytic institute. Training in psychodynamic psychotherapy is less intensive and may be obtained through institutes and professional associations as continuing education seminars and workshops.

Traditional analytic training has historically included these primary segments: academic instruction, personal psychoanalysis, and the psychoanalysis of several patients under the supervision of a qualified analytic supervisor (Dewald, 1997; Hyman, 2008; Zaphiropoulos, 1984). As the supervisee progresses, the three segments become integrated with the goal of developing the supervisee's "psychoanalytic instrument," that is, the use of self in clinical work (Dewald, 1997). To that end, the supervisory relationship becomes a primary focus in more contemporary psychoanalytic approaches to supervision (Frawley-O'Dea & Sarnat, 2001). Supervision thereby becomes a model for the teaching of the techniques of psychoanalysis.

Although supervision has long played an integral role in psychoanalytic training and practice, its formality and format have evolved considerably (Hyman, 2008; D. Jacobs et al., 1995; Rock, 1997). As early as 1902, Freud hosted what may have been the first group supervision. He held meetings of the Wednesday Psychological Society in his waiting room, where a small group of analysts consulted about their clinical work (Freud, 1914/1986).

A few years later, Freud conducted what D. Jacobs et al. (1995) have deemed the first documented account of individual psychodynamic supervision, published by Freud in 1909. The well-known case of Little Hans involved Freud's oversight of Max Graf in the treatment of his own son for his phobia of horses. The boy's mother was a patient of Freud, and so his collaboration with this patient's husband would clearly be problematic by today's ethical standards. Nevertheless, the patient reportedly improved, and Freud began what has become an integral part of psychotherapeutic training—clinical supervision (Bernard & Goodyear, 2009; Frawley-O'Dea & Sarnat, 2001). The now ubiquitous belief that psychotherapists in all mental health professions benefit from consultation with colleagues has its roots in psychoanalysis.

Several theoretical approaches to psychoanalysis have developed since Freud's initial work. Many intellectual splits occurred in the early to mid-1900s. Adler, Stekel, Jung, and Rank were some of the early defectors but among those who maintained their allegiance to fundamental psychoanalytic principles; first Klein (1930s and 1940s) and later the British Object Relations school (early 1940s) developed distinct theoretical perspectives (Wallerstein, 1992). Other derivations followed. Psychoanalytic training and education were increasingly provided by institutes whose admissions criteria and other policies varied considerably and resulted in a great deal of conflict. Hyman (2008) described the institute movement as "replete with incidents of internecine struggles, splits, and even dissolutions" (p. 99). The competition and conflict between psychoanalytic institutes has implications for trainees as "they will be expected to adopt, espouse, and defend the theories to which the institute subscribes, [and] subordinate themselves to the organization's needs" (Hyman, 2008, p. 100).

This "psychoanalytic pluralism" (Wallerstein, 1992, p. 5) is reflected in the literature on psychoanalytic supervision. Frawley-O'Dea and Sarnat (2001) have identified and provided thorough reviews of five such models, including their own:

- patient-centered (classical) model (Dewald, 1987),
- learning problem or supervisee-centered (ego psychological) model (Ekstein & Wallerstein, 1972),
- empathic (self-psychological) model (Brightman, 1984–1985),
- anxiety-focused (object relations) model (Jarmon, 1990; Newirth, 1990), and
- supervisory-matrix-centered (relationship) model (Frawley-O'Dea & Sarnat, 2001).

Unlike earlier models focusing on either client (Dewald, 1987; Freud, 1909/1973) or supervisee dynamics (Ekstein & Wallerstein, 1972), Frawley-O'Dea and Sarnat (2001) suggested that the supervisor focus on relevant data involving the client, the supervisee, and/or the supervision. The supervision includes the relationship between the supervisor and supervisee—of central importance in this model. Sarnat drew on her work with Frawley-O'Dea (2001) in a chapter coauthored by supervision experts representing two other theoretical models (Beck et al., 2008). She described one of the foundational concepts of the supervisory-matrix-centered model: "Client, therapist, and supervisor are viewed as co-creators of two reciprocally influential relationships, the clinical relationship and the supervisor relationship" (p. 69). Sarnat (1998) emphasized the importance of exploring supervisees' unconscious material as a means for informing the supervision.

The "teach–treat boundary" (Frawley-O'Dea & Sarnat, 2001, p. 140) is another important ethical concept in the supervisory-matrix-centered model. Supervisors must consider it when they embark on an exploration of supervisee dynamics with the ultimate goals of facilitating supervisees' professional development and helping them help their clients. Frawley-O'Dea and Sarnat (2001) described the distinction in this way:

> While in the analytic setting, the objective is to explore as fully as possible the genetic origins and range of potential meanings attributable to the transference–countertransference constellations. . . . In supervision, discussion of the supervisee's psychological functioning and its impact on relational patterns at play in supervision and in the supervised treatment is more limited in scope. Here, the goal is for supervisee and supervisor to pursue the supervisee's personality and character only in as far as is necessary to clarify the vicissitudes of the supervisory relationship and to promote effective psychoanalytic work with the supervised patient. (p. 140)

Four concepts that are incorporated in some form in most psychoanalytic approaches to supervision, including the Frawley-O'Dea & Sarnat (2001) model, are learning alliance, transference, countertransference, and parallel process.

Learning Alliance

The concept of a *learning alliance* (Dewald, 1997; Fleming & Benedek, 1964), *supervisory working alliance* (Bordin, 1983), or *supervisory alliance* (Teitelbaum, 2001) between supervisor and supervisee is analogous to the working alliance in a therapeutic relationship (Dewald, 1997). Teitelbaum (2001) asserted,

> For supervisees to learn in the context of supervision, they must trust that the supervisory atmosphere is a benign one, that they can feel safe in exposing themselves in spite of the evaluative component of the supervision, and that the supervisor is earnestly interested in being there for the supervisee in a way that meets her learning needs. (p. 10)

Dewald (1997) defined a learning alliance as

> a situation of comfort and safety that will allow the candidate [i.e., supervisee] openly and honestly to report the experience and interactions between him- or herself and the patient in a way that allows the supervisor a reasonable view and understanding of the analyst/analysis and interactions. (p. 33)

Clemens (2006) described the partnership between supervisor and supervisee as "a working alliance, devoted to understanding and resolving the patient's problems" (p. 42). The learning alliance concept has relevance for and has been incorporated into other models of supervision (Bernard & Goodyear, 2009).

Transference and Countertransference

The concepts of transference and countertransference are among the contributions of psychoanalytic authors. Definitions of these terms vary in breadth. Usher (1993) defined *transference* in psychotherapy as "conscious but more particularly unconscious repetitions of early important relationships" (p. 7). She clarified, "Transference is actually an inappropriate displacement onto the therapist . . . of the patient's at least partly unconscious perceptions of figures in their past" (Usher, 1993, p. 8). *Countertransference* has been defined as "a situation in which an analyst's feelings and attitudes toward a patient are derived from earlier situations in the analyst's life that have been displaced onto the patient" (Moore & Fine, 1990, p. 47).

Although some psychoanalytic-supervision literature focuses on how supervisors might help supervisees recognize and interpret transference and countertransference in the context of the therapeutic relationship (Clemens, 2006; Varghese, 2006), these phenomena also occur in supervisory relationships (Frawley-O'Dea & Sarnat, 2001). Supervisees may attribute characteristics to the supervisor that reflect their own experiences with authority figures (Grinberg, 1997; Issacharoff, 1984). Common transference themes in supervision include admiration, the wish to please, attraction, and a desire to emulate the supervisor (D. Jacobs, 2001). Negative transference is as likely. Supervisees are "placed in the metaphoric position of the dependent child needing and receiving help from the adult who is in a position of authority and responsibility" (Caruth, 1990, p. 181). Intimidation, resentment, fear of criticism, and feelings of being "seen through or diagnosed" (D. Jacobs et al., 1995, p. 210) are examples of feelings that may develop.

According to Frawley-O'Dea and Sarnat (2001), supervisors are "embedded participants" (p. 29) in the supervisory relationship and are therefore subject to their own countertransferential responses to supervisees. Supervisors may feel gratified by supervisee admiration, gratitude, deference, or idealization, for example. Their behavior may be motivated in part by the wish to impress, care for, and inspire their supervisees. Further, the job of supervisor includes a component of giving. The need to be seen as replete with resources such as knowledge, experience, and talent and to inspire gratitude in supervisees may fuel the desire to give generously (Schlesinger, 1981).

Sometimes supervisors' countertransference reactions are primarily related to the dynamic between themselves and a given supervisee and manifest as "relational enactments" (Frawley-O'Dea & Sarnat, 2001, p. 63). In other cases, supervisors introduce their own idiosyncratic, unexamined dynamics to the supervisory relationship. These dynamics interact with those of supervisees and, if not identified, may compromise the effectiveness of supervision or result in harm to supervisees. Taibbi (1993) provided an example of how unchecked countertransference on the part of one family therapy supervisor resulted in such destructive blind spots.

> She easily formed close relationships with young clinicians, who, within a few years, would serve as junior partners in her private practice. But then something would erupt: she would suspect some fraudulent behavior, a deception, a clinical impropriety. The relationship, once so close, would blow up, leaving her feeling betrayed and the junior therapists feeling deeply hurt and mystified. The problem was the supervisor's inability to deal with loss. The supervisory relationship was ending, as it must, but the supervisor could not accept this inevitability, so the death went unacknowledged, the grief unvoiced. Like parents who suddenly throw their teenager out of the house at three in the morning rather than acknowledge the developmental changes in the relationship, she used her power to banish the therapist rather than face the loss. (p. 55)

When transference and countertransference reactions occur in supervision, the supervisor bears the ethical responsibility of monitoring them. The supervisor must use his or her own countertransference responses as a resource to inform the supervision and consider them with the best interests of the supervisee and his or her patients as primary. Similarly, supervisors may monitor supervisee transference toward them and, when and if appropriate, consider interpretation. It is therefore critical that supervisors make such interpretations cautiously and judiciously, that they do not derail the supervision into a therapeutic interchange, and that they do not violate supervisees' privacy.

Parallel Process

As with the various theoretical approaches to family systems, psychoanalytic models share some basic concepts. Bernard and Goodyear (2009) described the concept of parallel process as "the best known single phenomenon in supervision: perhaps even the signature phenomenon" (p. 150). The concept of parallel process is derived from psychoanalysis (Doehrman, 1976; Ekstein & Wallerstein, 1958, 1972; Friedlander, Siegel, & Brenock 1989; Mueller, 1982; Sachs & Shapiro, 1976; Searles, 1955). Parallel process in supervision, as in psychotherapy, is an unconscious process in which the themes and dynamics in the therapeutic and supervisory relationships are parallel. Allphin (2005), building on Doehrman's (1976) conceptualization of parallel process, described the phenomenon in this way:

> Supervisees may treat their patients as their supervisors treat them or as the supervisees wish their supervisors would treat them. Or the supervisor may treat the supervisee the way the patient treats the supervisee. Or the supervisee may treat the supervisor the way the patient treats the supervisee. (p. 107)

This description makes clear that the process is bidirectional and that the origination point of a particular dynamic may be in either the therapeutic or supervisory relationship.

Kadushin and Harkness (2002) described a similar unconscious process:

> The supervisee, in attempting to understand the client's behavior, identifies with it and mimics it for presentation in the supervisory conference to obtain help in dealing with it. . . . What the client does with the supervisee, the supervisee will, in turn, do with the supervisor. (p. 209)

Kadushin and Harkness (2002) further indicated that a parallel process may occur "in reverse" (p. 210), with the supervisee acting out what is experienced in the supervisory relationship with clients. They offered examples in which supervisor indifference resulted in supervisee indifference with clients or a dominant supervisor led to the supervisee dominating his or her clients (Kadushin & Harkness, 2002). Alonso and Rutan (1988) have described this dynamic in cases in which the psychotherapy client has experienced abuse. They observed that psychotherapists may identify with these clients and act out with the supervisor the client's fears of abandonment and shame (Alonso & Rutan, 1988). Frawley-O'Dea and Sarnat (2001) described the phenomenon more succinctly as "the means by which the supervisor dyad enacts one or more key dynamics also alive in the treatment dyad" (p. 170).

Simplified examples of possible parallel processes follow:

- A supervisee presents the same overly dependent client in every supervision session and frequently contacts the supervisor between meetings to get "her take" on something related to the case, which is beginning to annoy the supervisor. The supervisee complains that the client relies too much on him for direction and says that he is beginning to feel resentful.
- A supervisor observes that his supervisee has become excessively and unusually directive, opinionated, and controlling with a particularly resistant patient. The supervisor points out this tendency on several occasions, without apparent impact. In a moment of frustration, the supervisor writes specific nondirective responses for the supervisee to memorize and deliver to the client. He further assigns her to create and submit a verbatim transcript of the next session for his critique.
- A new supervisor is assigned a novice clinician who happens to be an accomplished musician. The supervisor's undergraduate degree is in music, and she often inquires about her supervisee's performance experiences. The supervisee wanted to pursue a career in forensic psychology but was unable to secure a practicum in that area and so settled for this one in psychotherapy. One of his first cases is a recently widowed lawyer. The supervisee tells the supervisor that talking about this client's law career helps him to cope with the loss in another area of his life.

The source of the parallel in each of these cases arguably may be any member of the triad. In the first case, the dependent client likely is the origination point, but a supervisee bringing a strong desire to be needed might encourage this stance in the patient, thus setting the dynamic into motion. Perhaps in an unconscious attempt to convey his frustration, elicit empathy, or provoke a response he can emulate, the supervisee unconsciously replicates in supervision the dynamic that has developed in the psychotherapy. The supervisor begins to experience the feelings of the supervisee. If the supervisor fails to recognize and correctly interpret this countertransference, she becomes at risk for acting out in a way that undermines the supervision and forgoes a learning opportunity for the supervisee.

The behavior of the directive supervisor in the second case perhaps has developed in response to the overly controlling and directive supervisee, creating a parallel process. Or the supervisor may have sensed subtle resistance on the part of the supervisee and thus become more controlling, prompting the supervisee to become controlling with the client.

The supervisor in the third case seems to have developed a transference reaction to the supervisee (Stimmel, 1995), having become enamored of him, personally interested in his musical activities, and perhaps envious. Similarly, the supervisee's interest in learning more about law, rather than a legitimate therapeutic rationale, seems to have driven his pursuit of related topics. The transference in both cases apparently remained unconscious, uncontained, and unchecked. By her role model, the supervisor may have given implicit permission for the supervisee to engage his client in discussions born out of his own needs and interests rather than those of his client. Unchallenged, the parallel transferences could continue to develop unnoticed.

In real life, the parallel processes spawned in the context of supervision are typically more subtle and harder to discern than those in the examples, particularly for individuals unconsciously engaged in them. These cases are intended to provide illustrative, albeit oversimplified, examples.

Falender and Shafranske (2004) have cautioned that such dynamics in the supervisory relationship, if not identified "may result in ruptures in the therapeutic or supervisory alliance or may unwittingly produce iatrogenic effects through the perpetuation of maladaptive patterns of interpersonal relating" (p. 85). Stimmel (1995) has further cautioned supervisors about the risk of misinterpreting their transference responses to supervisees as a parallel process. She has demonstrated through several examples how "this sophisticated concept . . . can be used to avoid acknowledging an important component of the dyadic relationship between supervisee/supervisor, student/teacher—the transference" (Stimmel, 1995, p. 610).

Parallel processes can and often do work in the service of both the psychotherapy and the supervision (Russell, Crimmings, & Lent, 1984). Stimmel (1995) described how informative the emergence of such a process can be: "It [parallel process] is the closest living representative in the supervisor's consulting room of that which occurs in the supervisee's consulting room" (p. 617). Supervisee awareness of client pathology may increase through identification with client feelings and behavior. Similarly, when supervisors maintain appropriate boundaries with supervisees, they provide positive role models for recognizing, accurately interpreting, and effectively using these reactions and parallel dynamics and further the clinical work.

Despite its broad discussion in the literature, empirical research on the concept of parallel process in supervision has been criticized for design flaws, including small sample sizes and inappropriate generalization of results (Ellis & Ladany, 1997). Doehrman's (1976) frequently cited dissertation on the topic of parallel process, for example, included only four psychology trainee subjects. Although studies with larger sample sizes do exist (Patton & Kivlighan, 1997), design flaws make results and implication difficult to interpret and discern (Kadushin & Harkness, 2002).

Most of the literature on this topic is theoretical and based on anecdotal accounts of clinical observations. Authors debate about whether the phenomenon is a parallel or merely an analogous process, whether its existence is empirically provable, and whether it represents a displacement or a projection. Nevertheless, supervisors' awareness of and sensitivity to dynamics in the supervisory relationship will likely enhance their effectiveness and help guard against misunderstandings.

ETHICAL CONSIDERATIONS IN PSYCHOANALYTIC SUPERVISION

Psychoanalytic treatment and supervision are characterized by the extensive advanced training they require, their small professional communities, and their primary focus on relationships. Therefore, some of the most salient ethical challenges are related to competency, multiple relationships, and boundaries.

Psychoanalytic techniques are powerful, and relationships are emotionally intense. Strong fundamental and ongoing training are essential to establish and maintain competency in psychoanalytic treatment and supervision. As illustrated in the preceding examples, misuse of techniques or misinterpretation of intense emotions can set the stage for serious clinical and ethical errors and harm to clients and supervisees. Supervisors must not only maintain their competency in providing supervision but also remain current in the treatment areas in which their supervisees are engaged (AAMFT, 2001; AAPC, 1994; ACA, 2005; APA, 2002; CPA, 2000). Personal analysis or psychotherapy, as needed, will likely facilitate the self-awareness and self-monitoring essential to maintaining competence and minimizing the likelihood of clinical and ethical errors.

Many of the ethical challenges endemic in other small communities (Schank & Skovolt, 2006) occur among psychoanalytically oriented clinicians. It is not uncommon, for example, for supervisors to belong to the same associations and be in attendance at the same professional and social functions as their clients, supervisees, and their own teachers and analysts or psychotherapists. Analysts and psychodynamic psychotherapists and supervisors will likely acquire information about their patients and supervisees from out-side sources and will probably have friends in common. Those in training then likely will seek the required analysis from an individual who may have played a role in their academic training—perhaps as a lecturer, if not a for-mer professor or supervisor with evaluative authority. Ultimately, educators will become colleagues with whom they will have regular interactions within specialized professional societies and associations. The potential for bound-ary challenges in analytic communities is great, and all parties must be vigi-lant about protecting confidentiality, minimizing and effectively managing multiple relationships that arise, and monitoring their objectivity.

Psychoanalytic Supervision Case: Transitions in the Supervisory Relationship

Dr. Blake, a psychoanalyst, is part of a large group practice that offers supervised experience for analysts in training. She is flattered, albeit anxious, on learning that Chris, the son of her former, now-retired analyst, is enrolled at the local institute and has specifically requested her as his supervisor for postdoctoral training. Chris, in turn, is excited but a bit conflicted at the prospect of working with Dr. Blake. His father has described Dr. Blake as "brilliant" and strongly recommended her, although he has not, of course, dis-closed the nature of their relationship.

During their early sessions, Chris often asks Dr. Blake how she would handle some of the challenging dilemmas he has encountered. Dr. Blake offers input and generously shares examples from her experience. Chris is in awe of her ability to size up situations quickly and to generate such insightful responses, and Dr. Blake is pleased that he is finding her input helpful. She can't help but reflect on how much Chris reminds her of his father. Beyond the striking physical resemblance, Chris is exceptionally bright, intuitive, and kind—so much like his dad.

As the supervision progresses, Dr. Blake decides that she could be more effective in helping Chris with his countertransference if she knew more about his family of origin. Modeling self-disclosure by sharing some of her struggles with her own family, she decides, may encourage Chris to be more available in the supervision. Also, these disclosures could provide an oppor-tunity to practice his interpretation skills with her.

Chris feels some curiosity about Dr. Blake and is honored that she is interested in his perspective on these personal matters. Over time, however, Chris begins to feel that too much supervision time is allocated to Dr. Blake's clients and personal problems. He feels increasingly resentful and frustrated in his attempts to refocus the discussion. Further, Chris is feeling more con-fident in his own skills and begins to disagree with Dr. Blake's assessments.

Chris makes one attempt to discuss his concerns with Dr. Blake, but he feels misunderstood and fears that further challenge will negatively impact his evaluation. He then consults about the situation with a colleague who mentions hearing that Dr. Blake had been in analysis with Chris's father. On hearing this news, Chris is flooded with conflicting feelings. In addition to feeling foolish, he becomes angry with his father for recommending Dr. Blake and begins to question Dr. Blake's motives, particularly with regard to inquiries about his personal life. Chris knows that his father won't acknowledge whether Dr. Blake has been his client, and he thinks it would be inappropriate to raise the issue with her. He decides to keep the information to himself and "just get through" the training.

Chris begins to appear indifferent to Dr. Blake's self-disclosures and avoids talking about personal responses to his own clients. He opts to quietly ignore several of her suggestions and directives. In one instance, Dr. Blake tells Chris to obtain authorization from a client to speak to her psychiatrist. Chris feels this would undermine his client's trust and so does not discuss it with the client or mention it again in supervision. In another case, Dr. Blake instructs him to terminate with and refer a new client because of a possible multiple relationship that might compromise his objectivity. Given Dr. Blake's decision to accept him as a supervisee, this recommendation infuriates Chris. He enthusiastically invites the client to continue working with him.

Dr. Blake detects changes in Chris's receptivity to supervision and becomes concerned that he is developing "an attitude problem." She is shocked to discover, when reviewing a sample of Chris's treatment records, that the file on the first case contains no authorization and no notation regarding a consultation with the psychiatrist. Further, she learns that Chris has been treating the client she directed him to refer!

As angry as she is, Dr. Blake hesitates to report her concerns to the administration, knowing it would have repercussions for Chris's career. She considers that his father will be disappointed in him or, worse, angry with her. Dr. Blake elects to wait for his year-end evaluation, just a few weeks away, to discuss the matter with Chris. She uses the time to search for additional evidence, which she does indeed find. Ultimately, Dr. Blake writes in Chris's evaluation, "Although initially a very promising clinician, Chris has had increasing difficulty taking direction and has not met learning goals. His deception and insubordination suggest ethical deficits and do not bode well for his future as an analyst." Chris is furious and considers filing a complaint against Dr. Blake.

Psychoanalytic Supervision Case Discussion

The supervisory relationship between Dr. Blake and Chris initially appeared quite promising, but only on the surface. Dr. Blake's history as an analytic patient of Chris's father was a ticking ethical time bomb, unknown to Chris and unexamined by Dr. Blake. Perhaps it was not impossible for this supervisory relationship to work, but Dr. Blake should have considered the potential difficulties before accepting Chris for supervision (Gottlieb, Robinson, & Younggren, 2007). That Dr. Blake was oblivious to potential problems rendered her unable to mitigate them.

Dr. Blake's decision to accept Chris as her supervisee, despite her history as an analytic patient of his father, marks her first wrong turn. Professional ethics codes consistently caution psychologists and other mental health clinicians to consider the potential for other prior or concurrent relationships to compromise professional objectivity and effectiveness before deciding to engage in them (AAMFT, 2001; ACA, 2005; APA, 2002; ASPPB, 2005; NASW, 2008). To what extent did Dr. Blake's desire to impress Chris and his father affect her supervisory behavior? Were Dr. Blake's inquiries about Chris's family born solely of recognition of his need to hone his interpretation skills, or was her curiosity about her former analyst contributing to her decision? Did she use the supervisory relationship to maintain a connection with her unavailable analyst? Were her efforts to "model self-disclosure" (not grounded in psychoanalytic theory) part of a strategy for eliciting the comfort she experienced in her analysis? To what degree did her positive and apparently unresolved transference to Chris's father color her perceptions of Chris's attributes?

Dr. Blake was gratified by the vote of confidence from her former analyst and by Chris's initial admiration. She seemed to enjoy the opportunities to discuss her professional successes and personal challenges. There is no evidence that she examined the potential influence of these factors.

Chris did not have the same ethical responsibility as Dr. Blake for the supervisory relationship, yet his decisions to violate supervisory directives and deceive his supervisor about his work represent ethical infractions. Assuming that Dr. Blake obtained Chris's informed consent to participate in supervision, he knew of and agreed to keep her informed about his cases and follow or revisit clinical decisions with her. He must also have been informed of grievance procedures should he become dissatisfied with some aspect of supervision. Yet Chris elected not to pursue any of these avenues, instead acting out his anger by engaging in a multiple relationship with his client, ignoring signs of trouble, and proceeding without benefit of supervisory assistance.

The multiple relationship, known by Dr. Blake at the outset, set this supervision on a trajectory fraught with ethical land mines. Unchecked, the problems festered and multiplied. Dr. Blake's personal needs became inextricably entwined with Chris's supervisory needs, corrupting the supervision and compromising the welfare of Chris's clients. The learning alliance was destroyed, the transference and countertransference of both went unrecognized and uninterpreted, and a destructive parallel process was allowed to develop and thrive.

Failure to use these psychoanalytic concepts in the service of supervisory and treatment relationships, as they were intended, created both ethical and clinical problems. Yet these same concepts applied appropriately could have turned potential disaster into a positive learning opportunity, benefiting both the supervisee and his clients.

CONCLUSION: THEORY-BASED ETHICAL IMPLICATIONS

Numerous models of supervision as well as their subsets are described in the literature of psychology, marriage and family therapy, counseling, and other mental health professions. There is no consensus or empirical evidence indicating the clear superiority of any one model (Morgan & Sprenkle, 2007). Regardless of one's theoretical orientation to psychotherapy or clinical supervision, each model contains techniques, methods, strategies, and conceptualizations that stimulate thinking and illuminate and enhance supervision based in other orientations.

Although supervisors may identify with a specific theoretical model of psychotherapy, they may not have a clearly formulated approach to supervision. Only in recent years has specific course work in supervision become a common or required part of the education of psychotherapists (Falender & Shafranske, 2004). Falender and Shafranske suggested that for many supervisors, "behaviors are based on implicit models of supervision, culled from their experiences as a supervisee, from their identifications with past supervisors, or from skills derived from psychotherapy or teaching" (p. 7). Thus, eclectic or integrated models of are more commonly practiced (Bernard & Goodyear, 2009; Norcross & Halgin, 1997).

Given that many practicing supervisors have not had the benefit of specialized training (Norcross & Halgin, 1997), it is important that they understand the theoretical roots of their supervisory practices, maintain theoretical competence through continuing education, and remain cognizant of the ethical challenges associated with applying any theoretical approach.

4
DEVELOPMENTAL MODELS OF SUPERVISION

Many authors have proposed and advocated for supervision models describing the trajectory of professional development for supervisees learning to practice psychotherapy. These developmental models dominated the clinical supervision literature in the 1980s and were termed the "zeitgeist of supervision models" (Holloway, 1987, p. 209). Some of the earlier models (Alonso, 1983; Ekstein & Wallerstein, 1972; Fleming, 1953; Gaoni & Newmann, 1974; Harvey, Hunt, & Schroder, 1961; Hogan, 1964; Littrell, Lee-Bordin, & Lorenz, 1979; Loganbill, Hardy, & Delworth, 1982; Sansbury, 1982; Stoltenberg, 1981) provided a foundation for the subsequent developmental conceptualizations of supervision. More contemporary developmental models include those developed by Rodenhauser (1994); Skovolt and Ronnestad (1992); Stoltenberg and McNeill (2009); Stoltenberg, McNeill, and Delworth (1998); Taibbi (1995); and Watkins (1995).

Supervisors and consultants espousing any theoretical approach share the goal of positively impacting the professional development of their supervisees and consultees. To that end, a framework for conceptualizing and facilitating professional development is useful if not essential and is therefore included here.

Existing developmental models focus on students and supervisees and do not address consultees. Although these models might be used to conceptualize the characteristics and needs of consultees, supervision is the primary focus. Specifically, the goals of this chapter are to

- describe the basic assumptions underlying developmental models of supervision as well as their strengths, limitations, and related research;
- provide an overview of the Integrated Developmental Model (Stoltenberg et al., 1998), including the latest revision of the model (Stoltenberg & McNeill, 2009), and describe the characteristics and needs of supervisees at each of four developmental levels;
- discuss the ethical challenges encountered by supervisees at various stages of development and provide a case illustration for each level; and
- offer a framework for supervisors to conceptualize and effectively respond to supervisee's ethical errors and to anticipate and address their own ethical pitfalls.

OVERVIEW OF DEVELOPMENTAL MODELS OF SUPERVISION

Developmental models have been reviewed, critiqued, studied, and categorized extensively. E. L. Worthington (1987) compared 16 developmental models, and Watkins (1995) identified and critiqued 6 others, including his own. Stoltenberg and Delworth (1987) described 7 developmental models and then presented and later revised their own model (Stoltenberg & McNeill, 2009; Stoltenberg et al., 1998).

Developmental models share an underlying assumption that psychologists and other mental health clinicians progress through stages as they develop skills and become socialized into their professions. According to most developmental theories (e.g., Hess, 1987; Littrell et al., 1979; Stoltenberg et al., 1998), supervisees become increasingly competent, secure, and independent, and supervisors must make adjustments as supervisees evolve (Inman & Ladany, 2008; Kadushin & Harkness, 2002).

Some proponents of developmental models have argued against the adaptation of theoretical models of counseling and psychotherapy to supervision, noting the important differences between the two and suggesting that supervisory and psychotherapy models remain separate (e.g., Loganbill et al., 1982). Stoltenberg and McNeill (1997) explicated this argument:

"Unless one assumes that the issues faced by clients in psychotherapy and supervisees in supervision are fundamentally the same, which strikes us as flawed, we are left with the need to construct a model idiosyncratic to the supervision context" (p. 184). Other advocates for developmental models have described them as metatheoretical (Watkins, 1995), suggesting that they be used in combination with rather than in place of psychotherapy-based approaches.

Stoltenberg and McNeill (1997), authors of one developmental approach, claimed that "the research literature appears to support many of the key constructs of developmental models, including differential characteristics and training needs of supervisees, reactions to supervision, and behavior of supervisors across levels of experience" (p. 184). Studies of developmental models generally offer support for the existence of some developmental process evident in supervisees in terms of their intellectual and personal growth (Borders, 1990; B. L. Fisher, 1989; Krause & Allen, 1988; Lovell, 1999; Neufeldt, Karno, & Nelson, 1996; Skovolt & Ronnestad, 1992), though criticism of these studies, discussed subsequently, suggests caution in interpreting their conclusions (Ellis & Ladany, 1997; Inman & Ladany, 2008).

Despite their many proponents, developmental models also draw criticism. Russell, Crimmings, and Lent (1984) and Worthington (1987) have characterized developmental models as simplistic and incomplete. Conversely, Holloway (1987) has challenged the same approaches as being too complex to be useful. Patterson (1997), an advocate of a supervisee-centered approach to supervision, criticized what he characterized as disregard for the importance of theoretical orientation. He observed that although both supervisor and supervisee have a theoretical approach to psychotherapy, whether stated or implicit, developmental approaches "fail to consider how the supervisor and supervisee are to reconcile differences or reach agreement on what is expected of the supervisee—what the criteria for the supervisee's practice and performance are" (p. 134). Patterson (1997) further warned against supervision that is not grounded in a particular theoretical approach to psychotherapy: "My position on this is clear. It is not simply desirable or important, but necessary that the supervisor and supervisee be committed to a theory—the same theory" (p. 135).

Another criticism of developmental models, particularly the Stoltenberg and Delworth (1987) model, is their use of the "practicum level as a proxy for experience level" (Ellis & Ladany, 1997, p. 483). Further, developmental stages cannot be assumed to apply uniformly to all individuals. Falender and Shafranske (2004) cautioned, "In light of the unique strengths and competencies that supervisees, including novices, bring to training, a priori assumptions applied to individual supervisees are not particularly helpful" (p. 11).

Stoltenberg et al. (1998) acknowledged these criticisms; Stoltenberg and McNeill (2009) addressed them in detail.

Perhaps some of the harshest criticism of developmental models focuses on related research. Ellis and Ladany (1997) and more recently Inman and Ladany (2008) have not specifically criticized the efficacy of developmental models but rather have focused on methodological problems identified in research designed to demonstrate their utility and validity. Ellis and Ladany (1997) conducted an extensive "review-study" of clinical supervision research, including studies of developmental models. Some of the problems they have identified in studies focused on supervisee development and experience level include

> pervasive threats to the theoretical and hypothesis validities of the studies; the nearly exclusive use of cross-sectional research designs to test developmental inferences; the numerous conceptual, methodological, and statistical mismatches and confounds; the unacceptably high Type I and Type II error rates . . . the paucity of psychometrically sound measures; improper statistical analyses; and violations of statistical assumptions. (p. 482)

At that time, Ellis and Ladany (1997) concluded that developmental models of supervision were largely untested, simplistic, and only partially accurate. More than 10 years later, however, Inman and Ladany (2008) have acknowledged that

> the bulk of the studies suggest some support for the developmental process operating in supervisees. Furthermore, the research shows that supervisees not only need different types of guidance (e.g., there is a greater need for structure on the part of beginning vs. advanced supervisees), but also show a developmental increase in both personal (e.g., reflectivity) and intellectual (e.g., cognitive complexity) aspects of their growth. (p. 505)

Nevertheless, Inman and Ladany (2008) maintained that the frequent use of self-report as a measure, in combination with other methodological problems, renders conclusions based on research about developmental models tenuous. Bernard and Goodyear (2009), Falender and Shafranske (2004), and Watkins (1995) have provided thorough reviews of many developmental models of supervision, and therefore such a review is not attempted here. Rather, one model—the integrated/integrative developmental model (IDM; Stoltenberg & McNeill, 2009; Stoltenberg et al., 1998) is considered in the sections that follow in light of the ethical challenges encountered by supervisors and supervisees at each developmental level.

INTEGRATED/INTEGRATIVE DEVELOPMENTAL
MODEL OF SUPERVISION

Stoltenberg and Delworth's (1987) IDM is based on the earlier work of Hogan (1964), Loganbill et al. (1982), and Stoltenberg (1981). Stoltenberg et al. (1998) further developed the IDM, considered the best known and most widely used developmental model of supervision (Bernard & Goodyear, 2009; Stoltenberg, 2008). Falender and Shafranske referred to the IDM as the "most comprehensive model available" (2004, pp. 10–11), providing this description:

> This model considers the trainee's cognitive and affective awareness of the client, motivation relating to perceived efforts, enthusiasm, and investment across time, as well as the client's autonomy, individuation, and independence. It proposes a sequence of development from increasing autonomy to shifting awareness from self to client and finally to independent functioning. (pp. 10–11)

Stoltenberg and McNeill (2009) have further developed, refined, and expanded the IDM, taking into account research and criticism of earlier models. They also modified the name, changing *integrated* to *integrative*. A brief description of the model, including recent modifications (Stoltenberg & McNeill, 2009), follows.

OVERVIEW OF THE INTEGRATED/INTEGRATIVE
DEVELOPMENTAL MODEL OF SUPERVISION

Stoltenberg et al. (1998) conceptualized professional development in four levels: 1, 2, 3, and 3 integrated (3i). Supervisees at each stage are assumed to share certain characteristics and related needs. These characteristics are considered in terms of three overriding structures: self and other awareness (cognitive and affective), motivation, and autonomy. According to the IDM, Level 1 supervisees tend to be motivated, dependent, and focused on themselves and their performance. Level 2 supervisees experience fluctuating motivation, vacillate between dependency and autonomy, and tend to focus on and identify with clients. Level 3 supervisees evidence stable motivation, are generally autonomous, and are able to accurately assess their own strengths and weaknesses as well as those of their clients. Level 3i supervisees have integrated the Level 3 characteristics across domains of clinical activity described in the section that follows (see Stoltenberg & McNeill, 2009, for detailed descriptions of each developmental level; see also Stoltenberg et al., 1998).

Domains of Clinical Activity

Stoltenberg and McNeill (2009) have identified the following eight general domains of clinical activity:

1. intervention skills competence—application of theoretical orientation in providing psychotherapy in various formats (e.g., couples, individual, group therapy);
2. assessment techniques—use of psychological assessment instruments;
3. interpersonal assessment—incorporates the use of self in conceptualizing a client's interpersonal dynamics;
4. client conceptualization—diagnosis, case conceptualization;
5. individual differences—relevance of ethnicity, race, culture, and gender, and other individual differences;
6. theoretical orientation—theoretical models of personality and psychotherapy;
7. treatment plans and goal—organization of treatment including the sequencing of interventions and topics; and
8. professional ethics—integration of personal and professional ethics.

It is plausible—in fact likely, according to this model—that individual supervisees exhibit characteristics of different stages of development in different domains. The most recent publication emphasizes the variability of individuals both between and within domains (Stoltenberg & McNeill, 2009). Although many master's students beginning their first practicum are characterized as Level 1 supervisees on all domains, this is not always the case. A student in counseling, social work, or psychology may have worked as an addiction counselor for many years before resuming education, for example, and therefore be more advanced in related skill areas. Even those with no relevant professional experience may have personal experiences or age-related maturity that advance their development within a given domain.

Stoltenberg (2008) has described a case illustrating this complexity. In this case, a doctoral student is confident and basically competent in his work with individual clients, functioning at Level 2. At Level 1, however, in his work with couples, he is "experiencing cognitive confusion, anxiety, and a desire to depend more on guidance from the supervisor but highly motivated to learn and improve" (Stoltenberg, 2008, p. 52). Clearly, the supervisee benefits when the supervisor accurately perceives his or her strengths and limitations and tailors the supervision accordingly.

Stoltenberg and McNeill (2009) have acknowledged that the eight domains of clinical activity described are "overly large and inclusive" (p. 4). They clarified that these domains are "meant to highlight the need to attend to particular areas of practice in considering a trainee's development, rather than to broadly assume a level of professional development that lacks meaning and relevance" (Stoltenberg & McNeill, 2009, p. 4).

Another feature of the IDM (Stoltenberg & McNeill, 2009) is that it includes five categories of supervisory interventions:

1. facilitative (conveying warmth, respect, and nurturance),
2. confrontive (noting discrepancies between behaviors, beliefs, or emotions),
3. conceptual (using theoretical tenets to assign meaning to events),
4. prescriptive (developing action plans, offering supervisory directives), and
5. catalytic (actively promoting change).

Stoltenberg (2008) recommended each of these interventions as particularly useful with supervisees at various developmental stages:

> Facilitative interventions are appropriate across levels. For Level 1 trainees, in addition, prescriptive and conceptual interventions are useful. In late Level 1, catalytic interventions can be appropriate. For Level 2, in addition to facilitative interventions, confrontive, conceptual, and catalytic interventions are used regularly. For Level 3, facilitative interventions remain important; confrontive interventions are occasionally used; and conceptual and catalytic remain useful. (pp. 43–44)

Stoltenberg and McNeill (2009) further suggested strategies to help supervisees transition from each developmental stage to the next.

The following section describes the general characteristics of supervisees at each developmental stage, along with corresponding needs, possible interventions, and ethical challenges. Again, any given individual likely functions at different levels of development both between and within different domains of clinical practice (Stoltenberg & McNeill, 2009).

Level 1 Supervisees

Level 1 supervisees, according to the IDM (Stoltenberg & McNeill, 2009), are highly motivated to practice what they have been trained to do. Supervisees are understandably anxious, however, about the novel challenges they will face as they encounter new clients with great expectations. This anxiety can spawn a simplistic or naive view of clients and a tendency to over- or underpathologize problems so as to understand them. Yet anxiety fuels the desire for learning and the longing for a sense of competence, both of which are sources of motivation.

Dependence on supervisors and other outside resources is characteristic of Level 1 supervisees and, in fact, is necessary as they begin to develop skills. They are not skilled enough to function with much autonomy, and so supervisors must provide structure and guidance.

Level 1 supervisees are characteristically concerned about and preoccupied with their own performance. This self-focus may make it difficult for them to accurately recall in supervision the content of sessions, particularly in terms of the client's experience. Stoltenberg et al. (1998) cautioned that self-preoccupation not be mistaken for insightful self-understanding. Level 1 supervisees generally need the help of supervisors to accurately identify their strengths and limitations.

These characteristics—high motivation, dependency, and limited self-awareness—combine to produce particular needs. Structured learning opportunities and how-to materials may be helpful. Supervisees also may benefit from viewing recorded demonstrations of psychotherapy, observing test administrations, and reading others' reports. Stoltenberg and McNeill (2009) recommended that supervisors of Level 1 supervisees emphasize relationship skills and basic intervention strategies. The complexity of the work should be titrated through careful case assignment, manageable caseload size, and readily achievable goals. Feedback must focus primarily on strengths.

Similarly, Level 1 supervisees benefit from guidance regarding preparation for supervision sessions. Teaching supervisees how to present cases, perhaps by providing an outline for use as a guide, for example, likely will reduce anxiety and increase the utility of the supervision (see Appendix E, this volume). In short, Level 1 supervisees benefit when supervisors provide structure, support, and clear and reasonable expectations.

Ethical Considerations for Level 1 Supervisees

The ethical issues facing Level 1 supervisees are related primarily to competence, though ethical mistakes may occur in other areas as well. Such errors by novice clinicians operating under the supervision of a qualified professional are expected and generally are not considered ethical violations (see case examples that follow). Most ethics codes (e.g., APA, 2002; ASPPB, 2005; CPA, 2000) require that supervisors maintain responsibility for monitoring supervisees as closely as necessary and for delegating responsibilities appropriately. APA (2002) states, for example, that psychologists "authorize only those responsibilities that such persons can be expected to perform competently on the basis of their education, training, or experience, either independently or with the level of supervision being provided" (p. 5).

Novice supervisees are vulnerable to error because they lack the knowledge and experience to respond appropriately and reliably to complex clinical and ethical challenges. The self-focus and desire for simplicity characteristic of Level 1 supervisees puts them at risk for failing to recognize important indicators of pathology in their clients. They are more likely to perceive a problem they feel equipped to address than a more complex one. They may mistake a major depression for an adjustment disorder, or post-traumatic stress disorder for social anxiety, for example. A Level 1 supervisee, like anyone attempting to navigate a novel situation, tends to generalize from his or her own related experiences. Lacking clinical experience, however, the supervisee is at risk for making incorrect assumptions about how to proceed.

The following cases illustrate some of these challenges.

Case A

A supervisee tells his supervisor that he feels anxious at the start of every therapy session. He reports solving the problem by beginning each session with a 5-minute relaxation exercise, adding that his clients find it invaluable.

This intervention, clearly born of the supervisee's needs, likely is unrelated to the therapeutic needs of his clients. Although it does not rise to the level of exploitation, the case illustrates how the supervisee's focus on himself has resulted in his not stopping to consider his clients' needs.

Case B

A doctoral student intern explains to her supervisor that when she was in treatment, the most helpful intervention her psychologist used was to hug her at the end of a particularly difficult session. Reflecting on the power of that experience, she now hugs all of her clients at the end of each session.

Like the supervisee in the previous example, this student generalized from her idiosyncratic experience. She was apparently oblivious to the complexities considered by her psychologist in deciding to hug her at that particular point in time. Naïveté and self-focus led her to generalize inappropriately and draw incorrect conclusions about her clients' therapeutic needs. Given the context, it is inaccurate to characterize this behavior as an ethical violation, but certainly it underscores the supervisor's responsibility to monitor and sensitively challenge Level 1 supervisees.

Level 1 supervisees' lack of experience and knowledge also contributes to their not knowing what they do not know. In other words, they may not recognize a situation in which they should seek the input of a supervisor.

Or they may raise what they believe to be the main issue and overlook a more important one.

Case C

Christina, a doctoral intern in a college counseling center, comes to her supervisor with what she recognizes as an ethical dilemma. She references the center's policy of providing services only to current students and says she is clear about not violating that. Christina is also aware of the ethical mandate to protect client privacy.

With these factors in mind, Christina tells her supervisor she has responded cautiously to the request of a former client (now graduated) to meet for a "follow-up" to his counseling. She explained to him the policy and clarified that they could not, therefore, meet in the counseling center, but she offered to meet for lunch. To protect his privacy, Christina declined to meet in the college student center where he might be recognized. Instead, she arranged to meet him at a local restaurant. Now she wonders whether it is ethical to count the time toward the hours required for her internship.

The supervisor hearing this scenario might be alarmed and feel tempted to provide a rapid-fire review of the supervisee's errors. Perhaps more helpful, however, would be consideration of Stoltenberg and McNeill's (2009) recommendation for the supervision of Level 1 supervisees: to focus on the supervisee's strengths.

To her credit, Christina accurately detected an ethical issue. Her intent was to be helpful to the former client while conforming to counseling center policy and professional ethics codes. To that end, she tried to educate herself about both. Christina also was conscientious about counting only the hours that were legitimately a part of her internship. And finally, she had the good judgment to bring the situation to the attention of her supervisor before attending the planned lunch. The supervisor should commend Christina on each of these points.

Despite these positive steps, Christina did not discern the primary ethical issue—a possible multiple relationship (APA, 2002). The potential for the former client to be confused about the nature of this new relationship is significant. Christina seems to have agreed to something she did not think through. What was the client's agenda in requesting the follow-up? Is he interested in additional counseling? A friendship? A date? What does Christina imagine they will talk about in this setting? Will she record the event in his file? How will she respond to a request for further meetings? What alternatives might address the client's needs? Does the policy permit a single session with the objective of assessment and referral? If she cancels, how will Christina explain her decision to the client in a way least likely to cause hurt and further confusion?

Raising the issue with her supervisor affords Christina an opportunity to talk through these and other relevant questions in the safety and security of supervision and to identify a path out of the dilemma. This situation is rife with opportunities for developing skills that will serve Christiana well throughout her career.

General Considerations for Level 1 Supervisees

The supervisors in each of these cases must be aware that Level 1 supervisees have limited skills and experience and are likely to be anxious. Each of these factors makes them vulnerable to naive mistakes and to not knowing exactly what questions to ask their supervisors. Therefore, self-report alone is not a reliable supervisory technique. Close monitoring using a range of techniques is necessary. Observation, examination of records, and review of electronically recorded sessions in addition to supervisee self-report help supervisors to anticipate and attend to potential problems.

Level 2 Supervisees

As psychotherapists transition to Level 2, the self-focus and self-consciousness characteristic of Level 1 supervisees diminish and give way to increased ability to attend to and develop empathy for clients (Stoltenberg & McNeill, 2009). Supervisees' ability to recall and report clients' responses improves. As they gain experience, Level 2 supervisees recognize and tolerate greater complexity and ambiguity in their clinical work as well as more challenge from supervisors. Their ability to function more autonomously increases as they build skills.

Despite these milestones, Level 2 supervisees face challenges that make this time in their development difficult in other respects. As they acquire new skills and deepen their appreciation for clinical complexities, idealistic notions begin to dissipate (Stoltenberg et al., 1998). Their overaccommodations in relation to the client's perspectives and requests may begin to feel burdensome and may become increasingly unsound. Writing reports and case notes, negotiating with insurance companies for authorization of additional treatment, and the dissatisfaction or regression of clients contribute to periodic disillusionment and fluctuating motivation and confidence. Confronting their limitations may prompt supervisees to overwork. They may, for example, read books about incest or alcoholism while on vacation, work long hours to keep current with case notes, or become preoccupied with and distressed by clients' stories. They may revisit career choices as doubts about their ability to perform and questions about whether this work is as satisfying as anticipated arise.

The desire for autonomy coupled with the need for supervisory assistance may engender ambivalence and disagreements with supervisors. As Level 2 supervisees attempt to carve out their professional identities, they may unite with clients in opposition to supervisors and become evasive in supervision. They may become angry when a suggestion from the supervisor "doesn't work." Frustrated Level 2 supervisees may tell their supervisors that another staff member has given them contradictory advice about a case. Or they may victoriously present a published article in which the authors advocate a strategy that is in direct opposition to an instruction from the supervisor.

Taibbi (1993) described his experiences with supervisees at a stage comparable to Level 2 in the Stoltenberg et al. (1998) model:

> The therapist can become inflated with his or her own sense of power; new ideas can easily become too narrow, too quickly rigid. One therapist, for example, fascinated with bodywork, insisted that this was the most, perhaps the only *truly* effective technique with recent sexual abuse victims. Another wanted to use strong experiential approaches with clients who had fairly weak defenses. Supervision with these two therapists quickly assumed the form, if not the tone, of parent–adolescent confrontations. Both therapists probably thought I was stodgy and old-fashioned in my thinking; I thought they were naïve and still had a lot to learn. (1993, p. 55)

Stoltenberg et al. (1998) have recommended several strategies for supervising Level 2 supervisees: expressing support, inviting their ideas, offering alternatives rather than directives when possible, and collaborating with supervisees in planning interventions. Supportive supervisory interventions must be balanced with challenge. Despite the discomfort associated with conflict, Stoltenberg et al. (1998) have stated that "what is comfortable, reassuring, or viewed positively by supervisees is often not what produces further growth" (p. 81).

Ethical Considerations for Level 2 Supervisees

Like Level 1 supervisees, those at Level 2 encounter a variety of ethical challenges. The tendency to overidentify with and become overaccommodating of clients paves the way to ambiguous boundaries; for example, two of the most salient boundaries for Level 2 supervisees are those between their personal and professional lives and between their own issues and clients problems. An increased capacity for empathy, combined with an insufficiently developed filter as they hear about a client's experience of abuse and trauma, serious medical problems, or insurmountable financial difficulties may be overwhelming (Kaser-Boyd, 2008) and can lead to emotional exhaustion or vicarious trauma for the supervisee (Ladany, Friedlander, & Nelson, 2005). The desire to debrief (inappropriately) becomes strong, if not irresistible. Retelling client stories to spouses or partners or friends may become one way to manage the flood of feelings that is sometimes experienced.

Such an error is not primarily the result of naiveté, as with a Level 1 supervisee. Disclosing such information in a social context is more likely the result of the supervisee's inability to separate the client's experience from his or her own. Feelings of incompetence or impotence on the part of Level 2 supervisees may lead them to cope by making denigrating comments about a client. Referring to a client as "that borderline" or "a real piece of work" may help supervisees feel less responsible when there is little progress in a case. But they also cultivate an attitude of disrespect or even contempt for clients. Supervisors must address such comments in a nonshaming way to help supervisees develop clear boundaries between themselves and their clients. Such boundaries will help Level 2 supervisees learn not to personalize client's behaviors but rather to acknowledge their own emotional responses or countertransference and make good clinical use of this information.

Neither relieving anxiety nor shocking or entertaining friends or colleagues is a legitimate reason for discussing client stories. Supervisors must ensure that supervisees have appropriate places in which to process their thoughts and feelings about these stories, such as in a supervision group, with the supervisor, or with their own psychotherapists. The distinction between appropriate and inappropriate disclosures are complex, and supervisors may need to provide specific coaching to teach supervisees how to appropriately share something about their experiences with family and friends to obtain needed support. For example, it is not inappropriate to tell a spouse or partner something like "I've had a very difficult day. It's very painful to hear such sad stories" or to share that "a story I heard today reminded me of something that happened to me," followed by the sharing of that personal experience.

Level 2 supervisees working in settings in which clients probably have experienced trauma may be especially vulnerable. Chemical dependency treatment programs, rape crisis centers, domestic abuse programs, prisons, and residential treatment for children are examples of settings in which supervisees might experience secondary trauma and need to talk about what they are hearing (Kaser-Boyd, 2008).

A second area of potential ethical difficulty for Level 2 supervisees involves establishing boundaries within the context of client relationships. When a supervisor requires or models clear boundaries, this may be mistaken by a supervisee, particularly at Level 2, as a lack of empathy.

Supervisees must learn that taking on the client's feelings is not necessarily helpful and may, in fact, diminish their effectiveness. If the supervisee is obviously flooded with sadness in response to the client's story of abuse, for example, the client may feel a need to protect, comfort, or in other ways take care of the psychotherapist and may do so by minimizing his or her own feelings. Clients also may perceive this intense affect as evidence that the psychotherapist is troubled and not capable of helping them. Another possibility is that clients would mistake empathy for an indication of love or as a desire for friendship.

Any of these responses is clearly countertherapeutic and likely will confound the treatment process. Helping supervisees to recognize possible negative outcomes may inspire them to establish clear boundaries with clients. In addition to insight, they need support and understanding to accomplish the goal of constructing the necessary buffer between themselves and their clients.

Another strategy for helping Level 2 supervisees clarify boundaries is to monitor and encourage self-care. This might include suggesting that they take breaks or vacation time or seek psychotherapy. Learning to balance work and leisure is critical at this point in their development. These suggestions will not be persuasive if the supervisor does not model appropriate self-care.

A third area of ethical challenge involves the supervisor's ability to withstand challenges from the supervisee. Fear of or discomfort with conflict or with the supervisee's dissatisfaction or disappointment may result in a supervisor becoming overaccommodating with supervisees, ignoring questionable behavior, or capitulating to supervisee resistance to monitoring. The potential for conflict in the supervisory relationship is evident at this stage. Just as Level 2 supervisees are at risk for overaccommodating clients, supervisors are at risk for overaccommodating supervisees. Taibbi has stated, "The only protection against these dangers is sensitivity to them" (1993, p. 55).

The following example illustrates how overidentification with clients, separation from the supervisor, and good intentions associated with Level 2 can lead to ethical problems.

Case D: Dr. Chen and James: I Am More Culturally Sensitive Than You

James, a Caucasian man with European heritage, is working as a doctoral intern. He has completed a course in cultural diversity and tells his supervisor Dr. Chen, a Chinese American, that he hopes to apply what he learned in that course. He is committed to being sensitive to and embracing cultural difference, as recommended in the APA (1993) "Guidelines for Providers of Psychological Services to Ethnic, Linguistic, and Culturally

Diverse Populations." James is elated when Donny, a young Native American man, is assigned to him. Donny, whose father is Caucasian and mother is Ojibwa, was raised as a Catholic in a large metropolitan area, but he has relatives on the reservation and spent many summers there. He has recently completed chemical dependency treatment and was referred to psychotherapy for assistance in his adjustment to a sober lifestyle.

As part of his recovery, Donny decides to explore Native American spirituality, a decision enthusiastically encouraged by James. James looks forward to hearing about Donny's participation in sweat lodges, powwows, and other Native American rituals. Donny explains the importance of fire in his culture and tells how the burning of sage and visits from the great spirits comfort him. James is in awe of Donny's discoveries.

Donny often complains that the substance abuse counselor in his aftercare group does not understand his spirituality. James apologizes, noting that not all Caucasian people are as sensitive to cultural issues as he, and he encourages Donny to advocate for himself in that relationship. Donny adds that he feels betrayed by some of his Native American friends who apparently called this counselor to express concern about Donny. "Now they don't even get my unique spirituality. You are the only one who understands!"

Dr. Chen raises questions about Donny's mental health in light of some of his spiritual practices. James is defensive and suggests that despite her own bicultural experience, Dr. Chen's training on multicultural issues, and Native Americans in particular, may be a bit out-of-date. Dr. Chen is offended by this characterization but feels unsure of her perspective and uncomfortable with the conflict. She drops the subject and decides to consult with a colleague before pursuing it further. Given that Dr. Chen apparently lacks appreciation for Donny's spirituality, James quietly vows to be more cautious about what he shares.

The following afternoon, Dr. Chen receives a call from the substance abuse counselor expressing concern about James's management of the case. Donny, who had not slept in 2 days, had come to the counselor's home the night before. The counselor awoke to find a raging campfire built on her front lawn, and Donny chanting and dancing around it. Now hospitalized, he has been diagnosed with bipolar disorder.

Case D Discussion

In this case, James's good intentions about being sensitive to other cultures and his unclear boundaries eclipsed his clinical judgment. He found the relationship so personally gratifying that he was unable to question the client's reports of his spiritual activities. Further, his overidentification with Donny and conflicted relationship with Dr. Chen, both common with Level 2 supervisees

(Stoltenberg & McNeill, 2009), led him to conceal important information from her, which contributed to his mistaken diagnosis. Dr. Chen's insecurities about her own knowledge base in the face of confrontation from James led her to suspend her normally sound clinical judgment to avoid a conflict.

Supervision of Level 2 supervisees requires a willingness to challenge and to be challenged by supervisees. Avoidance of conflict can result in both clinical and ethical problems that have the potential to grow in the absence of close monitoring.

Level 3 and 3i Supervisees

Transition to Level 3 is marked by the emergence of a reliable awareness of both self and others, stable motivation, and greater autonomy (Stoltenberg & McNeill, 2009; Stoltenberg et al., 1998). Level 3 supervisees more accurately identify their strengths and weaknesses and use this self-knowledge to further the treatment they provide. They recognize their own affective and cognitive responses to clients, distill from those responses their clinical implications, and formulate more sophisticated and effective interventions. They now base clinical decisions on a greater understanding of human behavior that is grounded in theory, experience, and relevant data they are now able to solicit from clients. Level 3 supervisees focus simultaneously and effectively on clients, themselves, and the process evolving in each session. Motivation is no longer erratic, and confidence is not easily shaken by therapeutic setbacks or challenges from clients or supervisors. Significantly more independent, Level 3 supervisees generally have a solid sense of what they know and what they do not know, and they are not defensive about being challenged. Level 3i supervisees share these characteristics, but additionally, these attributes are integrated across several domains (Stoltenberg & McNeill, 2009).

Supervisors of Level 3 and 3i supervisees can be nondirective, encourage creativity and risk taking, and introduce challenging theoretical and clinical perspectives without fear of overwhelming or confusing supervisees. As supervisees evidence stable competence in one or more domains, individual goals for their personal and professional development dictate the focus of supervision (Stoltenberg & McNeill, 2009).

Ethical Considerations for Level 3 and 3i Supervisees

Supervisees at Level 3 and 3i are not typically vulnerable to ethical errors involving competence, as are Level 1 supervisees. Because they are generally aware of their strengths and weaknesses, Level 3 and 3i supervisees can reliably discern when they are out of their depth. They do not hesitate to refer prospective clients whose therapeutic needs are inconsistent with their clinical skills. Similarly, when a current client presents new issues or interpersonal challenges, Level 3 and 3i supervisees recognize the need for consultation and are open to input as well as to the possibility that clients may need referrals for more specialized treatment.

The exception to this general rule occurs when a supervisee develops a clinical blind spot, resulting in compromised objectivity or effectiveness. The source of this compromise may be a multiple relationship, the confluence of personal issues with those of the client, or the emergence of a medical or psychological problem. Perhaps some distressing life circumstance has impacted his or her normally sound judgment (see Chapter 5, this volume). Supervisors observing such atypical behaviors in their Level 3 or 3i supervisees must be willing to confront them and to consider possible ways of accounting for them. Of course, the supervisee should be included in the consideration of these issues.

As discussed, Stoltenberg and McNeill (2009) have emphasized the importance of considering the complexity of professional development when evaluating or interpreting supervisee needs and behavior. A well-educated, experienced psychotherapist who is beginning postdoctoral training in neuropsychological assessment likely would be considered a Level 1 supervisee in the domain of assessment and may be at risk for some of the same competency-based errors as novice clinicians. Although postdoctoral supervisees may be wiser about recognizing their limitations, they and their supervisors may also be vulnerable to overestimating their abilities and assuming or allowing greater autonomy than is warranted.

"Diagnosis" of Ethical Errors

Ethical missteps and serious mistakes are clearly not the exclusive purview of professionals at any developmental level. The types and etiologies of errors made by supervisees at different developmental stages vary. For example, errors by Level 1 supervisees are not always the result of a lack of knowledge and experience. Medical or mental health problems, characterological issues, addictions, or other factors can also be mediating or primarily causal.

Supervisors must consider the characteristics associated with each developmental stage in conceptualizing supervisees' needs and behavior and in identifying and tailoring supervisory interventions to particular individuals. A novice clinician who eats his lunch during a psychotherapy session or allows therapeutic dialogue to slide into a discussion about sports may need additional coaching and education. A Level 2 supervisee who suddenly initiates such behavior may be trying to forge her own professional identity, whereas an experienced clinician doing the same thing may be burned out, overworked, lonely, or facing some life crisis. This uncharacteristic informality may suggest that a supervisee is turning to clients to meet personal needs. Each of these developmental contexts requires a different supervisory response.

ETHICAL CHALLENGES FOR SUPERVISORS

The supervision of students or employees at each developmental level (Stoltenberg & McNeill, 2009) not only is likely to spawn related ethical issues for supervisees but may also set the stage for particular types of dilemmas for supervisors. Stoltenberg et al. (1998) addressed the subject of supervisor development, though they did not designate supervision as one of their eight domains of clinical activity. Supervision is nevertheless an area of practice requiring specialized education, training, and experience (Falender & Shafranske, 2004). Supervisors are likely to progress through a developmental trajectory similar to that of supervisees as they become increasingly competent (Stoltenberg et al., 1998), and the ethical challenges they encounter are likely to parallel and interact with those of the psychotherapists they supervise. As is the case with psychotherapists, supervisors bring their own idiosyncratic vulnerabilities to their work and therefore respond differently to challenges presented by supervisees at various developmental levels. Thus, another dimension to be considered involves the dynamics set in motion by the interaction of the developmental levels of both members of the supervisory dyad. The following examples illustrate such potential dynamics.

Some supervisors may find the deference, admiration, and dependency associated with Level 1 supervisees to be gratifying. This is particularly likely when a Level 1 (i.e., a novice) supervisor whose competence is insufficiently developed supervises a Level 1 supervisee. In this case, the supervisee's adulation and relative skill deficit may help to bolster flagging self-confidence and thus be attractive to the supervisor. The risk of the supervisor unconsciously reinforcing dependency, discouraging professional growth, and exploiting the supervisee's dependency is evident.

Supervisors who are conflicted about their own dependency needs, who have histories of complicated relationships with caregivers or dependents, or who have concurrent relationships imbued with similar themes may be at risk for experiencing negative feelings toward supervisees with developmentally normative dependency needs. Irritation or anger in response to supervisees' needs may result in supervisees feeling rejected and ashamed. In response to unrealistic expectations for autonomy, novice clinicians may find themselves floundering but reluctant to ask for help, fearing the supervisor's criticism. When supervision becomes inaccessible or limited in this way, the welfare of the supervisee as well as that of his or her clients is compromised.

The supervision of Level 2 supervisees brings another set of ethical challenges for supervisors. Fluctuating motivation, dependency–autonomy conflicts, overidentification with clients, and limited self-awareness on the part of supervisees may challenge supervisors (Stoltenberg & McNeill, 2009; Stoltenberg et al., 1998) and set the stage for ethical errors. The characteristic tendency of Level 2 supervisees to challenge supervisors and to question their authority may be threatening, particularly if the supervisor is at Level 1. Such challenges may illuminate the supervisor's vulnerabilities and amplify his or her insecurities, thus compromising objectivity. In fact, Stoltenberg et al. (1998) strongly cautioned against this pairing.

When Level 2 supervisors are assigned to supervise Level 2 supervisees, the risk of associated ethical challenges increases. Stoltenberg et al. (1998) identified some potential problems associated with this pairing. For example, Level 2 supervisors struggling with their own confusion and frustration may become angry with supervisees and withdraw their investment in the relationship. Or they may use evaluations in a punitive way, listing "global deficits" (Stoltenberg et al., 1998, p. 162) and establishing requirements that supervisees either cannot meet or are likely to exacerbate their characteristic resistance. When the personal problems or normative emotional responses of Level 2 supervisees become apparent, Level 2 supervisors may respond by subtly shifting into psychotherapy-like interactions, sliding into a role with which they are more comfortable and confident (Stoltenberg et al., 1998).

Some supervisors—at any level of development—respond to Level 2 supervisees by overaccommodating to avoid conflict. For example, supervisors may avoid challenging questionable behavior or not persist when the supervisee resists discussing ethically problematic decisions. Other supervisors may become rigid, authoritarian, and demanding so as to establish their authority and ensure compliance and so quell their anxiety. Neither stance facilitates the professional development of the supervisee, and either could result from the supervisor's level of development or from the alchemy of other factors characterizing the members of the dyad. Thus, the misuse of power, compromised objectivity, and insidious drift into multiple relationships are some ethical risks that must be monitored in working with Level 2 supervisees.

Level 3 and 3i supervisees are often considered a relative pleasure to supervise. They tend to be "lower maintenance" and more enjoyable for many supervisors, who may be overcommitted and who welcome the relative ease with which they can execute their supervisory responsibilities.

Therein lies the challenge. Supervisors must always remember that they are providing a service, and though more experienced supervisees may not require the degree of attention needed earlier in their development, the focus of supervisory meetings must remain on the needs of the supervisees. Meetings may include more collegial discussions, but time must be spent on supervisees' cases, questions, and on clinical and professional interests. Because Level 3 and 3i supervisees are less needy, supervisors may rationalize canceling supervision sessions, cutting the time short in favor of returning phone calls, or suggesting that they just go out for lunch instead. Although sharing a meal with a supervisee may be appropriate and even helpful, such social outings should not replace clinical supervision.

Another ethical challenge for supervisors of Level 3 and 3i supervisees is ensuring that their own feelings (or transference or countertransference) in response to the supervisee do not contaminate their objectivity. Themes of envy, competition, intimidation, or resentment may emerge in response to a supervisee's professional accomplishments. Learning that a supervisee has just signed a book contract or been invited to present at a major conference, particularly if the supervisor has tried unsuccessfully to do the same, could prompt the supervisor to become distant, discouraging, or denigrating of those accomplishments. Yet it is always the supervisor's responsibility, as it is the psychotherapist's in a treatment relationship, to contain and manage such feelings, with the help of a consultant if necessary.

Conversely, supervisors may idealize Level 3 or 3i supervisees and become oblivious to their needs. In this scenario, positive, collegial feelings might lead supervisors to use the relationship to meet their social or professional needs. Although advanced supervisees do not generally need the kind of support and frequent feedback about strengths so helpful to Level 1 supervisees, every professional needs recognition for his or her achievements and clinical successes; providing that is always part of the supervisor's responsibilities. Further, a supervisor's admiration of a supervisee's extraordinary competence in one domain may hinder awareness of deficits in other domains.

When supervisors experience a neutral or mild emotional response to manifestations of supervisees' developmental characteristics and needs, the work of the supervisor is simplified. Strong countertransferential feelings in the context of supervision are not in and of themselves ethically problematic. Yet unrecognized or misunderstood, they increase the risk of ethical errors related to compromised objectivity and diminished supervisory effectiveness.

Supervisees' level of development is certainly not the only factor affecting their work performance or the dynamics of a supervisory relationship. The context of the work setting, cultural and ethnic backgrounds of each member of the supervisory dyad, the client population, and the personalities of all parties influence the supervisory process.

CONCLUSION

Professionals at every level of development encounter ethical dilemmas, and no one is immune to error. Therefore, supervisees are best served by supervisors who rule out the more common factors leading to ethical errors and respond with sensitivity to their supervisees' individual needs in the context of developmental level: That is the core concept of developmental models of supervision.

5

BOUNDARIES AND MULTIPLE RELATIONSHIPS

Most of the time, supervisory and consultative relationships are just that. Providers of these services generally operate within the confines of appropriate roles and ensure that their charges are not confused by the demands and challenges of other roles. Challenges to these roles do sometimes occur, however, despite the best efforts of supervisors and consultants.

The zeitgeist regarding appropriate professional boundaries in psychology and other mental health professions has evolved in recent years, and opinions continue to be diverse (Pope & Vasquez, 2007). There is general agreement, for example, that sexual harassment, exploitation, and sexual contact between psychotherapists and clients are unethical (American Association for Marriage and Family Therapy [AAMFT], 2001; American Association of Pastoral Counselors [AAPC], 1994; American Counseling Association [ACA], 2005; American Psychiatric Association [ApA], 2009; American Psychological Association [APA], 2002; Association of State and Provincial Psychology Boards [ASPPB], 2005; Canadian Psychological Association [CPA], 2000, 2009; Center for Credentialing & Education [CCE], 2008; National Association of Alcohol and Drug Abuse Counselors [NAADAC], 2008; National Association of Social Workers

[NASW], 2008). However, the question of whether other diversions from the role of psychotherapist are problematic or unethical continues to be a subject of debate (Zur, 2007).

One point of view illustrating this controversy is that of Lazarus and Zur (2002). These authors have argued that the avoidance of dual or multiple relationships with clients has gone too far and may be countertherapeutic. They have claimed that psychotherapists' unwillingness to consider engaging in nonsexual dual relationships is based on "the fear of lawsuits and of many hypervigilant regulatory and consumer protection agencies" (Lazarus & Zur, 2002, p. xxxii) rather than on the unique needs of the individual patient or client. More recently, Barnett, Lazarus, Vasquez, Moorehead-Slaughter, and Johnson (2007) have supported Lazarus and Zur's views. Others have argued for greater sensitivity to the power imbalance in professional relationships and to the potential for exploitation and harm (Celenza, 2007; Gabbard, 1994; Gutheil & Gabbard, 1993; M. R. Peterson, 1992).

Much of the professional literature on boundaries and multiple relationships is focused on therapeutic relationships (Anderson & Kitchner, 1996; G. Corey, Corey, & Callanan, 2007; Cottone, 2005; Gutheil, 1993; Gutheil & Gabbard, 1993; Herlihy & Corey, 2006; W. B. Johnson, Ralph, & Johnson, 2005; Knapp & Slattery, 2004). Some of these articles address clinical supervision along with their focus on psychotherapy (Lamb, Catanzaro, & Moorman, 2003; Moleski & Kiselica, 2005; Nigro, 2004; M. R. Peterson, 1992; T. W. White, 2003). Other publications specifically consider boundaries and multiple relationships in the context of supervision (Bonosky, 1995; Falender & Shafranske, 2004; Gabbard & Lester, 1995; Gottlieb, Robinson, & Younggren, 2007; Haynes, Corey, & Moulton, 2003; Heru, Strong, Price, & Recupero, 2004; Slimp & Burian, 1994). Discussions of boundaries in clinical consultation are even more rare, and these authors most often address boundaries in organizational rather than clinical consultation (Bellman, 2002; Brown, Pryzwansky, & Schulte, 2001). Certainly there are similarities between psychotherapy, supervision, and consultation, but the relationships, boundaries, and ethical dilemmas differ. Separate consideration of boundaries in each is therefore warranted.

This chapter addresses these gaps in the literature, providing an opportunity to examine

- professional standards and guidelines pertaining to multiple relationships as well as seven specific topics related to multiple relationships in supervisory and consultative relationships (boundaries, exploitation and abuse of power, psychotherapy with supervisees, sexual harassment and sexual exploitation, sexual contact with supervisees, impaired objectivity and judgment, and unforeseen or unavoidable multiple relationships);

- the concept of social power and its implications for supervision and consultation;
- the potential impact of individual characteristics of members of the supervisor–consultant dyad, including gender, race, ethnicity, sexual orientation, religion, and physical ability;
- the roles and functions of supervisors and consultants and how secondary roles complement or compromise the primary roles;
- other types of relationships (e.g., social, sexual, collegial, psychotherapeutic) and interactions that may affect the primary supervisory or consultative relationship; and
- strategies and models for making decisions about engaging in alternate roles.

ETHICAL STANDARDS

Virtually every association of mental health professionals addresses the issues of multiple relationships, boundaries, and exploitation (AAMFT, 2001; AAPC, 1994; ACA, 2005; ApA, 2009; APA, 2002; ASPPB, 2005; CPA, 2000; NAADAC, 2008; NASW, 2005, 2008), yet only a few include specific definitions (APA, 2002; ASPPB, 2005). Many address supervision and consultation directly; others contain statements with indirect implications for these areas of practice. An overview of the seven primary boundary issues addressed in relevant codes and guidelines provides a context for further discussion (see Table 5.1).

Psychology Professional Associations

The language of the APA Ethics Code (2002) is general and covers supervision and consultation as well as psychotherapy and other professional functions performed by psychologists. The APA Ethics Code defines a multiple relationship as one in which a psychologist is in a professional role with a person while simultaneously engaging in another role with that individual or someone "closely associated with or related to" (2002, p. 6) that person. In addition, a multiple relationship occurs when a psychologist promises to engage in such a relationship in the future.

TABLE 5.1
Ethical Codes and Guidelines: Sections That Address Boundaries and Multiple Relationships Applicable to Supervision and Consultation

Code or guideline	Boundary issue						
	General boundaries and multiple relationships	General exploitation and abuse of power	Psychotherapy with supervisees	Sexual harassment and exploitation	Sexual contact with supervisees	Impaired objectivity and judgment	Unforeseen or unavoidable multiple relationships
			Psychology professional associations				
APA (2002)	7.05 (b)	3.03, 3.08	7.05 (a, b)	3.02	7.07	7.04	3.05 (b)
ASPPB (2005)	—	III.E.1.	III.B.2.b.	III.E.1.	III.E.1.	III.B.2.b.	—
CPA (2000)	—	I.4	—	I.4, III.31	II.28	III.33	III.34
			Counseling professional associations				
AAMFT (2001)	—	3.9, 4.1	4.2	3.8	4.3	4.1, 4.6	4.6
AAPC (1994)	V.	V.	V.A.	V.B.	V.C.	V.	—
ACA (2005)	F.3.a., F.3.d.	—	F.5.c., F.6.e.	C.6.a., F.3.c.	F.3.b.	—	F.3.a., F.3.e.
NAADAC (2008)	—	7	—	—	—	—	—

	Other mental health professional associations					
ApA (2009)	3.01(b)	4.14	—	4.14	—	—
NASW (2008)	—	1.06(b), 3.01(c), 3.02(d)	2.08	2.07(a)	2.09 (a, b)	2.07(b)
NASW (2005)	—	—	—	—	—	—
		Specialty guidelines				
AAMFT (2007)	pp. 11, 12, 15	—	pp. 11, 15	—	p. 15	3.2.2, 3.2.3
AAPC (1997)	—	3.2.1	3.3	—	3.2.3	—
ACES (1993)	3.12, 3.17	—	2.11, 3.17, 3.18, 3.19	2.10	2.10	2.09
ASPPBª (2003)	II.D.(1, 2, 3)	II.D. (1, 2, 3)	II.D. (1, 2, 3)	II.D. (1, 2, 3)	—	II.D. (1, 2, 3)
CPA (2009)	III. 7, 8	III.4	—	III. 8	—	—
CCE (2008)	5	5	5	5	5	—

Note. APA = American Psychological Association; ApA = American Psychiatric Association; ASPPB = Association of State and Provincial Psychology Boards; CPA = Canadian Psychological Association; AAMFT = American Association for Marriage and Family Therapy; AAPC = American Association for Pastoral Counselors; ACA = American Counseling Association; NAADAC = National Association of Alcohol and Drug Abuse Counselors; ApA = American Psychiatric Association; NASW = National Association of Social Workers; ACES = Association for Counselor Educators and Supervisors; CCE = Center for Credentialing & Education. Dashes indicate that no section of a code addresses a given issue. Although not numbered in the document, for clarification the parenthetical numbers refer to each of these sections: (1) doctoral level candidates, (2) credentialed nondoctoral personnel, and (3) uncredentialed personnel providing psychological services.
ªThe ASPPB *Supervision Guidelines* includes three sections, each focusing on a different type of supervisee.

The APA Ethics Code incorporates the concept of impaired objectivity when addressing the appropriateness or inappropriateness of multiple relationships:

> A psychologist refrains from entering into a multiple relationship if the multiple relationship could reasonably be expected to impair the psychologist's objectivity, competence, or effectiveness in performing his or her functions as a psychologist, or otherwise risks exploitation or harm to the person with whom the professional relationship exists. (p. 6)

The *ASPPB Code of Conduct* (2005) defines multiple relationships in a similar manner but also provides examples of additional relationships that might occur: "Psychologists recognize that multiple relationships may occur because of the psychologist's present or previous familial, social, emotional, financial, supervisory, political, administrative or legal relationship with the client or a relevant person associated with or related to the client" (p. 6). The ASPPB code further states that psychologists must "take reasonable steps to ensure that if such a multiple relationship occurs, it is not exploitative of the client or relevant person associated with or related to the client" (p. 6).

Thus, APA and ASPPB codes focus on relationships most likely to impair judgment or risk harm or exploitation. Multiple relationships without the potential for such impact are not prohibited by either code.

The *Canadian Code of Ethics for Psychologists* (CPA, 2000) does not include a definition of multiple relationships, but it does state that psychologists

> avoid dual or multiple relationships (e.g., with . . . supervisees, students, or trainees) and other situations that might present a conflict of interest or that might reduce their ability to be objective and unbiased in their determinations of what might be in the best interests of others. (p. 24)

Like the APA and ASPPB codes, the CPA code highlights the concept of impaired objectivity as a factor underlying the requirement that psychologists avoid certain multiple relationships. The second factor is that such relationships risk harm to consumers, including supervisees, and by extrapolation, consultees.

Each of these three sets of ethical standards also prohibits sexual harassment, exploitation, and related abuses of power (APA, 2002; ASPPB, 2005; CPA, 2000). The APA's specific prohibition of sexual as well as other types of exploitation of supervisees is underscored in other standards of its Ethics Code (3.08, 7.07).

Another standard of the APA Ethics Code, 7.04, states that supervisors must not require supervisees to disclose personal information in the context of training unless the supervisees are notified of the requirement in advance or the disclosure is necessary to evaluate and obtain assistance for the individual. Implicit is the idea that required disclosure of personal information may not only invade the privacy of supervisees but may also alter the nature of their relationships with the professors and supervisors charged with evaluating them. Further, there exists the potential for supervisors to solicit information for personal gratification (e.g., to satisfy curiosity or a need for friendship). When supervisors are privy to personal information unrelated to the work of supervisees, they must take deliberate steps to ensure that this knowledge does not contaminate their professional judgment when executing evaluations and other responsibilities.

Counseling Professional Associations

Several counseling associations address multiple relationships by providing specific examples rather than definitions (AAPC, 1994; ACA, 2005). The AAPC *Code of Ethics* (1994) acknowledges the power inherent in supervisory relationships and requires counselors to "avoid exploiting their trust and dependency" (p. 4) and "avoid dual relationships with such persons that could impair our judgment or increase the risk of personal and/or financial exploitation" (p. 4).

The ACA *Code of Ethics* (2005), in a section entitled Supervision, Training, and Teaching, does not use the term *multiple relationship* nor define the concept specifically. Rather, the code instructs counseling supervisors to "avoid nonprofessional relationships with current supervisees" and states that supervisors "do not engage in any form of nonprofessional interaction that may compromise the supervisory relationship" (ACA, 2005, p. 14).

The NAADAC *Code of Ethics* (2008) uses the term *dual relationships* (p. 3), but the context represents a sharp contrast to similar codes. The preamble to Principle 7 states, for example, "I understand that I must seek to nurture and support the development of a *relationship of equals* [italics added] rather than to take unfair advantage of individuals who are vulnerable and exploitable" (NAADAC, 2008, p. 2). This statement implies a dichotomy: Members develop "equal" relationships with those they serve, or by default, they will "take unfair advantage" (NAADAC, 2008, p. 2). Unlike other ethics codes, the NAADAC *Code of Ethics* implies that either the power differential does not exist or that it is something to be overcome.

Mental Health Associations

Like the counseling associations (AAPC, 1994; ACA, 2005), the AAMFT *Code of Ethics* (2001) does not define multiple relationships but offers examples of prohibited behavior. This code states that its members must not accept as supervisees "those individuals with whom a prior or existing relationship could compromise the therapist's objectivity" (AAMFT, 2001, p. 6).

The ApA (2009) and NASW (2005) have not defined or specifically addressed multiple relationships in supervision. In fact, aside from a discussion of sexual contact, the ApA (2009) *Principles of Medical Ethics With Annotations Especially Applicable to Psychiatry* does not mention boundaries or multiple relationships with supervisees. The NASW's *Standards for Clinical Social Work* (2005) addresses neither general boundaries and multiple relationships nor sexual contact with supervisees. The NASW *Code of Ethics* (2008), however, does state that "social workers should not take unfair advantage of any professional relationship or exploit others to further their personal, religious, political, or business interests" (NASW, 2008, p. 7). Section 3.01, Supervision and Consultation, includes another relevant statement: "Social workers who provide supervision or consultation are responsible for setting clear, appropriate, and culturally sensitive boundaries" (NASW, 2008, p. 15). Although lacking a definition, the code alerts social workers to the responsibility for managing boundaries in supervision.

ETHICAL AND SPECIALTY GUIDELINES AND ETHICS CODES

Several professional associations have addressed multiple relationships and boundaries in specialty guidelines. Unlike other guidelines, which are generally aspirational, AAMFT's "Responsibilities and Guidelines for AAMFT Approved Supervisors and Supervisor Candidates" (included in AAMFT, 2007) is detailed, specific, and binding. Supervisors are specifically prohibited from supervising current and former family members and therapy clients.

The supervisors of pastoral counselors are offered direction in the *Supervision Standards of Practice* (AAPC, 1997). Section 3, Managing the Supervisory Relationship, instructs supervisors to "limit the risk of exploiting supervisees" (AAPC, 1997, p. 3) by adhering to the AAPC *Code of Ethics* (1994). *Supervision Standards of Practice* also acknowledges (and therefore allows) that supervision may occur between individuals "who have social and collegial relations in addition to the supervisory relationship" (AAPC, 1997, p. 3). In such situations, supervisors are directed to "structure interactions so as not to interfere with the successful fulfillment of the supervisory contract" (AAPC, 1997, p. 3). Should such circumstances compromise supervisors' ability to discharge their responsibilities effectively, the *Supervision Standards of Practice* encourages them to terminate the supervisory relationship. Further, it distinguishes between therapy and supervision, discouraging supervisors from providing both to the same individual.

The ACES *Ethical Guidelines for Counseling Supervisors* (1993) provides a detailed discussion of boundaries in the context of supervision. The ACES recommends the avoidance of dual roles when possible and when those roles "might impair the supervisor's objectivity and professional judgment" (1993, p. 3) and that conflicts be minimized when additional roles are unavoidable (2.09). The combination of psychotherapy and supervision is specifically discouraged (2.11). Whether therapy may be provided in addition to supervision is not clear, but other recommendations suggest it may not. The ACES Ethical Guidelines also addresses personal growth activities that may be a part of a supervisee's training (3.17, 3.18, 3.19). Although supervisors may recommend such activities to supervisees, they should not themselves provide the services.

The ASPPB *Supervision Guidelines* (2003) simply states that "supervisors avoid entering into dual relationships with their supervisees" (p. 4). When they encounter "unforeseen interference which may be potentially harmful to the supervisory relationship" (p. 4), supervisors are to obtain consultation and resolve the problem "with due regard for the best interests of the supervisee" (p. 4). Like the ASPPB *Supervision Guidelines*, the CPA *Ethical Guidelines for Supervision in Psychology: Teaching, Research, Practice, and Administration* (2009) states that supervisors (and supervisees) should "avoid all forms of exploitation, or actions that harm the supervisor or supervisee and that do not serve the objectives of the supervision e.g., financial, sexual, gossip, blackmail, false allegations, and coercion in the supervisory and the work relationships" (p. 8). *The Approved Clinical Supervisor (ACS)Code of Ethics* (CCE, 2008) requires that supervisors "avoid all dual relationships with supervisees that may interfere with . . . professional judgment or exploit the supervisee" (p. 1).

In summary, all of these professional ethics codes (AAMFT, 2001; AAPC, 1994; ACA, 2005; ApA, 2009; APA, 2002; ASPPB, 2005; CPA, 2000; NAADAC, 2008; NASW, 2005, 2008) and specialty guidelines (AAMFT, 2007; AAPC, 1997; ACES, 1993; ASPPB, 2003; CCE, 2008; CPA, 2009) alert supervisors to the risks associated with engaging in multiple relationships with supervisees. Some include prohibitions of particular relationships (AAMFT, 2001; AAPC, 1994; ACA, 2005; APA, 2002; ASPPB, 2005; NAADAC, 2008; NASW, 2008), and others discourage such behavior (ApA, 2009; CPA, 2000). These codes and guidelines provide a foundation for the consideration of specific boundary and multiple relationships issues.

POWER AND INFLUENCE IN SUPERVISION AND CONSULTATION

The ethical dimensions of supervisory and consultative relationships are best examined in the context of power and influence. Although their roles differ, both supervisors and consultants are in positions of authority. But the magnitude of this power differential varies substantially from one such relationship to another. Some of the many factors determining the power differential in a given relationship are considered in the discussion that follows. The more omnipresent and pervasive issues of power and influence provide a context for their consideration.

French and Raven contributed seminal work on the issue of social power in 1959, and Kadushin (1992) later considered its applicability to supervision. Although more contemporary authors have described similar models to explain power in relationships (M. R. Peterson, 1992), French and Raven's (1959) robust, albeit theoretical, analysis is readily applicable to understanding the power inherent in both supervisory and consultative relationships.

French and Raven (1959, p. 151) defined the strength of power as the maximum potential ability of one social agent (O; "person, role, norm group, or part of a group") to influence a person (P), in this case, a supervisee or consultee. They identified five bases of social power:

1. reward power, based on P's perception that O has the ability to mediate rewards for him;
2. coercive power, based on P's perception that O has the ability to mediate punishments for him;
3. legitimate power, based on the perception by P that O has a legitimate right to prescribe behavior for him;
4. referent power, based on P's identification with O; and
5. expert power, based on the perception that O has some special knowledge or expertness. (French & Raven, 1959, pp. 155–156)

French and Raven's (1959) paradigm may be extrapolated to suggest that supervisors possess both reward and coercive power. Clinical supervisors generally have the power to pass or fail, to endorse or not endorse (for certification or licensure), and/or to hire or fire a supervisee. State and provincial licensing boards and employers sometimes mandate supervision as part of a rehabilitation plan. The supervisor in such a case may be in a position to make favorable or unfavorable recommendations regarding the individual's licensure or employment status. The appointment to and implicit endorsement of an individual in the role of supervisor by an agency, credentialing body, institution, licensing board, or professional association imbues the supervisor (O) with credibility in the eyes of the supervisee (P), adding legitimate power to any prescription for behavior. This implicit endorsement, in combination with possession of the required degrees and experience, affords the supervisor expert power.

French and Raven (1959) indicated that referent power "has its basis in the identification of P with O . . . a feeling of oneness . . . or a desire for such an identity" (p. 161). The degree to which a given supervisee (P) identifies with his or her supervisor (O) determines the existence and magnitude of referent power in that relationship. Many variables influence the extent of this identification. The degree to which supervisees perceive themselves to be like their supervisors or the degree to which they aspire to be like them affects the extent to which they identify with them. Members of the supervisory dyad may be similar or different in terms of factors such as gender, race, ethnicity, sexual orientation, religion, age, relationship status, physical size, and physical ability or disability. When the supervision is conducted across disciplines, the degree of identification may be influenced and the power differential affected, depending on the perceived status of the supervisor's profession. In addition to these characteristics, a supervisee may identify with the supervisor's theoretical orientation, preferred client populations, or research interests or be drawn to a charismatic personality. Beyond professional factors, supervisees may perceive similarities between themselves and their supervisors in innumerable other areas. The two individuals might share, for example, a mutual love of tennis or fishing, affiliation with the same political party or social cause, or enjoyment of the same authors. In addiction treatment settings, the supervisor and supervisee may both be in recovery and share similar personal histories.

Additionally, each of these variables must be considered in the light of their cultural context (Pack-Brown & Williams, 2003). If the dominant culture affords greater power to a particular gender or race, for example, then the gender and race of each dyad member will likely influence the relative power of the supervisor over the supervisee. When supervisees feel great admiration for their supervisors and therefore identify with them, they are more likely to emulate them and to conform to their requests and directives. Conversely, if cultural factors and personal characteristics align in an alternate way, the relative power of the supervisor may be diminished. It is possible that these factors could interact to potentiate, minimize, or in some other way influence the impact.

Consulting relationships generally involve a less potent power differential than their supervisory counterparts. This is particularly true when consultation is brief, circumscribed, and provided by a peer. The consultant's ability to dispense rewards or administer punishments, as defined by French and Raven (1959), is relatively minimal. Legitimate, referent, and expert power, on the other hand, are potentially as powerful in a consulting relationship as in a supervisory relationship, though not necessarily.

NATURE OF BOUNDARIES AND BOUNDARY VIOLATIONS

Many authors have drawn distinctions between boundary crossings and violations (Barnett, 2008; Barnett et al., 2007; Gabbard & Lester, 1995; Guthiel & Gabbard, 1993; Lazarus & Zur, 2002). Boundary violations are considered inherently unethical, and they have a high probability of causing harm. Conversely, boundary crossings may or may not be unethical. Both are departures from standard practice, but a boundary crossing may be a carefully considered exception to the general rule based on a low probability of harm and a high likelihood of benefit to the individual.

Except in cases of egregious boundary violations, knowing the specific action or behavior that falls outside of the supervisor's or consultant's role is rarely enough to definitively determine whether a boundary has been violated. Complicating such determinations is the fact that relationships are not static. The unique power differential in a given supervisory or consultative relationship is determined by the confluence of multiple factors—factors that continually evolve. Todd and Storm (1997), in their discussion of supervisory relationships, observed that "all relations of power are unstable and changeable" (p. 232). What might be highly inappropriate and even harmful with one individual at a particular time (e.g., the first week of supervision) might be highly effective and helpful with a different person or with the same individual at another time. Directly intervening with a supervisee's client may be necessary and welcomed early in the supervision but considered inappropriate and intrusive with a more seasoned consultee. A supervisee who has a history of difficulties with professional boundaries will require a more cautious approach. Asking such a supervisee to lunch could mislead the individual into perceiving a desire for friendship, whereas the same invitation, extended in the context of a longer term supervisory relationship in which the boundaries have been clearly established, may be a neutral or even helpful event.

The characteristics and vulnerabilities of the supervisor are also relevant (Barnett, 2008). Thus, a particular action by one supervisor at a certain time could be fraught with risk, whereas that same action by another supervisor might be quite safe. Supervisors' ability to accurately assess risk may vary. A supervisor with a history of alcoholism who is in the throes of a painful divorce will likely be at greater risk of impaired objectivity and of serious boundary violations if he or she invites a supervisee to meet at a bar to celebrate the completion of their conference presentation. A supervisor without those vulnerabilities will likely be better equipped to evaluate the risks and make a sound ethical decision, which may include having a drink with the supervisee.

Contextual variables must be considered not only in formal professional interactions but also in informal ones. Supervisors are more likely to share a meal or discuss politics and vacation preferences later in a relationship. Advanced supervisees are more likely to enjoy and appreciate these conversations (provided that they do not occur during the supervision sessions) and less likely to feel pressure to alter their opinions to accommodate the supervisor. Earlier, however, a supervisee with differing views is at greater risk for feeling intimidated, alienated, or uninformed or for questioning the supervisor's skills and abilities. Supervisors' responsibility to analyze these dynamics is complex, however, because the relationships are not static. It is possible for example, that as supervisees progress, they may identify more with their supervisors, thus increasing the referent power in the relationship. The AAPC *Supervision Standards of Practice* (1997) includes a statement acknowledging these changing parameters: "Supervisors attend to the evolution of power dynamics in the supervisory relationship" (p. 3).

Individual personalities and preferences are also factors in determining appropriate action. One person may appreciate an action or disclosure that offends the sensibilities of another. Further, the absence of a complaint by the supervisee or consultee or even expressed appreciation for a supervisor's or consultant's behavior is not the only filter through which a boundary decision must be sifted. Particularly in supervision, novice clinicians may not understand what is appropriate behavior for supervisors. It is therefore incumbent on those with more power to not only consider supervisees' or consultees' likely responses but to use their experience and expertise to anticipate possible repercussions that may not be readily apparent.

Whether a particular action on the part of a supervisor or consultant constitutes a boundary crossing, boundary violation, helpful intervention, or just a neutral, inconsequential interaction depends on many factors. The purposes, objectives, and anticipated duration and course of the relationship must be considered along with the specific roles, functions, and responsibilities associated with the relationship. As mentioned, consultation generally involves a less potent power differential, so boundaries in these relationships may be more flexible. If, for example, a consultation is provided to a colleague learning to administer a new version of a psychological test (for which he or she is competent to administer the previous version), the prior existence of a friendship likely presents minimal risks. In contrast, the purpose of the relationship may be to oversee the work of a previously impaired professional following a disciplinary order from their state licensing board. The board may permit the individual to resume a limited practice with consultation or supervision from a designated clinician for whom objectivity and sound judgment is critical to ensure client welfare. Particularly when the impairment has resulted in boundary violations, the risk of agreeing to supervise or consult with a person with whom one has a prior or concurrent relationship is significant. In addition to compromises to clinical work, the impact on the clinician of a confusing role model must be considered.

The supervisor's or consultant's knowledge and understanding of their supervisees or consultees' individual personalities, vulnerabilities, characteristics, needs, and history enables more accurate prediction of potential problems and risks. Conversations with previous employers and supervisors may be helpful in this regard. A previous professional connection with a prospective supervisee, assuming that role is not in conflict with the proposed one, might be helpful to the supervisor or consultant when deciding whether to work with a given individual.

ROLES OF SUPERVISOR AND CONSULTANT

To determine whether an action is consistent with the role of supervisor or consultant, it is helpful to first review the components of each of these roles (see Chapter 1, this volume). Certainly there is overlap in the actual tasks of a clinical supervisor and a clinical consultant, as conceptualized here. One fundamental distinction lies in the power, authority, and responsibility inherent in each role. Because supervision involves greater responsibility and because it is generally required, the roles in which the supervisor engages are more prescribed. Supervisors' responsibilities often include evaluation, passing or failing practicum students and interns, and endorsement for licensure or certification. Supervisors create records regarding the work performance of supervisees and the progress of their clients. On-site supervisors generally have access to information about clients as well as the authority to intervene with them directly if necessary. Supervisors may require changes in records, reports, and treatment plans and may trump the clinical judgment of their supervisees. Because supervisors are liable for the work of their supervisees, they have the authority to establish requirements and dispense meaningful consequences for noncompliance.

Conversely, consultants make recommendations, suggest clinical direction, and influence but do not direct consultees' behavior. The circumstances occasioning the consultation and specified in the consultation contract (see Chapter 6, this volume) determine the extent of their purview. Consultants may provide evaluative feedback, but that feedback does not typically determine whether the individual passes or fails the experience. Consultants offer opinions, but those opinions do not carry the same weight as the opinions of supervisors. In some cases, a consultant may have an educative role or even participate in the rehabilitation of a clinician. Yet the contract is different. Consultants have less responsibility, less authority, and therefore less power than supervisors.

ADMINISTRATIVE VERSUS CLINICAL SUPERVISION

Another area of responsibility sometimes listed in a clinical supervisor's job description, but not in a consultant's, is that of administrator. Although the separation of the two roles likely reduces complexity and the potential for compromised objectivity and effectiveness, in reality, administrative and clinical responsibilities are often combined (Kenfield, 1993; Tromski-Klingshirn & Davis, 2007). Therefore, responsibilities associated with both roles are delineated in the discussion that follows to facilitate examination of potential challenges and pitfalls inherent in their combination.

Bernard and Goodyear (2009) clarified that "the clinical supervisor has a dual investment in the quality of services offered to clients and the professional development of the supervisee" (p. 193). In contrast, administrative supervisors "focus on matters such as communication protocol, personnel concerns, and fiscal issues" (Bernard & Goodyear, 2009, p. 193). In addition to these generalities, specific responsibilities distinguish the two roles. Administrative responsibilities may include

- creating and implementing policies and procedures;
- hiring, firing, and disciplining employees;
- determining employee salaries, promotions, workloads, and schedules;
- monitoring productivity;
- developing and administering a budget; and
- advertising and marketing of services.

The tasks of clinical supervisors typically include

- reviewing and signing off on clinical reports and records,
- teaching clinical skills,
- providing formative and summative evaluations,
- facilitating the professional development of supervisees,
- passing or failing student-supervisees who are completing practicums or internships,
- endorsing (or electing not to endorse) supervises for licensure or certification, and
- attending to the supervisory relationship.

In summary, the primary concern of administrative supervisors is the management of the institution (Falvey, 1987), whereas the priorities for clinical supervisors are supervisees, their clients, and the profession.

Although combining the two roles may not be uncommon (Kenfield, 1993; Tromski-Klingshirn & Davis, 2007), doing so may increase the power differential and compromise the supervisors' effectiveness in each role. One disadvantage of combining these roles, for example, is that supervisees' tendency to inhibit disclosure of vulnerabilities and clinical errors may be enhanced when there are added implications for raises, promotions, or even employment.

Some responsibilities may be either administrative or clinical. Both administrative and clinical supervisors, for example, might evaluate employee-supervisees, write recommendations, and address their professional development needs. Both may oversee case assignment, though clinical supervisors are likely to be more familiar with the skills and interests of supervisees. Verification of practicum and internship students' hours is usually required, and either type of supervisor could provide this. Clinical supervisors, however, are more likely to keep detailed records of the content of supervisory meetings, including information about specific cases.

VARIATIONS IN THE SUPERVISORY AND CONSULTATIVE ROLES BY SETTING

Both clinical supervision and consultation are provided in a variety of settings. The relationship boundaries vary according to the unique aspects of these work environments. Academic, employment, and private practice settings are considered.

Academia

Master's and doctoral students in psychology and other mental health professions are typically required to complete practicums and/or internships as part of their academic training. Individual and group supervision are usually provided on-site, and supervisors are generally assigned the responsibilities and given the authority described previously. Additionally, students often participate in group instruction provided by program faculty, complementing the on-site supervision (Council for Accreditation of Counseling and Related Educational Programs, 2001; Riva & Cornish, 1995). Such groups in which students present cases are sometimes described as *supervision*. Faculty members conducting these groups, however, do not have access to client files nor do they have legitimate opportunities to intervene with clients in emergencies.

In short, they do not have the authority to assume liability for their students' professional decisions and behavior. When these educational or consultative groups are referred to as supervision, faculty members may unintentionally assume the liability of supervisors in the case of a malpractice suit. This type of oversight is more accurately described as *consultation* or *education* because these terms more clearly reflect the responsibility associated with the role and may therefore mitigate legal exposure for faculty.

Professional Employment

The duties of supervisors in employment settings may include administrative or clinical responsibilities and sometimes both. These settings often provide new professionals with a place to obtain the clinical supervision required for licensure. When supervisees are licensed, credentialed professionals, however, they are more likely to receive administrative supervision than the more intensive clinical supervision typically provided for prelicensure colleagues. Clinical management of cases is the ultimate responsibility of each individual professional, and assistance is sought as needed. Staff meetings are sometimes used for group or peer consultation, but when the meeting agenda is combined with administrative tasks, clinical work may be relegated to a lower priority.

Clinical supervision and consultation for credentialed professionals have many advantages (ACES, 1993). Although not generally required, either can be a strategy for maintaining and enhancing professional competence. Further, supervision and consultation facilitate the professional development of employee-clinicians, may improve the quality of services to clients, and can serve as a risk management strategy (Gottlieb, 1993; Gottlieb et al., 2007; Haas & Malouf, 2005; Younggren & Gottlieb, 2004). Unless clinical supervision is a high priority, the agency, program, or department may neglect these objectives. Therefore, despite the desirability of providing clinical as well as administrative supervision, the latter is probably more common in employment settings.

Private Practice

As discussed, mental health professionals seeking licensure or certification are often required by credentialing bodies to obtain supervised, postdegree experience. Although most obtain this supervision in their work settings, the employing agency may not always include staff members with the appropriate credentials. In that case, prospective licensees may seek supervision from an appropriately credentialed professional practicing privately in the community, assuming such supervisory arrangements are not prohibited by licensing boards as is the case in some jurisdictions. In California, for example, applicants accruing hours toward licensure are prohibited from paying for supervision and from obtaining it outside of an employment setting (California Board of Psychology, 2008). Another situation in which private supervision might be sought occurs when it is required as part of a prescribed rehabilitation plan following an ethical violation or period of professional impairment.

Perhaps the most important difference between privately arranged supervision and that which is provided by employers or as a part of academic training is who selects and hires whom. Typically, supervisors have the opportunity to interview, select (in the case of students), and hire supervisees. Of course, the other party in each case has the option to say no; a prospective intern or employee may withdraw from the application process or decline an offer. Similarly, a prospective supervisor might decide after an initial interview not to supervise an individual. Nevertheless, the opportunities for supervisees to make initial choices are greatest in privately arranged supervision.

Another distinguishing feature of privately arranged supervision is that supervisees pay directly for the supervision. The ASPPB *Supervision Guidelines* (2003) addresses this situation: "Payment for supervisory services by the predoctoral supervisee is not acceptable. If payment is required for supervision for postdoctoral experience, supervisors should pay particular attention to the impact of the financial arrangements on the supervisory relationship" (p. 4).

Supervisors offering their services privately must be exceptionally clear about the boundaries of the relationship. Although supervisees hire and pay the supervisors, it is the supervisor who is responsible for establishing and monitoring the boundaries. In this respect, offering supervision privately is not unlike private psychotherapy. Supervisors and psychotherapists alike must be vigilant to ensure that their need for business does not lead to their becoming inappropriately accommodating or to avoid confronting problematic behavior so as to dodge conflict. Supervisors in private settings must clarify the decisions for which they are responsible, the decisions the supervisee can make, and those they will make collaboratively.

THE RELATIONSHIP BETWEEN ROLES AND BOUNDARIES

Generally, the more power associated with a given role, the greater the caution that must be exercised by the supervisor or consultant. Because supervisors have more power and influence over supervisees than do consultants over consultees, supervisors must consider ethical dilemmas and make decisions involving boundaries more conservatively. Both supervisors and consultants provide a professional service and are therefore accountable for the relationships that develop, for their own behavior, and in the case of supervisors, for the behavior of supervisees.

Supervisors and consultants play both formal and informal roles relative to the individuals they serve. Teacher, mentor, evaluator, and endorser are examples of more formal roles appropriately associated with that of supervisor. Role model, advocate, support person, and career resource are examples of less formal roles that supervisors and consultants may fill. Each of these roles is generally compatible with the others, and engaging in them rarely presents a conflict that will compromise the individual's ability to execute other responsibilities.

Engaging in other less compatible roles and types of interactions, however, may present problems for supervisees and consultees and represent unethical behavior for supervisors and consultants. Generally, the more discrepant a secondary role is from the primary role, the greater the risk of harm. Because the role of supervisor involves greater power and responsibility compared with that of consultant, supervisors who engage in additional roles, concurrently or sequentially, may be more likely to encounter difficulties and risk harm to supervisees.

Some secondary roles are subtle and can come about in an instant out of a personal comment, request, or self-disclosure by the supervisor. Similarly, the supervisor's tolerance of out-of-role behavior on the part of the supervisee may indicate a subtle role shift. Other more high-risk roles are readily identifiable (e.g., business partner, money lender, babysitter). Sexual partner is certainly a role distinct from that of supervisor and so is discussed first.

SEXUAL RELATIONSHIPS WITH SUPERVISEES AND CONSULTEES

Much has been written about sexual exploitation of clients by psychotherapists (Benowitz, 1991; Borys & Pope, 1989; Celenza, 2007; G. Corey et al., 2007; Downs, 2003; Gonsiorek, 1995; Lamb et al., 2003; Pope, Keith-Spiegel, & Tabachnick, 1986; Rodolfa et al., 1994; Schoener, Milgrom, Gonsiorek, Luepker, & Conroe, 1989). Although sexual contact between supervisors and supervisees has received less attention, increasing recognition of the ethical dimensions of such relationships and of their implications for supervisees, other trainees, and clients has spawned many publications on the topic (Bonosky, 1995; Conroe & Schank, 1989; Glasser & Thorp, 1986; Lamb & Catanzaro, 1998; Miller & Larrabee, 1995; Sullivan & Ogloff, 1998; Zakrzewski, 2006).

Sexual Contact in the Context of Supervision

Professional associations and credentialing bodies agree that sexual harassment and sexually demeaning behavior in a supervisory relationship are unethical (AAMFT, 2001; AAPC, 1994; ACA, 2005; APA, 2002; ASPPB, 2003, 2005; CCE, 2008; CPA, 2000, 2009). Even among authors with diverse opinions about what constitutes appropriate professional boundaries, there is universal agreement that these behaviors are unacceptable (Bartell & Rubin, 1990; Hammel, Olkin, & Taube, 1996; Heru et al., 2004; Jacobs, 1991; Kolbert, Morgan, & Brendel, 2002; Lamb & Catanzaro, 1998; Miller & Larabee, 1995; M. R. Peterson, 1992; Rubin, Hampton, & McManus, 1997; Slimp & Burian, 1994; Sullivan & Ogloff, 1998; Zur, 2007). The issue of consensual sexual contact, however, is more controversial and so warrants additional discussion.

Sexual Contact in the Context of Consultation

The nature of relationships between consultants and consultees varies greatly, and boundaries may vary as well. Engaging in a brief, informal consultation with one's spouse or domestic partner is not without ethical challenges. Personal feelings about the other individual may stimulate protectiveness, defensiveness, or a tendency to be controlling, for example, and other perhaps unconscious agendas could come into play. Themes in the personal relationship have the potential to contaminate the consultation by diluting or exaggerating its perceived value, and a consultee may be more or less likely to follow advice based not on its efficacy but on the implications for the primary relationship. That said, such consultation probably is common among spouses and partners who are mental health professionals, and generally, it may be more helpful than problematic. Awareness of pitfalls, however, will decrease potential for problems.

Of course, this scenario presumes the sexual relationship precedes the professional one and that the consultation is brief and informal. When consultation is sought and a sexual relationship develops in that context, the potential for exploitation and harm is greater. Sexual relationships in the context of more formal consultative relationships and those that occur between supervisors and supervisees are very complex. All of the risks delineated regarding informal consultation most certainly apply and, in fact, are more salient in formal consultative and supervisory relationships.

ETHICAL STANDARDS REGARDING SEXUAL CONTACT IN SUPERVISION

The potential for compromised objectivity, exploitation, abuse of power, and harm to supervisees engaged in sexual contact with supervisors is significant, and these risks are reflected in professional ethics codes and literature. Gottlieb et al. (2007), for example, have stated that "the prohibition regarding sexual relationships with supervisees is now settled" (p. 241), citing the APA Ethics Code. APA prohibits psychologists from having sexual relationships with "students or supervisees who are in their department, agency, or training center or over whom psychologists have or are likely to have evaluative authority" (APA, 2002, p. 10).

With some exceptions (AAMFT, 2007; ASPPB, 2005; NAADAC, 2008; NASW, 2005), most professional ethics codes and specialty guidelines address the issue of sexual relationships in supervision (AAMFT, 2001; AAPC, 1994; ACA, 2005: ACES, 1993; ApA, 2009; APA, 2002; CCE, 2008; CPA, 2000, 2009; NASW, 2008). Some organizations specifically and categorically forbid them: AAMFT (2001), ACA (2005), CCE (2008), CPA (2000, 2009), and NASW (2008) all prohibit sexual relationships with current supervisees and do not allow for exceptions. Others include statements that may have implications for sexual contact between supervisors and supervisees. Table 5.2 provides a sampling of the most relevant statements from these publications.

The AAPC *Code of Ethics* (1994) is an example of a document that includes exceptions to the prohibition of sexual relationships between supervisors and supervisees. It specifies that "domestic partners" (p. 5) may supervise one another "in employee situations" (p. 5). The exception does not, apparently, apply to those supervising student trainees. Neither does the *ASPPB Code of Ethics* (2005) specifically prohibit sexual relationships per se between supervisors and supervisees, but rather it prohibits behavior that exploits supervisees as well as that which is "seductive, demeaning, or harassing" (p. 8). The ApA (2009) takes a slightly different approach, suggesting that sexual contact with supervisees "may be unethical" (p. 7) and may present possible risks to patient treatment and to supervisees. Although specialty guidelines do not carry the same weight as ethics codes, two such documents (ACES, 1993; ASPPB, 2003) recommend that supervisors avoid sexual contact with supervisees. The lack of complete uniformity among ethics codes and specialty guidelines suggests that some controversy remains.

Professional Literature on Sexual Contact in Supervision

The professional literature includes research and theoretical arguments regarding the incidence and impact of sexual contact with supervisors on supervisees, and most authors focus on the multitude of risks associated with such relationships (Bartell & Rubin, 1990; Bowman, Hatley, & Bowman, 1995; Gottlieb et al., 2007; Hammel et al., 1996; Miller & Larrabee, 1995; M. R. Peterson, 1992; Zakrzewski, 2006). Glasser and Thorp's (1986) seminal work in this area examined the incidence and impact of consensual sexual relationships between graduate psychology professors and their students and

TABLE 5.2

Ethics Codes and Guidelines Regarding
Sexual Contact With Supervisees

Code or guideline	Statement
Psychology professional associations	
APA (2002)	Psychologists do not engage in sexual relationships with students or supervisees who are in their department, agency, or training center or over whom psychologists have or are likely to have evaluative authority. (7.07, 10)
ASPPB (2005)	The psychologist shall not engage in any verbal or physical behavior with supervisees which is seductive, demeaning, or harassing or exploits a supervisee in any way— sexually, financially or otherwise. (p. 8)
CPA (2000)	In adhering to the Principle of Responsible Caring, psychologists would . . . not encourage or engage in sexual intimacy with students or trainees with whom the psychologist has an evaluative or other relationship of direct authority. (II.28, p. 17)
Counseling professional associations	
AAPC (1994)	All forms of sexual behavior . . . with our supervisees, students . . . and employees (except in employee situations involving domestic partners) are unethical. (V. C., p. 5)
ACA (2005)	Sexual or romantic interactions or relationships with current supervisees are prohibited. (F.3.a., p. 14)
Other mental health professional associations	
AAMFT (2001)	Marriage and family therapists do not engage in sexual intimacy with students or supervisees during the evaluative or training relationship between the therapist and student or supervisee. Should a supervise engage in sexual activity with a former supervisee, the burden of proof shifts to the supervisor to demonstrate that there has been no exploitation or injury to the supervisee. (4.3, p. 6)
	Marriage and family therapists avoid accepting as supervisees or students those individual with whom a prior or existing relationship could compromise the therapist's objectivity. When such situations cannot be avoided, therapists take appropriate precautions to maintain objectivity. Examples of such relationships include, but are not limited to, those individuals with whom the therapist has a current or prior sexual, close personal, immediate familial, or therapeutic relationship. (4.6, p. 6)

TABLE 5.2

Ethics Codes and Guidelines Regarding
Sexual Contact With Supervisees   *(Continued)*

Code or guideline	Statement
ApA (2009)	Sexual involvement between a faculty member or supervisor and a trainee or student, in those situations in which an abuse of power can occur, often takes advantage of inequalities in the working relationship and may be unethical because: a. Any treatment of a patient being supervised may be deleteriously affected. b. It may damage the trust relationship between teacher and student. c. Teachers are important professional role models for their trainees and affect their trainees' future professional behavior. (4.14, p. 7)
NASW (2008)	Social workers who function as supervisors . . . should not engage in sexual activities or contact with supervisees, students, trainees, or other colleagues over whom they exercise professional authority. (2.07a, p. 9)

Specialty guidelines	
ACES (1993)	Supervisors should not participate in any form of sexual contact with supervisees. (2.10, p. 3)
ASPPB (2003)	Supervisors avoid entering into dual relationships with their supervisees. (II. D., p. 7)
CPA (2009)	Supervisors and supervisees should: . . . be aware of professional boundaries in the supervisory relationship, and manage additional roles (e.g. social relationships) in a manner that does not compromise the supervisor relationship. Intimate sexual relationships, however, are prohibited. (III. 8., p. 7)
CCE (2008)	Avoid all dual relationships with supervisees that may interfere with the Approved Clinical Supervisor's professional judgment or exploit the supervisee. Sexual, romantic, or intimate relationships between an approved clinical supervisor and supervisees shall not occur. (5, p. 1)

Note. APA = American Psychological Association; ASPPB = Association of State and Provincial Psychology Boards; CPA = Canadian Psychological Association; AAPC = American Association for Pastoral Counselors; ACA = American Counseling Association; AAMFT = American Association for Marriage and Family Therapy; ApA = American Psychiatric Association; NASW = National Association of Social Workers; ACES = Association for Counselor Educators and Supervisors; and CCE = Center for Credentialing & Education.

between supervisors and supervisees. Their sample consisted of 464 female members of APA's Division 12, Clinical Psychology. About 5% of supervisees reported having had sexual contact with supervisors, and 17% reported sexual contact with professors during their graduate training (Glasser & Thorp, 1986). Perhaps Glasser and Thorp's (1986) most instructive finding illustrated how perceptions change over time: Although only 28% of subjects said that they felt coerced into the behavior at the time, in retrospect, 51% said they felt coerced to some degree.

Even more compelling is their finding that although 36% of subjects judged the sexual contact to be unethical when it occurred, at the time of the survey 95% thought it was unethical and harmful (Glasser & Thorp, 1986). Although faculty–student relationships are not identical to those of supervisors and supervisees, power differentials inherent in the two types of relationships are similar, and faculty can also serve as supervisors. Results are therefore relevant.

A more contemporary study, also using self-report, included 448 male and female student affiliates of APA (Zakrzewski, 2006). Only 2% of respondents, compared with 17% in the Glasser and Thorp study, reported having had sexual contact with psychology educators while they were students. Glasser and Thorp's (1986) subjects were all female, however, and Zakrzewski (2006), whose subjects were both male and female, reported that women were 2.5 times more likely than men to have had sexual contact with a psychology educator or to have experienced a sexual advance. This difference in sample characteristics could account for some of the differences in findings as well as the more optimistic possibility that the incidence actually decreased. Regarding their perceptions of that sexual contact, 88% of subjects felt that during the professional relationship, it was "highly inappropriate" (Zakrzewski, 2006, p. 726). These subjects did not have the benefit of hindsight afforded to the Glasser and Thorp (1986) subjects, who were surveyed as professionals rather than while they were still students.

Whether consent is possible in the context of a relationship of unequal power is debatable. The power differential in a supervisory dyad can "create unique vulnerabilities for supervisees" (Gottlieb, Robinson, & Younggren, 2007, p. 242). This vulnerability is reflected in data indicating that many students and supervisees who have had sexual contact with professors and supervisors report that they felt coerced (Glasser & Thorp, 1986; Zakrzewski, 2006). Fear of retaliation, feeling special or flattered by the attention, the desire to please superiors, and anticipated risks to their careers are all factors relegating students and supervisees to positions of diminished consent, if true consent is possible at all. At the very least, fear of ridicule or being ostracized by peers and reluctance to cause problems for the supervisor may lead supervisees to keep the relationship a secret, sometimes resulting in isolation, shame, and ambivalence.

Another issue not specifically addressed in the ethics codes is the impact of sexual relationships with supervisees on other students, supervisees, and employees. In Zakrzewski's (2006) study, 25% of his student subjects reported knowing about sexual contact between professors and students in their department, and 88% viewed such sexual contact as "highly inappropriate"

(p. 726). If graduate students perceive such sexual behavior as unethical and inappropriate and they are aware that their professors or supervisors are engaged in it, what is the message to them about the importance of ethical standards? Koocher and Keith-Spiegel (2006) asserted that such behavior teaches that "it is acceptable to gratify one's own needs with minimal regard for maintaining objectivity and clarity in professional relationships with those over whom they have substantial power, influence, and responsibility" (p. 227).

Beyond the impact of such role models, observing these relationships may cause other supervisees to wonder about the fairness of their supervisor's evaluations of both the supervisor's sexual partner-supervisee and of themselves. Observing this behavior also may cause supervisees to question the supervisor's credibility in general, diminishing their compliance and possibly compromising their clients' welfare. Concern about favoritism may compromise other supervisees' sense of safety in the program and their trust in other supervisors and professors (Burian & Slimp, 2000; Kolbert et al., 2002). Observers who are not mental health professionals may question the integrity of the professionals involved, and sexual behavior with students or supervisees may jeopardize public trust in the profession.

Filtering decisions through concerns about their impact on personal relationships challenges a supervisor's ability to accurately assess the skills of their supervisee–sexual partner. If conflicts occur in the personal relationship, particularly if that relationship is a secret, the supervisor may fear angering or disappointing the supervisee and risking that the individual will complain to his or her employer, academic department chair, or licensing board, thus compromising the supervisor's ability to challenge the professional behavior of the supervisee. The potential for overaccommodation with the supervisee is great. Similarly, the supervisee may feel dissatisfied with the supervision, the personal relationship, or both but fear negative evaluation if he or she should complain. The supervisee may also question the professional input of the supervisor, wondering whether it is the personal or professional agenda that is informing his or her judgment (M. R. Peterson, 1992). The ability of both parties to accurately interpret the behavior of the other, to express dissatisfaction, and to fully benefit from the relationship is significantly impaired.

Focus on a personal relationship also has the potential to detract from time and energy spent on discussing the clinical management of client cases, the supervisee's professional development, and other educational issues. Further, when a romantic relationship is developing, both parties usually work to present their best selves. Supervisees may then be more reluctant to reveal errors or more at risk for responding to perceived demand characteristics posed by their supervisors. Further, partners in new romantic relationships are typically infatuated and so are likely to overestimate positive characteristics and underestimate shortcomings of their new partners (Love, 2001). Such a stance certainly has the power to compromise the ability of a supervisor to judge accurately the competence of the supervisee. Similarly, the supervisee may have difficulty assessing whether the supervisor's behavior is appropriate and whether his or her own best interests are being served.

Arguments in favor of permitting concurrent sexual relationships between supervisors and supervisees are rare. Gordon (2005), however, made a case for allowing a psychologist to supervise a spouse, "as long as the supervising psychologist does not have or is not likely to have evaluative authority over his or her spouse" (p. 5). He presented the following case example:

> Dr. D's wife, a doctoral student in psychology, wanted to gain additional psychotherapy experience and work in her husband's private practice. His role as "supervisor" would be one of responsibility and overseeing and not one of evaluative authority. He would not be supervising his wife as part of a requirement to fulfill hours for licensing or certification or for the purposes of a course or fulfillment of a practicum or internship. . . . He would be taking legal and professional responsibility for his wife's work with a few patients on Saturdays when he was the most consistently available psychologist if something went wrong. (p. 5)

Gordon highlighted the benefits of such an arrangement: "The experience can be mutually rewarding, the wife could gain additional experience and skills, and the practice could provide low cost therapy for patients" (p. 6).

Although there may be benefits for the couple, how such an arrangement would result in low-cost therapy is unclear. Further, the risks to the supervisee and the potential for compromises in the supervised treatment are not identified or accounted for.

The APA Ethics Code (2002) states that psychologists are prohibited from engaging in sexual relationships with supervisees "who are in their department, agency, or training center *or* [italics added] over whom psychologists have or are likely to have evaluative authority" (p. 10). In Gordon's (2005) example, the spouse would be working in the psychologist's private practice, and so such a relationship seems contrary to the APA Ethics Code. Additionally, Gordon indicated that the husband-supervisor would assume "legal responsibility" (p. 5) and oversight of but not evaluative authority over the wife-supervisee's work. The distinction between these two roles is unclear. If this supervisor maintains legal responsibility for his supervisee's work, then he must have the authority to evaluate the correctness of her clinical decisions. If he does not agree, he should have the authority to trump those decisions. Although the supervisor in this case may not be required to submit a formal written evaluation to his wife's academic program or a credentialing body, the execution of his supervisory responsibilities requires that he serve in an evaluative capacity on a continual basis. Further, as discussed in the context of providing clinical consultation to a spouse or partner, the dynamics of the personal relationship may intrude on the professional relationship and compromise the integrity of the supervision. The possible impact on other staff members must also be considered.

Sexual Contact Before or After Supervision

Most ethics codes and specialty guidelines do not specifically comment on sexual contact with former supervisees; only the *AAMFT Code of Ethics* (2001) directly addresses the issue. According to the AAMFT (2001), if a supervisor engages in a sexual relationship with a former supervisee or accepts a current or past sexual partner as a supervisee, the burden of proof falls to the supervisor to demonstrate that there is no exploitation, seduction, harassment, or demeaning behavior. Although other professional associations do not discuss sexual contact with former supervisees, the advice offered by the AAMFT warrants consideration because of the risk of exploitation. Other sections of these publications dealing with multiple relationships may also be informative.

Can a clinician accept a former sexual partner as a supervisee? As with any multiple relationship, when a request for supervision comes from such an individual, the prospective supervisor must evaluate the potential for compromised objectivity and effectiveness as well as for exploitation. When contemplating the possibility of a romantic or sexual relationship with a former supervisee, supervisors might ask themselves the following questions:

- How much time has elapsed between the conclusion of the supervision and the proposed romantic relationship? (The greater the elapsed time, the less likely are problems.)
- Were any statements made during the supervisory relationship that indicted interest in a romantic relationship? (Regardless of who made such a statement initially, this suggests the likelihood that the supervisor's objectivity and effectiveness may have been compromised during the supervision by his or her desire for another type of relationship.)
- What is the current professional status of the former supervisee? (If the former supervisee is still a student or is seeking licensure, for example, he or she is more likely to need references, endorsements, or other further professional assistance from the supervisor.)
- What other risks might this particular situation entail, and what precautions might be taken to mitigate their likelihood?
- What is the potential impact on other supervisees and employees should they become aware of the subsequent relationship? (Will this cause them to reevaluate the perceived fairness and effectiveness of the supervision they received, perhaps undoing some of their gains?)

There are other questions that should be considered by a prospective supervisor before accepting a former sexual partner for supervision.

- Were there significant unresolved issues from the earlier relationship that might interfere with effective supervision?
- What is the potential impact on other supervisees and employees when they become aware of the history? (Any relationship that requires secret keeping or lying about such a history will likely impact morale, safety, and trust.)
- In what ways might the supervisor's objectivity and effectiveness be impaired by personal knowledge and feelings about the supervisee?
- To what degree is the prospective supervisor confident that the mutual history will not contaminate evaluative judgments or other supervisory responsibilities?

Perhaps the most obvious question to be considered in both cases is, "Why not someone else?" Clearly, the least complicated and risky course of action is to avoid mixing personal and professional relationships altogether.

In summary, engaging in a sexual relationship with a current supervisee is considered at least problematic by some mental health professional associations (AAPC, 1994; ApA, 2009; ASPPB, 2005) and clearly unethical by most (AAMFT, 2001; ACA, 2005; APA, 2002; CPA, 2000; NASW, 2008). Supervisors must be cognizant of the potential for harm to supervisees, supervisees' clients, other students, employees, and to the public trust in the profession. Although not specifically prohibited by any professional ethics code or guideline, sexual contact with former supervisees and supervision with former sexual partners warrant caution and consideration of the welfare of supervisees and all other parties for whom there may be negative consequences. Consultation with objective colleagues, both in advance of and throughout the supervision as needed, provides an additional safety net and may mitigate risks.

SIMILARITIES AND DIFFERENCES BETWEEN SUPERVISION AND PSYCHOTHERAPY

To appreciate the risks of combining the roles of psychotherapist and supervisor, consideration of their similarities and differences is necessary. Psychotherapy and supervision share some characteristics. Both involve the provision of a professional service to a consumer, and the provider in each case is usually compensated. Both relationships are governed by ethics codes, licensing board rules, and in some areas, law. The provider is imbued with more power than the individual receiving the service. Both relationships are structured, with the purposes and objectives of the relationship determining the focus of interactions between members.

There are also differences between psychotherapy and supervision with significant implications for the boundaries of these relationships. Psychotherapy clients generally are encouraged to raise any issue they deem relevant, whereas the agenda of supervision is far more circumscribed. Unlike psychotherapy clients, supervisees are limited to raising issues related in some way to their clients, work performance, or to other professional and work-related matters.

Perhaps the most significant difference between psychotherapy and supervision involves the purposes, responsibilities, and priorities of each. The general purpose of psychotherapy is to address the mental health needs of clients. The responsibilities of the psychotherapist include identifying mental health problems, assessing needs, formulating treatment plans, and implementing appropriate interventions. Clients are encouraged (in most types of treatment) to present their concerns, and the psychotherapist functions as a nonjudgmental helper. The primary, if not the only, concern is for the welfare of the client, the recipient of the service.

Barnett (2008) identified two fundamental differences between relationships with clients and those with students (a group that includes supervisees). First, academic settings tend to be more structured, and relationships between faculty and students are more public. Second, he observed that relationships with students evolve as training progresses, and the power differential often diminishes. Following completion of training, students become colleagues and sometimes friends. Unlike former clients who may later return for additional treatment, Barnett (2008) noted that graduates of an academic program are less likely than clients to return.

In contrast to psychotherapists' relationships with clients, the supervisor's highest consideration is the welfare of the supervisee's clients, who are not present and are not the direct recipients of the supervisor's services. The professional development of supervisees and gatekeeping for the profession are important but secondary to client welfare (Bernard & Goodyear, 2009). The appropriateness of particular topics of discussion must be weighed against these criteria. The supervisee's personal issues are pertinent only to the degree that they impact or might impact the treatment that the supervisee provides to others. When personal issues emerge through clinical work, the supervisor and supervisee might discuss them to a point, but if necessary, the supervisor can refer the supervisee for psychotherapy to allow more thorough exploration. The supervisor must evaluate the professional competence of the supervisee, a role that is most certainly not nonjudgmental in the same sense as is called for in psychotherapy.

THE PSYCHOTHERAPY–SUPERVISION BOUNDARY

The boundaries between therapy and supervision sometimes represent a grey area. Delineating precise lines between the two is complex because talking about personal issues and feelings is sometimes appropriate and necessary to supervision. And, of course, work-related concerns are commonly discussed in psychotherapy. Also, because supervisors are psychotherapists first, their more extensive training and experience in this realm might render them more comfortable providing therapy than supervision. Novice supervisors may be particularly vulnerable to making this shift. By allowing or inviting personal disclosures (e.g., about personal problems, traumatic experiences), supervisors introduce the risk that supervisees may experience the supervision as psychotherapy and develop unrealistic expectations about confidentiality, loyalty, and future interactions. When a supervisor includes personal information about the supervisee in an evaluation or expresses concern about a supervisee's mental health based on such information, the supervisee may feel betrayed, exposed, and vulnerable.

Of course, assuming appropriate informed consent is obtained at the outset of supervision, addressing relevant personal characteristics in an evaluation is useful, but covertly engaging in psychotherapy and assessment of a supervisee's mental health status is not. The APA Ethics Code (2002) further clarifies this distinction in Standard 7.04, Student Disclosure of Personal Information:

> Psychologists do not require students or supervisees to disclose personal information . . . either orally or in writing, regarding sexual history, history of abuse and neglect, psychological treatment, and relationships with parents, peers, and spouses or significant others except if (1) the program or training facility has clearly identified this requirement in its admissions or program materials, or (2) the information is necessary to evaluate or obtain assistance for students whose personal problems could reasonably be judged to be preventing them from performing their training- or professionally related activities in a competent manner or posing a threat to the students or others. (pp. 9–10)

Similarly, the ACES *Ethical Guidelines for Counseling Supervisors* (1993) recommends against supervisors providing psychotherapy: "Personal issues should be addressed in supervision only in terms of the impact of these issues on clients and on professional functioning" (p. 3).

Taibbi (1993) captured the difficulties associated with establishing the psychotherapy–supervision boundary. He defined the role of the psychotherapist as bringing the supervisee "right up to the crossover, to the point of recognizing the link between personal reactions and clinical behavior" (p. 53). Taibbi (1993) acknowledged the challenges:

> It often doesn't work so smoothly, however, and suddenly, after asking two or three relatively innocuous questions ("Is this dad making you feel anxious?"), I find the therapist railing against an old injury or crying over a long-forgotten hurt. I offer support, help sift and sort the past from the present and tactfully, gently, re-clarify the parameters of our relationship. Most of all I use the occasion to look back and reassess whether I have sent out unclear messages about my role or somehow encouraged the therapist to become my client. (p. 53)

Taibbi's description illustrates how difficult it can be to maintain this boundary and demonstrates the need for vigilance and self-reflection when it is crossed.

Like Taibbi (1993), Berman (1997), a psychoanalyst, cautioned supervisors about addressing personal issues in supervision. He was clear that when personal issues arise in the context of supervision, particularly when they are likely to affect the treatment, the supervisor must address them. Berman described the distinction as follows:

> The analyst attempts to reach the deepest and broadest understanding, proceeding open-mindedly with no immediate goals; the supervisor is much more selective and goal oriented, focusing on these aspects of the personal theme which can be directly related to consequences and actual dilemmas in the trainee's work with patients. (p. 182)

Efforts to ensure that the supervisor does not inadvertently slip into a psychotherapeutic role must be balanced with attention to the impact of personal issues on an individual's work performance. Too rigid a boundary likely will keep supervisees from acknowledging personal issues that affect their work, an important part of becoming an effective psychotherapist.

CONCURRENT SUPERVISION AND PSYCHOTHERAPY

Complexity is greatly reduced when, as generally occurs, the roles of supervisor and psychotherapist remain completely separate. Can one individual provide both psychotherapy and supervision to another? Can a psychotherapist accept a former client as a supervisee? Can a former client make the transition to supervisee? The following case illustrates how a supervisor might be persuaded to consider providing psychotherapy to a supervisee.

Case A: Limited Resources, Significant Needs

Dr. Davis has been supervising Mark, a doctoral intern in a marriage and family therapy training program. In his work with increasingly challenging families, some of Mark's own family issues have emerged and, at times, seem to have compromised his ability to respond objectively to his clients. Recognizing this obstacle, Dr. Davis suggests that Mark consider psychotherapy to address his personal issues. Because Mark is in a family systems training program, it seems important that he work with a therapist who shares this theoretical orientation. Unfortunately, there are no such readily accessible resources outside of the clinic in which they work.

Mark suggests the possibility of working with Dr. Davis. Mark points out that Dr. Davis not only has the appropriate theoretical orientation but also understands the issues that Mark needs to address, Additionally, Mark doesn't want to start over with someone new, sharing his personal story with yet another professional in their small community. Dr. Davis concurs with these points and feels that he could be helpful to Mark. Further, he enjoys providing psychotherapy to other professionals but rarely gets the opportunity.

Dr. Davis ultimately decides to provide the psychotherapy, but to ensure a clear boundary, he says he will do so only under specified conditions. Dr. Davis proposes that therapy sessions occur on Mark's day off and that they make every effort to keep the two relationships separate. They will confine discussions of Mark's work to supervision meetings and discussions of his personal issues to therapy sessions. Because of Mark's limited income, Dr. Davis offers to see him privately at a reduced fee. To protect Mark's privacy and because he would not want other students to perceive preferential treatment, Dr. Davis suggests they meet at his home and conceal the arrangement from other employees, students, and faculty. Mark expresses admiration for Dr. Davis's careful consideration of his needs, and he gratefully agrees to the arrangement.

Case A Discussion

Although not apparent to either party, this arrangement is fraught with risks. Dr. Davis will likely have difficulty keeping separate information obtained in each context. There is significant potential for knowledge of Mark's personal struggles to contaminate his evaluation. As his supervisor, Dr. Davis is liable for Mark's clinical work and serves as a gatekeeper for the profession. Concern about Mark's work performance could cause Dr. Davis to listen to Mark's personal disclosures with a different filter than if he were concerned only about his mental health. Dr. Davis's business interests, in addition to his desire to be a psychotherapist for other professionals, also may compromise his objectivity in responding to Mark's needs as a client and as a supervisee.

This dual role has the potential to negatively affect Mark in both roles as well. Whereas clients can generally count on and take comfort in their psychotherapists' nonjudgmental, supportive stance, Mark may feel particularly wounded by challenging feedback about his work in the context of supervision. Mark's awareness of the risks to his career may inhibit him in his role as a client and result in his withholding information that might negatively affect Dr. Davis's perceptions of his professional competence. If dissatisfied with some aspect of the treatment, Mark may be hesitant to offer what might be perceived as criticism of his supervisor's clinical skills. Mark's confidence in Dr. Davis as a supervisor might be negatively impacted if he observes what he perceives as errors in his treatment. If dissatisfied, Mark may not feel free to quit, fearing the real or imagined repercussions of angering the supervisor. If Mark decides to seek services from another clinician, fearing repercussions, he may not want to tell Dr. Davis and so would relinquish opportunities for coordination of his care. As a supervisee, Mark may also feel increased vulnerability due to Dr. Davis's knowledge of personal information about him. He may be reluctant to discuss his clinical mistakes so as to mitigate this vulnerability.

Dr. Davis has some vague awareness of these risks, as reflected in his decisions not to allow consideration of Mark's work issues in therapy and to avoid discussion of personal issues in supervision. His solution, however, introduces an artificial boundary that is likely to diminish the effectiveness of both the psychotherapy and the supervision.

In addition to the potential impact on Dr. Davis and Mark, the existence of this "secret relationship" will likely affect others in the agency, whether or not they know the exact nature of the connection (M. R. Peterson, 1992). Competition, envy, and mistrust may arise. In addition, although psychotherapists and supervisors have obligations (albeit different ones) to protect the privacy of clients and supervisees, asking the consumer of these services to refrain from revealing such information to others is unfair and creates an inappropriate obligation. Doing so may cause Mark to feel guilty for deliberately deceiving his colleagues and may result in isolation from them. If difficulties arise in either relationship, the other is likely to suffer.

In short, attempting to manage the roles of supervisor and psychotherapist simultaneously creates an untenable multiple relationship that compromises Dr. Davis's objectivity and effectiveness, exponentially magnifies Mark's vulnerability in both therapy and supervision, and negatively affects the work environment for other trainees and employees.

Sequential Engagement in Psychotherapy and Supervision

Engaging in these roles sequentially is likely to carry similar challenges, though the potential consequences may be different. For example, a clinician might request psychotherapy from a former supervisor. When training is complete, supervisors are no longer responsible for their supervisee's professional behavior and so have less investment in their professional functioning. Further, a supervisor's power, relative to a former supervisee's career, is likely limited to providing references for subsequent academic training or employment.

Although the risks of engaging in psychotherapy are diminished after the supervision ends, they are not eliminated. A supervisee-turned-client may be reluctant to ask for a letter of recommendation or, if one is provided, may be exquisitely sensitive to the former supervisor's comments. Anticipation of the need for a reference could inhibit the client's disclosures in the psychotherapy. Similarly, concern about the impact on the therapy relationship could compromise the ability of the supervisor-turned-psychotherapist to provide a candid reference while ensuring that it is based exclusively on perceptions formulated in the supervision.

Another problem with providing professional references involves differences in the limits to confidentiality between supervision and psychotherapy. If a former supervisee–current client believes that the supervisor's assessment of his or her skills reflects impressions gleaned from the psychotherapy, he or she may object that such disclosure was not authorized. Supervisors in this circumstance would find it difficult to demonstrate that they have clearly separated these two sources of information in their minds. A related challenge occurs when a prospective employer requests an opportunity to speak directly with the former supervisor to ask questions more informally. If the former supervisee is not offered the job, he or she may wonder whether something the supervisor-psychotherapist said has affected that outcome, which may impact treatment and create legal exposure for the supervisor-psychotherapist. A written release authorizing the desired communication may mitigate liability and provide an occasion for review of associated risks and benefits in the context of psychotherapy.

These risks notwithstanding, the transition from a less intimate relationship, supervision, to a more intimate one, psychotherapy, is not impossible. Factors for consideration include the time lapsed between the two relationships, the supervisor's assessment of the likelihood of conflict, and each party's preferences. Risks and benefits should be thoroughly delineated as part of the informed consent process at the outset and throughout the psychotherapy as needed.

Making the transition from psychotherapy client to supervisee is even more complicated. Clients, particularly those aspiring to be psychotherapists, may feel a great deal of admiration for their psychotherapists. The idea of becoming more of a peer, a fellow professional, likely holds some appeal. Yet, the shift from supportive person concerned primarily with the welfare of the individual to supervisor whose primary concern is that individual's clients is challenging and may be hurtful to the client. If, in the future, the supervisee needs treatment again, will the supervisor be available to provide it, or does engaging in the other role preclude a resumption of the previous one? Supervisors wanting to make this transition effectively must ensure that they do not inadvertently slide into a therapeutic discussion of personal issues in the context of supervision and that any consideration of supervisees' personal issues be appropriate to supervision. A clear informed consent will include a thorough discussion of these risks.

Clearly, numerous challenges are inherent in the transition from supervisor to psychotherapist, psychotherapist to supervisor, and in engaging in the two roles simultaneously. These challenges likely represent some of the reasons that any of these relationships are specifically prohibited by licensing boards in some jurisdictions (California Board of Psychology, 2008). Responsible contemplation of such a shift requires thorough consideration of the possible pitfalls as well as deliberate efforts to prevent or mitigate negative outcomes. The least complex option is to avoid the problem completely and refer the individual to a colleague.

OTHER MULTIPLE RELATIONSHIPS AND BOUNDARY CHALLENGES IN SUPERVISION

Opportunities for the development of other roles and relationships, both concurrent with and subsequent to supervision, are not uncommon and warrant careful consideration.

Collegial Relationships With Supervisees and Former Supervisees

As supervisees develop professionally, their needs and therefore the boundaries of the supervisory relationship will necessarily evolve to more effectively address these needs. At some point in the process, supervisors, particularly those who are also faculty in training programs (Biaggio, Paget, & Chenoweth, 1997), may consider proposing collaboration with supervisees on research, a conference presentation, writing for publication, or some other professional endeavor. Such activities have the potential to be enormously beneficial to supervisees. Encouragement and direction from an experienced mentor can provide supervisees with opportunities to build the skills and confidence needed to subsequently engage in such activities independently and may inculcate them with a desire to actively contribute to their profession. Further, these experiences may complement supervisees' professional repertoire and allow them to compete more effectively for other positions. Such endeavors also create networking opportunities that could lead to jobs or other chances for collaboration with a broader range of colleagues.

In spite of these benefits, there are many reasons that a given supervisee may not wish to participate at a particular time. Other personal or professional commitments may represent time constraints. The supervisee's interests and career goals may not be consistent with the supervisor's proposed project. Or, the individual may not particularly enjoy working with the supervisor and so not want to extend their contact. If these additional activities are not stated requirements of the position, then the supervisee must be free to refuse to participate. Yet, supervisees may fear negative repercussions or even reprisal if they decline (Sullivan & Ogloff, 1998). Therefore, supervisors must make their options clear.

It must also be acknowledged that such collaborative activities may benefit supervisors. If the supervisor is in academia and in a tenure-track position, for example, the pressure to conduct research, present, and publish is great. Collaborating with another person may make such an activity more appealing and even more possible. Many of the benefits for supervisees are also available to supervisors (e.g., networking, job opportunities). Because of these benefits, the potential for exploitation exists, and supervisors must be cautious to ensure that their own needs do not create an ethical blind spot for them in assessing the advisability of the proposed arrangement. They must make deliberate efforts to reassure supervisees of their freedom to choose whether to participate.

Former supervisees are likely to feel less of an obligation to respond affirmatively to supervisors' requests to work together on special projects. Yet, when former supervisors are the ones initiating the proposed activity, they must bear in mind that supervisees' gratitude and sense of diminished power may persist, and they must proceed cautiously. Consultation with a colleague or supervisor can help the supervisor sort out the complexities of such a decision.

When an idea for professional collaboration comes from a current supervisee, supervisors must consider not only whether the proposed activity appeals to them but also whether they believe it is in the best interest of the supervisee. Are there are risks for harm or exploitation? Will the supervisor's objectivity and effectiveness be compromised as he or she executes other responsibilities vis-à-vis the supervisee? When the proposal comes from a former supervisee, these complexities are diminished but, as stated previously, supervisors must consider their decisions carefully.

Friendships With Former Supervisees

As supervisees develop professionally and as they work more collabora-tively with supervisors, their relationships generally become more collegial and may evolve into friendships. If this occurs during the supervision, the potential for compromised objectivity is greater, and as with romantic rela-tionships, supervisors' effectiveness is diminished. Following the supervision, however, supervisees become colleagues and may even work together or be members of the same professional associations. Friendships are not uncom-mon and are generally not problematic. When developing such a friendship, however, former supervisors must be sensitive to any residual power imbal-ance and should consider factors mentioned previously, such as the time elapsed since the supervision, the individual vulnerability of the former super-visee, and the potential for exploitation.

Rural and Small Community Challenges

Although boundary challenges are endemic to any mental health practice, they seem to occur with greater frequency in rural and small communities than in larger urban areas (Campbell & Gordon, 2003; Helbok, Marinelli, & Walls, 2006; Schank & Skovholt, 2006). Supervisors and consultants in such communities face some of the same issues as psychotherapists.

The problem of limited resources represents perhaps one of the great-est challenges for supervisors and those needing supervision in small com-munities. Small communities (such as those consisting of individuals sharing a racial or ethnic identity, sexual orientation, faith, or specialty) may limit prospective supervisees' preferences for a supervisor with whom they share cultural or other aspects of their identities. Often other more practical matters move these preferences down on individual priority lists. Prelicensure professionals seeking employment and students seeking practicum or internship opportunities often must consider other factors such as location, learning opportunities, and availability. Further, there is a greater likelihood that prospective supervisees will have a preexisting rela-tionship with someone who shares an important aspect of their identity and is a member of a related small community or group.

The options for supervisees in rural communities are similarly limited in that there are fewer individuals with the necessary credentials in their geo-graphical area or work setting. The need for mental health professionals in underserved areas and limited training opportunities are just two of many fac-tors that may motivate credentialed psychotherapists to consider supervising someone with whom they have another relationship. Although these factors create challenges for rural practitioners, they do not justify disregard for ethical standards or the risks they may incur (Schank & Skovholt, 2006). That said, such circumstances may require more creative thinking about whether and how the supervision might be provided and what safeguards might be employed to minimize risk. In another area, where less complex options are readily available, it is generally simpler and safer to use an alternative resource.

Case B: No Choices?

Jane completed a master's degree in marriage and family therapy about 20 years ago. At the time of her graduation, licensure was not available in her state. Jane recently assumed a position as clinical director of a private clinic in a small rural community where she provides administrative supervision to 12 licensed mental health professionals in various professions. Two of these individuals are licensed marriage and family therapists. In this capacity, Jane determines agency policies, oversees billing for services, and manages personnel. Her responsibilities include hiring and firing employees, determining raises and employment status, monitoring employee compliance with policies and procedures, and scheduling.

Wishing to broaden her career options, Jane investigates the requirements for obtaining a license at this point. She is disappointed to learn that only part of her previous supervised experience will count toward licensure and that she will need 6 more months of clinical experience supervised by another licensee of the marriage and family therapy board. There is only one other mental health clinic in this community—her employer's main competitor. For Jane, this competition eliminates clinicians in that clinic as potential providers of the supervision she needs.

Jane considers the two licensed marriage and family therapists in her clinic and decides to ask her newest employee, Bill, to consider meeting with her weekly to discuss her cases and, ultimately, to sign off on her application for licensure. The other licensee, Patricia, has more experience, but Jane enjoys Bill's company more and has greater respect for his professional skills. Bill is flattered to be asked and agrees to provide the supervision without hesitation.

Case B Discussion

These two roles—administrative supervisor and clinical supervisee—are both professional roles, yet they contain responsibilities likely to be in conflict with one another. Particularly because the proposed relationship would exist primarily, if not exclusively, for the benefit of the current supervisor, the potential pitfalls must be carefully examined, ideally with a consultant, before raising the possibility with the supervisee/proposed supervisor. This benefit to Jane increases the risk that she may rationalize, perhaps unconsciously, about the advisability of this arrangement. Bill in this case, may feel some indebtedness to Jane or may fear repercussions for refusal. Given these factors, he may not be able to accurately assess the risks or feel completely free to decline. Further, the impact on Patricia, the other qualified employee, must also be considered. Jealousy, perceptions of unfair treatment, and negative implications of this role model are all possible outcomes.

Perhaps more important, there is no indication that Jane has attempted to identify alternatives after ruling out colleagues at the other clinic. Some options include

- consulting a professional directory or the licensing board to identify other appropriately credentialed colleagues in the region,
- arranging a combination of telephone and in-person supervision to decrease travel needed,
- using teleconferencing technology through a library or hospital to access a supervisor,
- meeting less frequently for long periods, and
- changing work hours to allow travel time to access supervision in another community.

Some of these alternatives may not meet the requirements outlined by the licensing board, but some boards might consider granting a waiver allowing an alternative means of meeting the requirement. If a waiver is requested and not granted, the individual may need to decide whether it is worthwhile or even possible to obtain the new credential, given the hardship involved. In short, living in a rural community may represent a significant challenge for those attempting to meet such licensing requirements. The risks associated with engaging in multiple relationships must not be overlooked. An objective consultant with appropriate expertise in ethics could assist in the process of identifying and evaluating the risks, benefits, and potential efficacy of alternatives. The decision-making models described in the discussion that follows provide additional guidelines.

An assessment of the similarities and differences between the role of supervisor and another proposed role is warranted to understand the risks of combining them. Previous relationships are one category of potentially, though not necessarily, problematic relationships. When the supervisor is a former professor, colleague, supervisee, psychotherapist, friend, or acquaintance, efforts to clarify the new parameters of the relationship are necessary.

Sequential, Subtle, and Transient Role Shifts

Subtle boundary crossings and role changes in supervision or consultation can occur insidiously and may even develop outside of the conscious awareness of the provider. Identifying the more common types of boundary crossings will help supervisors and consultants anticipate and guard against these risks. Gutheil and Gabbard (1993) elucidated seven aspects of therapeutic relationships that may be vulnerable to boundary crossings and violations. Each has a counterpart in supervision and consultation: time, place and space, money, gifts, clothing, language, and physical contact (Gutheil & Gabbard, 1993). Acknowledging that these boundaries differ from those in psychotherapy, these factors are relevant. Supervision and consultation are generally conducted at a designated time and in a professional office setting. Yet, in addition to the scheduled time, a supervisee or consultee may be permitted, or in fact encouraged, to seek additional assistance when the need is more urgent, as might occur in client emergencies.

If not prohibited by an applicable regulatory or a credentialing body or by policies of the employment setting, supervision or consultation may legitimately occur on the phone, in another office, or in some cases, another setting. A supervisor observing in-home treatment may very appropriately provide supervision in a car, for example. Inviting a supervisee to the supervisor's home to review clinical cases, discussing private information in a public setting where it could easily be overheard, or conducting supervision while taking a recreational drive, however, are more likely to represent boundary crossings (Gutheil & Gabbard, 1993; Gutheil & Simon, 2002; Smith & Fitzpatrick, 1995) or in some cases may be violations. Similarly, physical contact is not typically a part of supervision or consultation, as it is generally associated with greater intimacy than usually characterizes such relationships. Although not always problematic, touch initiated by the supervisor will likely exacerbate the supervisee's vulnerability. Because of the power difference, it may be awkward, if not very difficult for supervisees to object to being touched or hugged by a supervisor, even if they were uncomfortable. It is therefore incumbent on supervisors to carefully consider this vulnerability before initiating physical contact with a supervisee. As Slimp and Burian (1994) noted, "Even seemingly benign social relationships with positive intentions can still have an adverse effect on the training process" (p. 41).

Certainly, there are times and circumstances that call for flexibility in these areas. But, when exceptions are made, they must be considered thoughtfully and cautiously, reviewed with a trusted consultant, if possible, and discussed with the supervisee. Taking these steps will help ensure that the supervisor's judgment is objective and sound and will minimize confusion about the meaning of the interaction as well as the supervisee's expectations about future interactions.

Self-Disclosure

One function of supervisors and consultants is to provide a role model. To this end, self-disclosure about one's professional background, interests, theoretical orientation, and areas of expertise is helpful, if not essential. Sharing the supervisor's or consultant's experience as a supervisee, relevant personal experience, cultural or religious background, or clinical cases may be ethically appropriate and effective interventions. Even small talk with no direct relevance to the primary relationship may be appropriate and facilitative of supervision or consultation goals. Yet, in any of these examples, the same information disclosed at a different time, in a different context, or to a different individual may have a neutral, negative, or even harmful impact. Appreciation of the nuances and complexity of self-disclosure will allow supervisors and consultants to use it to enhance the quality and benefits of their services while minimizing risks.

As mentioned, supervisees and consultees are legitimately interested in learning about their supervisor's or consultant's professional background. This information may assist them in choosing, to the extent possible, individuals who are most likely to provide them with the desired knowledge and skills. Yet supervision and consultation can also offer providers a forum in which to showcase their successes, debrief, or obtain consultation about their own work. Novice trainees are particularly likely to respond with great interest, admiration, and even awe to these stories. They also may feel flattered to be asked for their opinions. Supervisee's anxiety about exposing their work may contribute to a preference for focusing on supervisors' or consultants' experiences. The personal gratification that can come from such interaction is undeniable, and a supervisor or consultant who lacks confidence or is feeling unappreciated, for example, may be particularly vulnerable to finding justification for using formal meetings in this way.

The content of the disclosure also requires consideration. How much time will be consumed by sharing this anecdote? How personal or intimate is the information? The sharing of either party's personal experiences or mental health issues may be pertinent and useful, or it may be distracting, irrelevant, or detrimental to the primary objectives of the relationship. Similarly, information about the supervisor's or consultant's medical history may helpful in understanding a client's condition. Acknowledging a history of childhood cancer, for example, could be very useful, assuming clinical relevance, whereas talking about having had a vasectomy or an abortion may be considered too personal or emotionally loaded. Disclosing a past clinical error could be instructive, comforting, and encouraging. However, if the disclosure is poorly timed or too serious an error, it has the potential to frighten the supervisee or consultee and may diminish confidence in the supervisor or consultant. Variables that should be considered include individual characteristics, history, and developmental stage of the supervisee or consultee.

That such interactions could also be both personally gratifying and efficacious increases the complexity of these decisions. Thus, skilled supervisors and consultants must be vigilant about assessing the legitimacy and relevance of disclosures in light of supervisee or consultee needs and motivations as well as of their own. They must continually evaluate the nature of their interactions to ensure that supervisee or consultee learning and client needs remain primary.

Requesting or Granting Favors

Similar ethical challenges occur when supervisors or consultants ask for personal favors or make suggestions that are not part of the requirements. When the person in power requests a favor, whether this is a requirement or an option may be unclear. The consequences for saying no may be ambiguous and difficult to anticipate. A supervisor, for instance, may be involved in a writing project and ask the supervisee to search for related professional articles. There may be some legitimate justification for the assignment that is not readily apparent to the supervisee. Or, perhaps, the objective is only to save the supervisor work. The supervisor in this case must have a clear understanding of the objectives and communicate their reasoning to the supervisee. Requesting more personal favors, such as running errands, babysitting, or organizing the supervisor's or consultant's office, are unrelated to the professional objectives of the relationship and should be avoided. Most important, supervisors and consultants must be conscious of the risks, vigilant in their self-assessments and monitoring, and clear in their communications with supervisees and consultees.

When supervisees or consultees make special requests, the implications of granting or refusing the request must be considered. Responding affirmatively, particularly if the favor is primarily personal, may contribute to a supervisee's or consultee's perception of a special connection, or it may engender indebtedness, particularly when the outcome is positive. The resulting dynamic may diminish such individuals' ability to advocate for themselves. The nature of the favor also is an important factor. Responding affirmatively to a request for the name of a good book on treatment of anxiety disorders is different from recommending a babysitter or lawyer. If the individual dislikes the book, a follow-up discussion is likely to result in a fruitful learning experience. If, however, the person has a negative experience with the endorsed child-care provider or lawyer, the repercussions for the relationship will be more complicated.

Business and Financial Interactions

When the recipient pays directly for supervision or consultation, there exists a legitimate fiduciary relationship. Beyond these interactions, however, supervisors and consultants must be cautious about financial involvements. For example, inviting supervisees or consultees to contribute to a political campaign or asking them to make a purchase for the supervisor's or consultant's children's school fundraiser may result in the supervisee or consultee feeling coerced into responding affirmatively. These situations may seem innocuous, but supervisees and consultees may feel unable to say no, regardless of their desire to contribute or not. Clearly, supervisors and consultants must anticipate such responses and proceed in ways affording the maximum opportunity for benefit, minimal risk of negative outcome, and built-in safety nets to encourage the discussion and correction of problems when they do arise.

Outside Social and Professional Interactions

Professional socialization and mentoring are important tasks associated with the supervision of trainees and novice professionals. Professional meetings and conventions can be intimidating for first-time attendees, and the company of a veteran can go a long way toward reducing anxiety and encouraging participation. Supervisors might coach their supervisees about everything from appropriate attire to navigating a convention program schedule. Supervisors might introduce supervisees to colleagues with similar professional interests. Collaborating on a conference program proposal and presentation, involving supervisees or consultees to the extent that they are capable, may have a profound effect on the individual's ability to make such professional contributions independently in the future. Clearly, there are many legitimate and beneficial ways in which these relationships may exist outside of the formal confines of scheduled meetings. In fact, although such additional involvement is generally not required of supervisors and consultants, it reflects generosity and commitment on their part, and it can be rewarding for both parties.

Again, however, the risk of exploitation is present. Supervisees and consultees may not feel free to decline offers that are not consistent with their professional objectives and interests or when other commitments would make such participation a burden. A supervisor's enthusiasm for a project or opportunity may diminish his or her ability to accurately assess its relevance for the supervisee, and he or she may neglect to make clear the individual's option to decline. There is also the risk that supervisees or consultees may feel they've been assigned an unfair portion of the work associated with a project and that the supervisor or consultant is benefiting disproportionately. If participation in such a project is required and may be considered in supervisee evaluation, the supervisor must clarify this as part of the informed consent process.

Students and trainees learning to supervise or consult as well as those currently providing these services may benefit from considering various hypothetical but not uncommon situations that arise in a supervisor or consultative relationship.

ETHICAL DECISION-MAKING MODELS

Relationships between supervisors and supervisees and between consultants and consultees are complex; related decisions require serious consideration. When members of these dyads enter into an additional role, supervisors and consultants must evaluate the extent and nature of the impact on the primary relationship. Additional roles or interactions include friendship; professional collaboration on research, publications, presentations, or projects; discussion of topics that are unrelated to supervision or consultation (e.g., personal problems of either individual); and incidental or planned interactions outside of formal meetings (e.g., at an agency party, a professional conferences, school function, or community event). Combining any of these roles with supervision or consultation is not necessarily problematic. The effect may be neutral or even overwhelmingly beneficial for the supervisee or consultee. If not considered and implemented thoughtfully and judiciously, however, each of these combinations has the potential to engender boundary violations.

The professional literature is replete with ethical decision-making models and sets of questions primarily designed to assist psychotherapists in their work with clients. Feminist models generally advocate significant involvement of the client in ethical decisions (Hill, Glaser, & Harden, 1995; Walden, 2006). Other models emphasize multicultural factors (Frame & Williams, 2005; Garcia, Cartwright, Winston, & Borzuchowska, 2003). Many of these models are general and may be adapted for supervision and consultation (G. Corey et al., 2007; Cottone & Tarvydas, 2003; Ebert, 2002; Gibson, 2008: Gottlieb, 1993; Knapp & VandeCreek, 2006; Sonne, 2006; Sperry, 2007; Welfel, 2006; Younggren & Gottlieb, 2004).

Haas and Malouf (2005) have provided an example of one such model. Writing for mental health practitioners in various disciplines, they proposed a "framework for ethical decision making" (p. 7). Their model includes three phases of information gathering as the first step: (a) "identifying the ethical problem" (p. 8), (b) "identifying legitimate stakeholders" (p. 9), and (c) "identifying relevant standards" (p. 10). Following this initial step, Haas and Malouf have described a "process of ethical decision making" (2005, p. 11). More specifically, they have recommended that mental health practitioners ask themselves a series of questions and engage in several activities:

- Does a relevant, professional, legal, or social standard exist?
- Is there a reason to deviate from the standard?
- What are the ethical dimensions of the issue?
- Can a primary ethical dimension be specified?
- Consult and review codes of ethics: Review literature; consider ethical principles.
- Generate a list of possible actions.
- Does the new course of action appear to satisfy the needs/ preferences of affected parties?
- Does the course of action present any new ethical problems?
- Can the course of action be implemented?
- Implement the chosen course of action. (Haas & Malouf, 2005, pp. 11–18)

Sonne (2006) offered a similar model that includes four general categories of factors for clinicians to consider in making ethical decisions about nonsexual multiple relationships: "therapist factors, client factors, therapy relationship factors, and other relationship factors" (p. 188). Some of the specific factors she described are also important considerations for supervisors and consultants. Culture, gender, specific profession, theoretical orientation, power differential, potential for benefit and harm to all parties, and potential for role conflict are some examples (Sonne, 2006). An advantage of this nonlinear model is that it encourages users to consider—and reconsider—a broad range of factors throughout the decision-making process.

DECISION-MAKING MODELS FOR RELATIONSHIPS WITH SUPERVISEES AND CONSULTEES

When contemplating a new type of role, interaction, or disclosure, supervisors and consultants may benefit from considering these decisions in light of the following:

1. To what extent would engaging in this relationship or connection meet the needs of the supervisee or consultee? How would this individual likely benefit?
2. To what extent would it meet my needs? How might I benefit?
3. Are the needs in question primarily personal or professional?

4. What could go wrong if I decided to do this? What harm could result and to whom (e.g., the supervisee or consultee, other supervisees or consultees, other employees, clients)?
5. What is the worst-case scenario, and how likely is it to occur? If it did occur, what could be done to ameliorate the negative or harmful effects? What can I do in advance to decrease the likelihood of a negative outcome?
6. What are the unique characteristics of this individual and of our particular relationship that should be considered? For example, is he especially admiring or deferential toward me? Is she struggling with trusting me?
7. What particular vulnerabilities or needs do I have that have the potential to create a blind spot for me in objectively evaluating this decision?
8. From whom did the initiative for this connection come? If the idea was mine (i.e., supervisor or consultant), to what extent is that individual likely to feel free to decline, given my responsibility for him or her?
9. What are the alternatives? What risks and benefits do they pose?

Considering these questions in consultation with a colleague will likely increase their usefulness.

CONCLUSION

Supervisors and consultants must be mindful of the obvious as well as the more subtle boundary crossings and violations that may occur in their relationships with the people they serve. They must make decisions thoughtfully and consciously, with the best interests of supervisees and consultees in mind. The consent or even preferences of supervisees and consultees is a necessary but not sufficient condition for engaging in an additional role or behavior in a supervisory, consultative, or therapeutic relationship. The buck stops with the person in charge—always.

6

INFORMED CONSENT TO
SUPERVISION AND CONSULTATION

The concept of informed consent has become an integral aspect of forming relationships with clients for the purpose of psychotherapy and assessment. Psychologists and other mental health professionals are trained to anticipate the risks and benefits of treatment and assessment, identify alternatives, understand reporting obligations and other limits to privacy, explain these factors to prospective clients, and assist them in making decisions about their participation. Professional ethics codes address the need for obtaining informed consent before providing clinical services (American Association for Marriage and Family Therapy [AAMFT], 2001; American Association of Pastoral Counselors, AAPC [1994]; American Counseling Association [ACA], 2005; American Psychiatric Association [ApA], 2009; American Psychological Association [APA], 2002; Association of State and Provincial Psychology Boards [ASPPB], 2005; Canadian Psychological Association [CPA], 2000; National Association of Alcohol and Drug Abuse Counselors

Portions of this chapter originally appeared in "Informed Consent Through Contracting for Supervision: Minimizing Risks, Enhancing Benefits," by J. T. Thomas, 2007, *Professional Psychology: Research and Practice, 38,* 221–231. Copyright 2007 by the American Psychological Association. Reprinted with permission of the author.

[NAADAC], 2008; National Association of Social Workers [NASW], 2008). The professional literature also discusses of the applications of these codes (C. B. Fisher, 2003; Haas & Malouf, 2005; Herlihy & Corey, 1996; Knapp & VandeCreek, 2003; Nagy, 2005; Welfel, 2006). Fewer publications, however, address informed consent as it applies to supervision, even though the need to do so is clear in many professional ethics codes (AAMFT, 2001; ACA, 2005; ACES, 1993; APA, 2002; ASPPB, 2003; Center for Credential & Education [CCE], 2008; CPA, 2009). Informed consent to clinical consultation, as described in this context, is discussed even less frequently.

In this chapter, the following issues are addressed:

- applicability of informed consent to supervision and consultation,
- purposes and objectives of obtaining informed consent to supervision and consultation,
- related ethical standards and guidelines, and
- elements of an informed consent document or contract for supervision and consultation.

Also included is the information needed by clinical supervisors and consultants to develop informed consent contracts for specific types of supervision and consultation. Because the ethics codes and professional literature primarily address supervision rather than consultation, this chapter focuses primarily on the former. Adaptations for consultation are described when applicable.

APPLICABILITY OF INFORMED CONSENT TO SUPERVISION AND CONSULTATION

Several of the issues addressed in obtaining informed consent for treatment or assessment are also applicable to supervision and consultation: Anticipated length of service, limits to privacy, fees and related policies, risks and benefits, and maintenance and storage of records are some examples. Further, consumers of both treatment and supervision benefit from obtaining information about the provider's professional background, theoretical approach, and credentials.

To make sound decisions about their participation in therapy, clients must receive at least minimal information about the implications of agreeing (Knapp & VandeCreek, 2006). Ethically, consent must be truly *informed* (the prospective client is provided with enough information to make a reasonable decision) and *voluntary*, and the individual must be *competent* to make a decision (Haas & Malouf, 2005). These concepts, however, are only partially applicable to supervision. Consent for any psychological service—psychotherapy, supervision, consultation—must be informed; consumers must receive enough relevant information about all factors that might reasonably influence their decisions. The other two components, voluntariness and competence to consent, apply differently to supervision and consultation.

Consumers of treatment or assessment must be free to accept or decline services without undue influence or coercion (legally mandated services notwithstanding). If after reviewing informed consent materials prospective clients are dissatisfied and unwilling to participate, they may elect to seek services from a different provider or agency or a different type of professional, or they may decide not to receive any services. In some circumstances, there may be negative consequences (e.g., refusal to participate in a fitness-for-duty evaluation may result in a person's not being considered for a position). Consultation, unless it is mandated, is similarly elective. Conversely, supervisees' alternatives are necessarily restricted by the requirements of their graduate programs, licensing boards, or other credentialing bodies (e.g., AAMFT, 2007)

One limitation for supervisees is that fewer qualified supervisors than therapists are likely to be available. Further, to obtain their degrees, students must participate in supervision, and they may have limited or no choices about who will supervise them. Student trainees generally are assigned to specific supervisors. Still, when provided with all relevant information, supervisees can decide whether to apply for a particular graduate program, internship, license, certification, or job. If they want to enter the profession, however, they must agree to certain parameters.

Finally, consumers of treatment and assessment services must be deemed competent to make decisions about those services (Haas & Malouf, 2005). They must be capable of evaluating risks and benefits to decide whether to engage in the proposed relationship. Mental or physical illness and intellectual or cognitive impairment may compromise an individual's capacity to accomplish this task. Supervisees and consultees are, presumably, mentally competent enough to understand what they are agreeing to and, if provided with adequate information, should be able to make reasonably informed decisions. Nevertheless, providing supervisees and consultees with relevant information at the outset of supervision helps to minimize risks and to maximize benefits for supervisees and consultees as well as for those they serve.

OBJECTIVES OF INFORMED CONSENT

Many authors have recommended an informed consent process for supervision (Barnett, 2000, 2005; Bernard & Goodyear, 2009; Bradley & Ladany, 2001; Brown, Pryzwansky, & Schulte, 2001; Cobia & Boes, 2000;

Fall & Sutton, 2004; Falvey, 2002; Guest & Dooley, 1999; Harrar, Vande-Creek, & Knapp, 1990; Haynes, Corey, & Moulton, 2003; Kaiser, 1997; Knapp & VandeCreek, 2006; McCarthy et al., 1995; Osborn & Davis, 1996; Prest, Schindler-Zimmerman, & Sporakowski, 1992; Remley, 1993; Sutter, McPherson, & Geeseman, 2002; Tanenbaum & Berman, 1990; J. T. Thomas, 2000, 2007; Vasquez, 1992; Welch, 2003). An effective informed consent, particularly when communicated both orally and in writing, improves the effectiveness of both supervisor and supervisee (Archer & Peake, 1984; Guest & Dooley, 1999; Osborn & Davis, 1996) and enhances the satisfaction of both parties. The same is likely true for consultants and consultees.

Cobia and Boes (2000) identified three ways in which obtaining the informed consent of supervisees positively affects the process. They asserted that having both professional disclosure statements and formal plans for supervision will "increase the opportunities for learning the skills necessary for professional collaboration; establish an environment conducive to open, honest communication; and promote the development of rapport and trust in the supervisory relationship" (p. 293). McCarthy et al. (1995) indicated that an effective supervisory consent acquaints supervisees with their supervisors, involves supervisees in structuring their experience, and provides an opportunity for questions. Several authors have pointed out that having a clear informed consent process affords the opportunity to clarify goals, methods, structure, and purposes of supervision (Barnett, 2000; Guest & Dooley, 1999; Keel & Brown, 1999; Liddle, Breunlin, & Schwartz, 1988; Prest et al., 1992; Rønnestad & Skovholt, 1993; Teitelbaum, 1990). An informed consent also helps to establish a clear structure and boundaries (Welch, 2003). Tanenbaum and Berman (1990) suggested that an informed consent document can help prevent misunderstandings, increase the accountability of both supervisees and supervisors, and provide a mechanism for monitoring the effectiveness of the supervision. Written contracts may also clarify the roles and responsibilities of the supervisor and supervisee (Osborn & Davis, 1996).

Supervisees benefit by having clear information about their roles and their supervisors' expectations (Fall & Sutton, 2004). Archer and Peake (1984) suggested that nonproductivity and negative reactions may result when a supervision contract is not used. With the information provided in a contract, the supervisee is more likely to effectively meet supervisor expectations.

Supervisors and consultants who go through the exercise of preparing clear informed consent materials are forced to think through and articulate what they have to offer and what they are committing to provide. Stating that supervisees must arrive on time, be prepared, and actively participate in 1 hour of supervision each week might, for example, make supervisors more conscious of their commitment to doing the same. Consultants and consultees are generally freer to design a plan that addresses the particular objectives of that relationship, and establishing a contract provides an opportunity to define the parameters. In either case, a clear document or contract helps ensure that important issues are covered (Sutter et al., 2002).

In short, an informed consent allows contracting parties to elucidate expectations and identify mutually agreed-on goals (Guest & Dooley, 1999), to anticipate likely and unlikely difficulties, and to discuss in advance how such problems might be addressed and/or avoided. The process of discussing these expectations and potential difficulties also sets a precedent of addressing related issues as they arise (Prest et al., 1992) and establishes a clear professional boundary that will set the tone for the relationship. Ideally, an informed consent will both decrease the likelihood of misunderstandings, impasses, and dissatisfaction for both parties and establish a strategy for efficiently addressing problems when they do occur (Tanenbaum & Berman, 1990).

Cobia and Boes (2000) described additional benefits. They suggested that providing such information to supervisees in advance will "increase the opportunities for learning the skills necessary for professional collaboration; establish an environment conducive to open, honest communication; and promote the development of rapport and trust in the supervisory relationship" (p. 293). Finally, taking supervisees and consultees through the process of obtaining their informed consent provides a model for them to use in obtaining the consent of those they serve.

INFORMED CONSENT AND THE MITIGATION OF PROBLEMS

Most of the time, supervisory and consultative relationships proceed uneventfully. Supervisors are reasonably pleased with supervisees' performance, and supervisees are generally satisfied with the supervision they receive. Consultants typically enjoy the opportunity to share their expertise and to assist a colleague. Learning problems and minor misunderstandings, when they do occur, are typically navigated effectively, and in spite of inevitable moments of dissatisfaction, the experience concludes pleasantly.

Imagine, however, a supervisory or consultative relationship that does not go exactly according to plan. Surprises are generally not welcome, and they often provide the seeds of irreconcilable impasses. Any unanticipated circumstance, outcome, or action on the part of the supervisor or consultant may result in a misunderstanding or conflict that culminates in a painful ending or develops into a board complaint or lawsuit. Consider the following cases that at the outset appeared to portend rewarding, satisfying, and fruitful learning opportunities for the consultee or supervisee and gratifying mentoring and teaching opportunities for the consultant or supervisor. Following these cases, preventative strategies are suggested.

Dr. King and Julia

Julia completed her doctorate in counseling psychology 6 years ago and had some training and experience in psychological assessment in that context. She has not had subsequent opportunities to use those skills, however, until now. Julia recently accepted a new position in a hospital where she is expected to conduct assessments of children suspected of having learning disabilities and attention-deficit/hyperactivity disorder, an area of competence she has claimed on her application. After reviewing some of her first reports, Julia's supervisor expresses concern that she seems to have misrepresented her qualifications. He tells her that as a condition of continued employment, she must arrange individualized consultation at her own expense to help her remediate what he sees as a significant skill deficit before doing any more assessments independently. He stipulates that the consultant must approve any reports she writes and that she must complete this consultation within 6 months.

Julia thinks her supervisor is being rigid and intolerant of her unique style. But she is also panicked at the possibility of losing her job. She contacts Dr. King, a clinical psychologist in independent practice, to inquire about arranging the required consultation as soon as possible. Dr. King has been conducting psychological assessments for nearly 20 years and is excited about the prospect of sharing her expertise and mentoring a colleague. Additionally, her practice has been slow lately and a regular self-pay appointment will be helpful. She readily agrees and sets their first appointment for the following day. The supervisor had not specified the frequency of the consultations, so Julia suggests 1-hour monthly meetings. In her haste to get started, Dr. King agrees. The first meeting goes well. Both are pleased with the arrangement and are looking forward to next month's meeting.

Before their second meeting, Julia sends four 20-page reports to review and requests that Dr. King call her with feedback as soon as possible because she has promised to have these reports out by the end of the week. Recognizing the short timeline, Julia suggests that Dr. King just inform her about any concerns via e-mail or voice mail and that if she doesn't hear from Dr. King by Friday, she'll assume the reports were fine and will go ahead and send them.

Dr. King has a busy week and isn't sure how she will have time to review all of these reports. She begins reading the first one and finds it incoherent, poorly written, and replete with inherently conflictual impressions and unfounded conclusions. Some of the inconsistent scores make her wonder about the conditions of the administration and the accuracy of the scoring. Dr. King also notes that the reports were not redacted, as she anticipated they would be, and that they include identifying information. Dr. King is concerned that the clients have not consented to these disclosures. She had imagined that they would discuss the reports during meetings and had not considered that it might make sense for her to read them in advance. Further, Dr. King had not thought about the amount of time it would take her to critique the reports and hadn't discussed related charges. Beyond all of these concerns, Dr. King becomes very anxious about what she has agreed to and thinks about how she could withdraw now.

Dr. King leaves Julia a message indicating that they will need to discuss the reports in person, that she is unable to read them this week, and that she will need to charge for time spent reviewing them. Dr. King also mentions that she is in the process of trying to reach Julia's supervisor for some clarification.

Julia leaves her an angry message stating that "client welfare is at stake." She adds that client-families are counting on receiving these test results to arrange urgently needed academic services. Julia says that she cannot afford to pay any more than what they clearly agreed to during their meeting. Finally, she says she has not given permission for Dr. King to speak to her supervisor and feels that such a conversation would represent a violation of her privacy. Julia reiterates her plan to mail the reports at the end of the week if she does not receive feedback before then.

Shortly into this arrangement, the unclarified assumptions on the part of all parties became obvious. The nature and extent of the skill deficit that the consultation was supposed to ameliorate was unclear. A representative work sample along with a conversation with the supervisor might have allowed Dr. King to more accurately assess the problem and to make an informed decision about whether the proposed intervention was adequate and appropriate. An authorization from Julia allowing communication between the supervisor and consultant would also have allowed Dr. King to report back regarding Julia's compliance, progress, and competence. Julia's privacy and that of her clients could have been addressed along with each person's responsibilities, fees, and conditions that might result in termination of the consultation. A short-term contract might have given all three parties an opportunity to reevaluate the efficacy of the original plan. Even after this difficult start, the consultant could attempt to clarify misunderstandings and begin again.

Dr. Woods and Sam

Dr. Woods, the local expert in eating disorders, has supervised interns and practicum students in the past, but after adopting a baby 3 years ago, he decided he was spread too thin and so pulled back from supervising. Sam, a master's student searching for a practicum, contacts Dr. Woods and lobbies him to consider taking him on. He has a strong interest in eating disorders and ultimately would like to work in their small community, but he has been unable to find anyone else in the area who could provide him with the training he needs to develop this specialty. Dr. Woods is concerned about the limited resources for clients with eating disorders and would like to see them expanded. He hesitates, though, because he and his wife have plans to adopt a second baby from another country, but because they have been told that the wait could be as long as 2 years, they have decided not to tell anyone, including the agency director. Dr. Woods agrees to provide the supervision.

Sam begins his practicum in September as planned, and by November, he is conducting assessments and individual and group psychotherapy with clients with eating disorders. He is enjoying the work, and Dr. Woods is pleased with his progress. This mutually satisfying and productive supervision continues smoothly until February when Dr. Woods tells the agency director that he and his wife have just been notified that a baby has unexpectedly become available for adoption and that they must travel to South America this week. The adoption agency requires them to remain in the country for 6 weeks, after which Dr. Woods plans to take another 6-week leave to care for the child. The director is supportive but says there is no one else in the agency with the appropriate credentials, expertise, or time to provide the supervision that Sam needs.

In this case, Sam is counting on being able to complete his practicum in time to graduate in the spring. A 12-week interruption in his training is also impractical for his clients. Had Sam been made aware of the possible interruption, he might have elected not to pursue a practicum at this site. Further, when a practicum is offered to a student, both the agency and the supervisor must make the commitment to provide resources needed for the student to complete that practicum. Of course, an unforeseen illness, accident, personal crisis, job change, or move could disrupt any supervision, but others at the training site must be prepared to find alternative ways of meeting the supervisee's training needs. Contracting with an outside expert might allow the student to continue with those cases but not accept any new ones. Another staff member or a faculty member in the student's academic program may also be able to supplement the supervision. In any case, such contingency plans must be considered before supervision begins.

In both of these cases, obtaining the clear informed consent of supervisees at the outset of the consultation or supervision would have afforded opportunities to clarify the parameters of the relationship in advance and avoid or mitigate misunderstandings.

INFORMED CONSENT WITHIN ETHICAL STANDARDS AND GUIDELINES

Most professional mental health organizations have ethical standards or guidelines addressing informed consent, particularly as it relates to treatment, assessment, and other clinical and forensic services. A few have specifically addressed, explicitly or implicitly, the need for informed consent to supervision. Some are ethics codes promulgated by professional associations (AAMFT, 2001; ACA, 2005; APA, 2002; CPA, 2000). Some are guidelines or ethics codes developed specifically for clinical supervision (ACES, 1993; ASPPB, 2003; CCE, 2008; CPA, 2009). Others include supervision requirements for various types of certification (AAMFT, 2007).

The APA Ethics Code (2002) addresses informed consent in terms of "consulting services," which may apply to supervision as well. Psychologists must obtain informed consent from recipients of consulting services and "appropriately document written or oral consent, permission, and assent" (APA, 2002, p. 6). The APA Ethics Code further addresses the required disclosure of personal information by students and supervisees:

> Psychologists do not require students or supervisees to disclose personal information in course- or program-related activities, either orally or in writing . . . except if (1) the program or training facility has clearly identified this requirement in its admissions and program materials. (APA, 2002, p. 9)

Implicit in this statement is the assumption that having such information in advance may influence prospective students' decisions about whether to apply to a particular graduate program. Therefore, student-supervisees must be provided with information about requirements for self-disclosure in advance of their matriculation. Also, supervisors are required to "establish a timely and specific process for providing feedback to students and supervisees. Information regarding the process is provided to the student at the beginning of supervision" (APA, 2002, p. 10). The APA Ethics Code further requires that supervisees inform their clients or patients about their status and the fact that they are being supervised and that they protect their clients' identities in supervision or obtain their authorization to discuss their cases with supervisors.

Like the APA Ethics Code, the ACA *Code of Ethics and Standards of Practice* (2005) includes specific protections regarding students and supervisees: "Supervisors are responsible for incorporating into their supervision the principles of informed consent and participation" (ACA, 2005, p. 14). Supervisors are further required to inform supervisees about any policies and procedures to which they are bound and about due process options in addressing complaint about their supervisions (ACA, 2005). Also similar to the APA Ethics Code, the ACA code addresses the rights of clients whose cases are supervised; counselors must inform clients about their qualifications and protect the client's privacy in supervision.

The *Canadian Code of Ethics for Psychologists* (CPA, 2000) addresses the issue in another way. The mandate is to "be particularly cautious in establishing the freedom of consent of any person who is in a dependent relationship to the psychologist" (p. 12). This code specifically includes students, employees, and by extrapolation, supervisees. The issues to be addressed as a part of this informed consent, however, are not specified.

The *AAMFT Code of Ethics* (2001) specifically addresses the need for informed consent to supervision in two general areas. First, supervisors must avoid disclosing information about supervisees "unless they have obtained the prior written consent of the . . . supervisee" (AAMFT, 2001, p. 8). The second aspect of supervision requiring informed consent involves financial arrangements. Section 7.2 states that prior to beginning supervision supervisors must

> clearly disclose and explain to . . . supervisees: (a) all financial arrangements and fees related to professional services, including charges for canceled or missed appointments; (b) the use of collection agencies or legal measures for nonpayment; and (c) the procedure for obtaining payment. (AAMFT, 2001, p. 8)

The CCE (2008) is not a professional association but a certification board that has established an ethics code for "Approved Clinical Supervisors" (ACS) with that certification. The *ACS Code of Ethics* addresses informed consent specifically, thoroughly, and prominently in its first three sections. Supervisors are charged with ensuring that supervisees' clients are informed about limitations to their privacy and "any status other than [their] being fully qualified for independent practice" (CCE, 2008, p. 1). In addition to disclosing their status, supervisees with restricted licenses must inform clients about the existence and nature of those restrictions. A parallel code requires supervisors to inform supervisees about their "credentials, areas of expertise, and training in supervision" (CCE, 2008, p. 1). Other protections for supervisees are addressed: They must be informed about supervision goals, evaluation processes, and the supervisor's preferred theoretical models (CCE, 2008).

Other organizations, in addition to their general ethics codes addressing informed consent to supervision, have developed specialty guidelines for supervisors. The ACES, a division of the ACA, has published a set of guidelines including attention to informed consent. As guidelines, they are considered aspirational and not enforceable. The *Ethical Guidelines for Counseling Supervisors* (ACES, 1993; hereinafter referred to as Ethical Guidelines) suggests that supervisors "incorporate the principles of informed consent . . . into the policies and procedures of their institutions, program, courses and individual supervisory relationships" (p. 7). Specific issues that should, according to the ACES, be incorporated into an informed consent agreement include "requirements, expectations, roles and rules; and due process and appeal" (p. 7).

The ACES Ethical Guidelines further recommends that supervisors inform supervisees about the "goals, policies, theoretical orientations toward counseling, training, and supervision model or approach on which the supervision is based" (p. 7). Supervisors are encouraged to communicate "in a timely way" (p. 7) in writing about the professional competencies and experiences that are required. When supervision occurs in the context of a university training program, the ACES recommends that supervisors "establish and communicate specific policies and procedures regarding field placements of students. The respective roles of the student counselor, the university supervisor, and the field supervisor should be clearly differentiated in areas such as evaluation, requirements, and confidentiality" (p. 8).

The AAMFT has established education and training standards for association members who want to become "approved supervisors." The *Approved Supervisor Designation Standards and Responsibilities Handbook* (AAMFT, 2007; hereinafter referred to as the Handbook) is comprehensive in that it includes information about supervisor training requirements and responsibilities as well as tools for supervisors. The AAMFT members providing supervision for clinical membership or marriage and family therapy licensure must develop a supervision contract, a tool for obtaining informed consent. The Handbook states that a supervision contract should include information about "fees, hours, time and place of meetings, case responsibility, caseload review, handling of suicide threats, and other dangerous clinical situations" (AAMFT, 2007, p. 12). The Handbook also includes other issues that might be addressed in a contract as well as a sample supervision contract.

The ASPPB has published a set of *Supervision Guidelines* (2003) to assist supervisors working in three contexts: doctoral level candidates for licensure and credentialed and uncredentialed nondoctoral personnel providing psychological services. Guidelines for doctoral level candidates suggest that prospective supervisees be provided with

> a written document specifying the rules and regulations of the program, as well as the roles, goals and objectives expected from both supervisees and supervisor. At the onset of training, the supervisor will be responsible for developing, along with the supervisees, a written individualized training plan which meets the needs of the supervisees and is consistent with the purpose of the setting. (ASPPB, 2003, p. 3)

The ASPPB *Supervision Guidelines* (2003) also addresses the need for written informed consent with regard to evaluation:

> At the outset of the supervisory period each supervisor together with the supervisee shall establish a written contract which specifies a) the competencies to be evaluated and the goals to be attained; b) the standards for measuring performance; and c) the time frame for goal attainment. (p. 4)

TABLE 6.1
Issues Addressed in Terms of Informed Consent

Issue	Organization
Supervisee privacy	AAMFT (2001), ACES (1993), NASW (2008)
Job duties, required experiences	ACES (1993)
Supervisor's credentials or orientation	ACES (1993), CCE (2008)
Due process for supervisees	AAMFT (2001), ACA (2005), ACES (1993), ASPPB (2003), CCE (2008)
Supervision boundaries, multiple relationships, exploitation, power	ACA (2005), CCE (2008)
Documentation of consent	APA (2002), ASPPB (2003)
Evaluation	ASPPB (2003), CCE (2008), NASW (2008)
Required self-disclosure and personal growth activities	APA (2002), ACES (1993)
Fees	AAMFT (2001), ASPPB (2003)
Conditions of supervision	AAMFT (2002), ASPPB (2003), CCE (2008)
Client privacy in supervision[a]	APA (2002), ACA (2005), AAMFT (2001), CCE (2008), NASW (2008)
Disclosure of trainee status[a]	APA (2002), ACA (2005), CCE (2008), CPA (2000), NASW (2008)

Note. AAMFT = American Association for Marriage and Family Therapy; ACES = Association for Counselor Education and Supervision; CCE = Center for Credentialing & Education; NASW = National Association of Social Workers; ACA = American Counseling Association; ASPPB = Association of State and Provincial Psychology Boards; APA = American Psychological Association; CPA = Canadian Psychological Association.
[a]These items involve the informed consent that supervisees obtain from their clients or patients regarding their supervision.

Table 6.1 is a summary of issues that may be included in an informed consent to supervision and the ethics codes and guidelines that specifically address them.

SUPERVISION CONTRACTS

Obtaining the informed consent of supervisees at the outset, if not in advance, of the supervisory relationship is critical to minimizing misunderstandings and to setting the tone for a supervisory relationship (Studer, 2005). The following are examples of the types of issues that might be addressed in an informed consent contract for supervision. This is not exhaustive, nor is it intended to imply that all of these issues must be in every contract. Rather it is a menu of topics designed to help supervisors choose areas that are pertinent to their particular settings and types of supervision. Fees, for example, are not generally relevant to the supervision of students.

Establishing a contract for supervision or consultation is one strategy for obtaining informed consent from supervisees. The contract may take various forms. Cobia and Boes (2000) suggested two interventions for obtaining the informed consent of those receiving postdegree supervision: "professional disclosure statements" and "formal plans for supervision" (p. 293). The first describes the service being offered and addresses the "mutual rights and responsibilities of all parties, the parameters of supervision, methods of evaluation, desired outcomes, and potential risks and benefits of participation in supervision" (pp. 293–294). The second, the formal plan, is essentially an individualized learning contract, a corollary to the treatment plan used in psychotherapy (Barnett, 2005; Tanenbaum & Berman, 1990).

An informed consent document might include all of the necessary information with a place for the signatures of both members of the dyad (Fall & Sutton, 2004; McCarthy et al., 1995; Osborn & Davis, 1996; Sutter et al., 2002) Or the consent form could be a separate page that refers to the primary document and includes signatures. A learning contract could be attached if needed. Whatever form it takes, such a contract might include relevant portions of the following types of information.

Supervisor's Background

Supervisees make the best use of supervision when they know something about their supervisors' backgrounds. Minimally, supervisees should know about their supervisors' academic degrees, certifications, and clinical specialties. Supervisors should also share their theoretical approaches to both supervision and psychotherapy orally, if not in writing.

Supervisory Methods

Supervisors use a broad range of methods in their work with supervisees. They might, for example, review electronic recordings, observe individual and group counseling sessions and test administrations, and evaluate clinical records and reports. Some supervisors provide cotherapy with supervisees, conduct site visits (if the supervisee works off-site), or in other ways monitor their cases. Supervisors should describe each of these to supervisees in advance.

Confidentiality Policies

Supervisees are entitled, as are their clients, to a degree of privacy. The precise limits of that privacy, however, are dependent on variables including state or provincial law, policies of the training program or agency, relevant ethics codes and licensing board rules, and the specific contract written by the supervisor. The circumstances under which the supervisor is obligated to breach the supervisee's confidentiality—to report unethical behavior, for example—must also be communicated (J. T. Thomas, 1994). Additionally, supervisors should ask supervisees, when appropriate, to provide written authorization for the supervisor to communicate with others about particular aspects of the supervision. Whenever two supervisors are involved, coordination of their services is necessary to ensure continuity and minimize confusion.

Regarding privacy, supervision contracts should address the following:

- who will have access to information about the supervisee's work performance, personal disclosures, and supervisor's assessments (e.g., academic or site or field supervisor, employer, licensing board, or other third party);
- which types of records will be kept regarding the supervision; and
- what will happen to supervisor's records (see the discussion that follows) and to recordings submitted for review (e.g., who is responsible for erasing or disposing of electronically recorded clinical material, who has access to that material, and under what circumstances).

Financial Issues and Policies

Supervisees must be informed about charges for which they are responsible. Fees may be charged for various related services such as supervisory sessions, report preparation, phone consultation, evaluation preparation, document review, tape review, observations of clinical work, joint sessions, and missed appointments. Agencies in which students participate in practicum or internship experiences do not generally charge a fee for supervision, in part because students typically contribute a service from which the agency benefits financially. Students obtaining supervision outside of the agency, however, may be required to pay a fee. Those seeking supervision to accrue hours for licensure or certification in a specialty area or to comply with requirements of a licensing board order in a disciplinary matter may need to obtain supervision independently, particularly if they are in independent practice. It should be noted that charging for prelicensure supervision is prohibited by some licensing boards (e.g., California Board of Psychology, 2008) and by the ASPPB *Supervision Guidelines* (2003).

Documentation

Supervisors should inform supervisees about the types of records they will create and maintain. An informed consent to supervision should specify exactly who, including the supervisee, will have access to that documentation; how and under what conditions it may be accessed; the length of time the documentation will be maintained; and how it will be secured. Records may include a narrative description of supervision discussions, a log of hours, dates of meetings, copies of evaluations, and so forth (see Chapter 9, this volume).

Risks and Benefits

Supervisors must inform supervisees about the potential risks and benefits of participation in supervision. One risk, for example, is the emotional discomfort and vulnerability associated with being scrutinized. Further, supervisees are encouraged to candidly discuss their work, including their mistakes. Doing so, however, creates the possibility of the appearance of that information in a performance evaluation or a report to an outside authority for unethical conduct. Supervisees may not realize that they have committed errors and may not know when they are admitting to having done so. Their evaluations may or may not be favorable, and they may impact supervisees' current or future licensure status, their ability to be certified in the future, or whether they are allowed to pass their practicum or internship. Further, the consequences of termination of the supervision by either party should be considered.

The potential benefits of supervision should also be addressed as part of informed consent. Supervision is likely to provide opportunities for supervisees to reflect on their clinical work and professional functioning and to obtain corrective feedback needed to improve their skills. Greater insight may increase supervisees' understanding of the ways in which their personal experiences may impact their work and thereby increase clinical effectiveness. Exposing one's clinical work to the scrutiny of a supervisor may decrease the likelihood that the individual will commit an ethical or legal error leading to a complaint or a lawsuit. Of course, other factors may also be included.

Evaluation

Evaluation of a supervisee's job performance is an integral aspect of supervision, particularly in student training or in the rehabilitation of an impaired professional (see Chapter 8, this volume). Informing supervisees about this process in advance is required by many professional ethics codes (AAMFT, 2001; ACA, 2005; APA, 2002) and is recommended by supervisory guidelines (ACES, 1993; ASPPB, 2003; CPA, 2009). Further, doing so increases the likelihood of supervisee compliance with expectations. Supervisees also benefit when supervisors elucidate evaluation methods (oral, written, completion of a form, inclusion of a self-evaluation); timing (midterm, semester-end, quarterly); criteria for successful completion; and, if applicable, the particular skills and responsibilities on which the individual will be evaluated. Supervisors should provide to supervisees any forms that will be used so they know exactly what they are required to do to succeed. According to Keith-Spiegel and Koocher (1998), a lack of timely feedback is the subject of many ethics complaints filed against supervisors. Supervisees are especially likely to be dissatisfied when they are abruptly terminated or given an unanticipated, poor evaluation.

Complaint Procedures

Supervisors must anticipate the possibility that supervisees might at some point in the process feel dissatisfied with their supervision. Acknowledging that possibility at the outset and instructing the supervisee about how to address such dissatisfaction may prevent a relatively small problem from developing into a serious impasse or complaint against the supervisor. Detailed due process procedures should be described in a consent document or referenced if they are contained in a student intern handbook or human resource policy manual (Cormier & Bernard, 1982). Generally, the first step is to talk directly with the supervisor. Supervisors should commit to providing opportunities for supervisees to discuss their feelings about their supervision. These opportunities may be provided both informally on a continuing basis and in conjunction with scheduled evaluations. Supervisees ought to be informed of their recourse should they be dissatisfied with the outcome of efforts to resolve a problem with their supervisor or if the nature of the issue makes impractical or onerous the prospect of addressing it directly with the supervisor.

Duration of the Contract and Criteria for Termination

Sometimes a contract clearly determines the length of the supervision. A 12-month internship, a 9-month practicum, and a required length of supervision for licensure or certification are examples. When supervision is required as part of a disciplinary order issued by a licensing board or employer, the duration may be specified or contingent on the achievement of particular goals. In some cases, duration is contingent on the supervisor's determination that supervisory goals are met or on the licensing board's decision to lift sanctions on the basis of that recommendation.

Sometimes supervisors wish to offer a shorter duration contract or probationary period with an option to extend it. Supervisees are free to discontinue at will, but supervisors should address the consequences of doing so in the discussion of risks and benefits. When supervisors elect to discontinue supervision because of the supervisee's failure to meet obligations agreed to at the outset (see examples that follow), the consequences to supervisees may be significant. The completion of their degrees or requirements for licensure, for example, may be delayed by a year or more. Therefore, supervisors must state at the outset the criteria for a supervisor-initiated termination. Examples of such criteria include

- noncompliance with supervisory directives;
- withholding or misrepresenting relevant information about themselves or their clients;
- failure to pay bills, if there is a fee for supervision;
- violations of specified ethics codes;
- failure to regularly attend supervision sessions and/or repeated tardiness; and
- consistent failure to prepare for supervisory sessions.

Supervisor's Responsibilities

Supervisees also should know about the services the supervisor is offering and how they will be provided. Supervisors are often expected to provide verification of the hours worked and the time spent in supervision. They may asked to endorse supervisees for licensure or certification. The supervisor may not feel comfortable endorsing a supervisee when there are concerns about professional competence, impairment, boundaries with clients, or any other ethical issue that becomes apparent in the course of the supervision. Of course, supervisors should bring these concerns to the attention of the supervisee in a timely fashion, but doing so may not be enough to eliminate the problem.

Sometimes, despite efforts to address such problems, concerns are not resolved to the satisfaction of the supervisor by the conclusion of the supervision. The emergence of such concerns may occur with any supervisee with no indication of such at the outset. Supervisors must therefore address this possibility in the supervisory contract. Stating what they will do if they have concerns about the individual's ability to function effectively will alert the supervisee and provide an agreed-upon guideline as well as some legal protection for the supervisor should the supervisee later object. Supervisors might say, for example, that they will verify their supervisees' participation in the supervision and the hours worked but will also attach a letter describing any persisting concerns.

Supervision Session Content

The frequency, duration, and format of supervisory meetings must be delineated. Meetings may occur weekly, biweekly, or at some other interval and can last for 50 minutes or for another agreed-on time period. They may be individual or group meetings. The meeting time may be spent on any of various activities—discussing clinical cases, the supervisee's professional development goals, or assigned readings. Supervisors might also use the time for role-playing client interactions, reviewing electronic recordings of clinical work, viewing and discussing educational videos, or examining the supervisee's case notes, testing reports, or other written work. A supervisory contract should include examples of how such sessions will be structured and what activities are likely to occur.

Supervisor Accessibility

Supervisors' availability is a critical issue, particularly for novice supervisees. Mental health emergencies generally require rapid decision making, taking into account multiple complex factors. These situations are stressful and challenging for even the most seasoned therapists, and consultation with colleagues, when possible, is standard procedure. The welfare of clients and supervisees as well as the liability of supervisors suggests that supervisees should never be required to navigate these challenging situations alone. Of course, supervisees should be trained to respond to crises. Part of that training should include a clear set of guidelines for accessing assistance. Supervisors' telephone numbers should be provided along with instructions for determining when it is appropriate to use those numbers outside of regular business hours. If the supervisor will be unavailable for any period (vacation, illness) or cannot be located immediately, another appropriately trained colleague should be identified and confirmed as willing to substitute for the primary supervisor. This information should be provided in writing and reviewed with the supervisee.

Supervisee's Responsibilities

The supervisee's specific job duties should be clearly described in writing and made available to supervisees in advance of their agreement to perform them. Responsibilities may be outlined in a job description, learning contract, and/or as part of the supervision contract. Their responsibilities vis-à-vis the supervision should be described as well. Supervisees might be expected, for example, to attend supervisory sessions, arrive on time, and be prepared to present cases for discussion. They might also be required to bring specified written material or to cue recordings to sections that will be reviewed during supervision.

Supervisors may wish to specify the requirements and obtain the supervisee's commitment to follow them. Supervisees might be asked to sign an agreement to perform all specified job duties, prepare for and participate in supervisory sessions, and follow specified ethics codes, licensing board rules, and relevant laws. Supervisors might also require supervisees to maintain and provide documentation of their malpractice insurance coverage. Minimum coverage limits could also be specified. In the case of a lawsuit, the supervisor's liability may be limited when the supervisee also has insurance coverage.

Agreement to Keep Supervisors Informed

Supervisors are generally held legally responsible for their supervisees' clinical work (Falvey, 2002; Harrar et al., 1990; Knapp & VandeCreek, 2006; Saccuzzo, 2003). This responsibility may encompass all of an individual's work or be confined to a circumscribed area of practice that the supervisor agrees to supervise. The contract should include clarification of such. To assume responsibility for a supervisee's clinical work, supervisors must have a strategy for monitoring client care (see Chapter 8, this volume). Whatever methods are used, supervisors must ensure that supervisees have a clear understanding of which cases they must present, how to prioritize these cases, and when they must notify their supervisors.

Sometimes supervisors assume that supervisees will inform them about any event, personal experience, or problem they would want to know about. Exactly which events this includes, however, is not always apparent until after they have occurred. Supervisees are even less likely to know what they are to report and at what point they are expected to do so. Sometimes supervisors complain that supervisees are not autonomous enough and that they ask for help with decisions they should be able to make independently. Conversely, some supervisees overestimate their ability to function independently. To the degree that such situations are anticipated and discussed in advance, both problems are minimized or avoided. Supervisors may wish to stipulate that they be informed about the following circumstances:

- disputes with clients or impasses in the therapy;
- allegations of unethical behavior by clients, colleagues, or others (e.g., a client's family members);
- threats of a complaint or lawsuit;
- mental health emergencies requiring immediate action;
- high-risk situations or cases in which clients evidence suicidal thoughts, gestures, attempts, or a significant history of attempts or those presenting with a history of, propensity for, or threats of violence;
- contemplated departures from standards of practice or exceptions to general rules, standards, policies, or practices;

- suspected or known clinical or ethical errors;
- contact with clients outside the context of treatment, incidental or otherwise; and
- legal issues such as possible reporting obligations related to suspected abuse of a child or vulnerable adult and ethical violations by other professionals.

Supervisees must agree not only to keep their supervisors informed but also to follow through on any recommendations or directives made by the supervisor. Here is an example of one such statement, to be signed by the supervisee: "I agree to keep the supervisor informed about all aspects of my clinical work (as specified above) and to implement any decisions or, if I believe circumstances warrant reconsideration, to discuss them with the supervisor."

Professional Development Goals

When the supervisee is not a student and a learning contract is not used, supervisory goals may be incorporated into the supervision contract or, minimally, discussed as part of the informed consent process. The following are examples of issues that might be addressed:

- specific skills and techniques that the supervisee wants to learn (e.g., to administer, score, and interpret particular psychological tests);
- particular deficits that the supervisee wants or needs to ameliorate, especially when the primary goal of the supervision is rehabilitation (e.g., a tendency to avoid interventions or topics that might cause discomfort, difficulty setting appropriate limits with clients, or problems with staying current with documentation of clinical work); and
- short- and long-term professional development goals (e.g., developing expertise with certain populations or learning the applications of a particular theoretical orientation).

INFORMED CONSENT TO CONSULTATION: DISTINCTIONS FROM SUPERVISION

Because of similarities in the work of clinical consultants and supervisors, many of the previously listed issues should be included in contracts for consultation. Adjustments may address primary differences between the two types of service. Supervisors maintain both responsibility for and authority over their supervisees' work; consultation is a relationship between "legal equals" (Knapp & VandeCreek, 2006, p. 151). Further, the responsibilities of a supervisor are generally broader than those of consultants. Contracts for consultation should delineate what the consultant agrees to do. Rather than take responsibility for a therapist's entire caseload, a consultant might agree to field particular questions or cases that the consultee chooses to raise. Or the consultant might offer an educational consultation focused on the use of a particular type of assessment instrument, learning to apply a particular theoretical orientation, or improving boundaries with clients. Such a contract need not then specify which issues the consultee must inform the consultant about. Rather, the consultee chooses which issues he or she wishes to raise. And, unlike supervisors, consultants are not ultimately responsible for decisions. Therefore, the contract should include a clear statement, signed by the consultee, emphasizing that the consultee is ultimately responsible, such as the following: "The consultant will offer suggestions and ideas. I may choose to accept and implement, modify, or ignore these suggestions. I understand that responsibility for clinical decisions regarding my clients rest solely with me."

CONCLUSION

Obtaining informed consent at the outset of supervision or consultation means securing a supervisee's or consultee's agreement to participate in light of all relevant factors. The specific information included in a supervision contract or other informed consent document varies according to the setting, context, and purpose of the supervision or consultation; supervisor's or consultant's preferences; supervisee's or consultee's needs; and other factors.

When supervisors and consultants prepare clear informed consent materials and address these issues at the outset, both orally and in writing, all parties benefit. Supervisors and consultants become clear about their commitments. Supervisees and consultees know what will be expected and exactly what they must to do to succeed. Both parties are likely to function more effectively, encounter fewer misunderstandings, and experience more satisfaction in their respective roles.

7

CONSULTATION AND SUPERVISION GROUPS

Psychologists provide consultation and supervision in the context of both individual meetings and in groups. The requirements of academic programs as well as those established for postdegree licensure or certification typically include a specified amount of individual supervision (Goodyear & Nelson, 1997; Milne & Oliver, 2000). According to Goodyear and Nelson (1997), group supervision is second only to individual supervision as the most commonly used modality. Having met supervision requirements for licensure or certification, many psychologists choose to seek individual consultation, group consultation, or both.

Consultation and supervision groups take several forms. Four categories of groups are considered here: supervisor led, consultant initiated and led, invited consultant, and peer consultation. Despite overlap, formats vary according to purpose and structure. The objectives of this chapter are to

- distinguish between types of consultation and supervision groups;
- describe the need for professional consultation and supervision beyond initial training and illustrate ways in which both can mitigate clinical and ethical errors;

- identify the potential risks and benefits of group consultation and supervision;
- present various models and formats for consultation and supervision groups;
- outline common scenarios with the potential to undermine the efficacy of such groups;
- outline ethical issues inherent in group consultation and supervision; and
- offer strategies for starting, structuring, sustaining, and improving consultation and supervision groups.

DISTINCTIONS BETWEEN CONSULTATION AND SUPERVISION GROUPS

Generally, some outside entity requires supervision for a particular purpose. Supervision may be required for a practicum, an internship, licensure, certification, as a condition of employment, or as part of a disciplinary action. The supervisor and supervisees are generally members of the same profession. As is the case with individual supervisors, group supervisors assume ultimate responsibility for the supervisees' professional decisions and behavior.

Bernard and Goodyear (2009) offered a comprehensive definition of group supervision:

> Group supervision is the regular meeting of a group of supervisees (a) with a designated supervisor or supervisors, (b) to monitor the quality of their work, and (c) to further their understanding of themselves as clinicians, of the clients with whom they work, and of service delivery in general. These supervisees are aided in achieving these goals by their supervisor(s) and by their feedback from and interactions with each other. (p. 244)

This definition delineates the significant responsibilities of a group supervisor. Conversely, consultation groups may or may not have a designated leader, and the format is generally more flexible and variable. A consultation group consists of peers who share common professional goals or interests. Each individual retains complete legal and clinical responsibility for his or her own work.

Supervision Groups

Supervision groups commonly exist in academic programs as well as in agencies and institutions where mental health professionals are trained or employed. The supervisor is responsible for determining the group's purpose, goals, content, format, and membership. The supervisor's responsibilities also include evaluation of group members' professional skills.

Consultant-Initiated and Consultant-Led Groups

Sometimes one person with particular expertise leads a consultation group. Consultants may advertise the group to colleagues and establish a fee for each group member. Without assuming legal responsibility for members' work, the consultant leads the group and determines its focus, format, schedule, and ground rules and screens and selects members. The consultant may offer information and recommendations but does not have the responsibility or authority to require particular actions or to determine which cases are presented.

Invited Consultant Groups

Members of an established peer consultation group may decide to invite a colleague possessing desired expertise to meet with the group for one session or on a continuing basis. An emissary group member likely would extend the invitation to a prospective consultant to meet with the group. If the proposal is for a one-time meeting, the negotiation generally occurs in advance by phone. If the group is looking for an ongoing connection, the consultant is asked to participate in a discussion to consider the feasibility of continuing. The fee, focus, format, and schedule usually are negotiated rather than unilaterally determined by the consultant. The responsibility and liability for clinical and ethical decisions rests with individual group members.

Peer Consultation

Peer consultation groups generally consist of colleagues with similar levels of professional experience. They function without a designated leader. Psychotherapists in independent practices, for example, may decide to assemble a group of colleagues to discuss their cases. Depending on their needs and objectives, they may choose to collaborate with colleagues located in the same office or building, or they may seek out colleagues who share a theoretical orientation or who engage in a particular type of work.

Employed psychologists sometimes have consultation groups available in their work settings. They may be referred to as *staffing groups, team meetings,* or by some other label. Such groups have many of the same potential benefits as other groups. But, unlike an autonomous, independent group initiated by and designed for the members, staff groups are preexisting. Employees may be required to attend, but they may have minimal input regarding the size, focus, and format of the group and nothing to say about its composition. The consultations may be combined with administrative staff meetings or squeezed into a lunch hour. When consultation is not afforded a high priority, attendance is likely to be erratic; people will arrive late (after preparing their lunches) and leave early to return calls, and members will be more reluctant to candidly share their cases. Personal vulnerability may be enhanced by historical or ongoing conflicts among members, competitive themes, personality conflicts, or fears about candidly exposing their mistakes to colleagues and to those with authority over their employment status.

Another potential limitation of group consultation in an employment setting, particularly one that is multidisciplinary, is that the focus must be broad enough to accommodate mental health staff from various professions with different types of expertise and needs. Despite advantages of these diverse perspectives, these factors can limit the utility of such groups.

For these reasons, employed psychologists may prefer to participate in a consultation group outside of their work settings. Individual employees may want to consult with colleagues in the same profession or those who share their particular clinical interests or are using similar specialized techniques. They may also prefer to be in a group with colleagues who have no authority over their employment status. For these reasons, employed psychologists may choose to supplement work site consultation with an outside group.

THE FUNCTION AND UTILITY OF GROUP SUPERVISION

Data supporting the efficacy of any type of supervision for improving treatment outcomes is sparse (Bernard & Goodyear, 2004), and studies supporting group supervision are even more rare (Goodyear & Guzzard, 2000; Holloway & Johnston, 1985; Prieto, 1996). Much of the existing research relies on the self-reports, perceived satisfaction, and preferences of supervisors and supervisees (Gonsalvez, Oades, & Freestone, 2002; McCarthy, DeBell, Kanuha, & McLeod, 1988; Milne & Oliver, 2000; Romans, Boswell, Carlozzi, & Ferguson, 1995). Because practitioners of group supervision have presented numerous and compelling arguments for its use, Bernard and Goodyear (2004) argued that "it would seem ill advised to forgo the use of group supervision while we await data concerning its processes and outcomes" (p. 236).

Benefits of Group Supervision

Most authors address group supervision in terms of its utility relative to individual supervision, particularly in the training of students. Group supervision is less costly in terms of time, money, and use of supervisors' time (Bernard & Goodyear, 2009; Haynes, Corey, & Moulton, 2003). When supervisees pay privately for supervision, the cost of group supervision is less.

In addition to these practical considerations, supervisees can benefit from exposure to a much greater breadth of client characteristics in terms of culture, race, ethnicity, age, diagnosis, and presenting problems (Bernard & Goodyear, 2009; Proctor & Inskipp, 2001). Further, group supervision affords supervisees opportunities to observe the impact of various types of interventions and to receive input about their cases as well as their strengths, growth areas, and skills from a broader range of colleagues. Thus, the opportunities to develop a more realistic sense of themselves may be enhanced (Bradley & Ladany, 2001). Membership in a group can also be a source of personal support, which can encourage appropriate risk taking, normalize supervisees' experiences (Bradley & Ladany, 2001; Counselman & Gompert, 1993; Yalom, 1995), and offer a venue for processing emotional responses to clinical work. Several authors have noted that supervisees' dependence on supervisors will be diminished when they can rely on a larger group of individuals (Bernard & Goodyear, 2009; Getzel & Salmon, 1985). For supervisees who are concurrently or will be conducting group therapy, membership in a supervision group will provide an opportunity to observe and experience the group process and, to the degree that the supervision group is effective in navigating the stages of its development (Bernard & Goodyear, 2009; Haynes et al., 2003; Tuckman & Jensen, 1977; Yalom, 1995), a model that can enhance their skills (Epstein, 2001; Hawkins & Shohet, 2006).

Limitations to Group Supervision

Despite the numerous advantages, group supervision also has inherent limitations that must be considered. Diminished confidentiality, for example, is a concern whenever the number of people who have access to information is increased (Bernard & Goodyear, 2009). When supervisees are novices, they also may be less informed than a more experienced individual supervisor might be about the nuances of confidentiality, and so the risk of inappropriate disclosure of private information is increased. When group is a substitute for individual supervision, it is also possible that it may not offer adequate time for attending to all of the needs of members, particularly when supervisees are new clinicians with complex and high risk cases. Altfeld and Bernard (1997) discussed "the potential for discord, competition, shame, humiliation, isolation, and feelings of inferiority and incompetence before one's peers" (p. 384).

Unaddressed group dynamics can diminish the value of any supervision group. Themes of competition, jealousy, and resentment, for example, can be destructive to individual members and to the group process (Ogren, Jonsson, & Sundin, 2005). Scapegoating and gossip outside of the group are similarly problematic (Yalom, 1995). Another potential problem occurs when a group of inexperienced supervisees support one another in arriving at an inaccurate diagnosis, case conceptualization, or intervention plan. The power of the group has the potential to mislead a clinician and result in harm to clients. When the group is too diverse in terms of professional experience and skill level, the focus of attention can be diverted to the conflicts that develop around these disparities. Finally, Bradley and Ladany (2001) pointed out potential problems that can result when multicultural issues are neglected or mismanaged.

These limitations of group supervision, however, are not entirely endemic. Awareness and appropriate intervention by a skilled supervisor or by one or more members has the potential to minimize if not ameliorate these problems. Group dynamics are inevitable, but they can provide a valuable opportunity for personal and professional growth, which can enhance the quality of the groups that the member will ultimately facilitate themselves. A skilled supervisor can choose to intervene when the group is off course and can do so in a way that preserves the dignity of members while challenging erroneous thinking. Multicultural issues within the group and those that involve clients can and should be attended to regularly (Bradley & Ladany, 2001; Lopez, 1997). Finally, a sensitive supervisor will be attuned to signs of interpersonal conflict and other problems among members. Dominance or withdrawal by a particular member and resistance to feedback are examples of dynamics that are not unlikely but are generally amenable to intervention.

THE FUNCTION AND UTILITY OF CONSULTATION GROUPS

Psychotherapists for whom supervision is not required may choose to organize and participate in a consultation group. Such participation has both benefits and limitations.

Benefits of Membership in a Consultation Group

Professionals may elect to participate in voluntary consultation with a variety of goals. Employed psychologists may, for reasons described previously, want to participate in a group outside of their work setting. An outside consultation group can consist of colleagues who have made deliberate decisions to work with one another. The increased trust associated with handpicked colleagues provides a safe forum for candidly discussing clients' transference responses as well as psychologists' own countertransference reactions.

Private practitioners obtain additional benefits. Fellow members can provide practical assistance by suggesting referral alternatives, providing referrals, and by helping one another manage their caseloads during temporary or permanent absences from practice. Consultation groups also offer members an economical professional development opportunity. Although time away from a full practice to travel to and attend a consultation group means lost revenue, there is typically no charge for participation (unless an expert is hired). Such groups offer members a chance to develop and enhance clinical skills, deepen knowledge, and be self-reflective in a supportive and challenging environment. Members can learn from colleagues' cases and their particular skills and areas of expertise. A peer consultation group has the additional advantage of allowing more candor. A group that consists of colleagues who do not have power over other members can have a disinhibiting influence, allowing members to discuss their ethical dilemmas, mistakes, questions, and challenges. All of these benefits may be enhanced because such groups typically consist of licensed, experienced professionals.

Consultation groups can serve as a source of both professional and personal, emotional support. Clinical work can be stressful (Barnett & Hillard, 2001; Sherman, 1996; Sherman & Thelen, 1998). Suicidal clients, threats of violence, and clients who frequently challenge their therapists can add to the difficulty of this work. Further, distressing events in a psychologist's personal life can negatively affect his or her effectiveness (Coster & Schwebel, 1997). Significant losses, illness, divorce, malpractice suits, and unanticipated absences from practice, for example, can create challenges for professional practice (Sherman & Thelen, 1998). Such support might also be available in an employment setting, but psychologists may find personal disclosure to fellow employees to be more risky than confiding in chosen colleagues. The presence of a group of colleagues with whom to share the emotional challenges of clinical work can help manage the associated stress and mitigate burnout.

A consultation group can also serve as a risk management strategy, particularly during personally difficult times. Exposing clinical work to colleagues allows opportunities for intervention when judgment is compromised by the stress of life events, health problems, or countertransference.

Limitations of Membership in a Consultation Group

The main limitation to participation in a consultation group is that the needs of a particular individual may not be met. In some cases, there is a poor fit from the outset, and in other cases, members' needs evolve and diverge over time. Careful planning and articulation of expectations, both initially and on a continual basis, can help to mitigate such problems. The following section describes strategies for minimizing limitations and maximizing benefits of consultation groups.

CONFIDENTIALITY IN SUPERVISION AND CONSULTATION GROUPS

Psychologists, like other mental health professionals, are required to protect as confidential any client information obtained in the course of consultation or supervision (American Psychological Association [APA], 2002). In other words, supervisors and consultants as well as members of supervision and consultation groups should not disclose client information obtained in these contexts (e.g., Canadian Psychological Association [CPA], 2000, I.43). Nevertheless, if identifying information about clients will be shared in consultation or supervision, the clients must be informed and consent to participation in treatment with an understanding of this condition (APA, 2002). Even when identifying information is not used, clients should be informed that their cases may be shared in a consultation or supervision group. In either case, clinicians should be judicious in their disclosure of client information.

Group consultation and supervision pose additional risks for client privacy. In small communities (geographic, ethnic, professional, etc.), the risk may be intensified (Schank & Skovolt, 2006). As the number of group members increases, so does the likelihood that an individual client will be known to a group member (if identifying information is used) or that a client's identity will be inadvertently recognized despite efforts to conceal it. When this occurs, the group should have a clear policy. At the moment a member realizes that he or she knows an individual being discussed, he or she should step out of the group and then not participate in any subsequent discussions regarding that case. This solution is not perfect, however. Sometimes a case is presented several times before a client is recognized. By that time, the individual who knows the client may have already obtained significant information. Ethical dilemmas arise about whether the client should be informed at that point about the error. In any case, the person who now has the information must commit to containing it to prevent further disclosures.

Disguising Clients' Identities

Efforts to disguise clients' identities should go beyond excluding an individual's last name. As a general rule, group members should present only what is necessary. If a referral for a grief group is needed, stating only that the client is an adolescent grieving the death of a grandparent, for example, would probably be adequate. When input about the general management of a case is needed, however, more information will be required. Sometimes nonessential details can be deliberately altered while still preserving the integrity of the case. Changing the age, number of children, marital status, hometown, or occupation could serve to protect the client's identity. Again, this is not a perfect solution, particularly for psychoanalytic supervision in which the details may be significant even when the presenter does not immediately recognize their relevance. Thus, the need to obtain assistance with a case must be weighed against the potential risk to the client's privacy, and every reasonable effort to minimize that risk should be used.

Privacy of Group Members

Privacy of group members must be considered in addition to that of the clients they present. Certainly, the leaders of consultation and supervision groups are obligated to group members in the same way they are responsible for anyone to whom they are providing a professional service. But what are the responsibilities of individual members? Discussions of group rules regarding confidentiality of clients should include expectations regarding information about group members. Further, there are no laws or rules that specifically address the privacy of members in a peer consultation group. In these groups, members need to discuss their preferences about that issue to ensure that all members' expectations are consistent. For example, members may feel fine about others sharing the identities of members and perhaps their areas of expertise and location of their practices. But they may not want any other personal information about them shared beyond the group. Members may not want others to disclose information about their plans for retirement, conflicts in their work settings, or about an illness resulting in an absence from practice, for example. There is no one correct way to handle such information, but advanced agreement about these and similar issues will minimize the likelihood of problematic disclosures that compromise the trust in the group.

ACTIVITIES OF CONSULTATION AND SUPERVISION GROUPS

Consultation and supervision groups provide a flexible venue for professional development limited only by the creativity of their members. The goals and objectives of a group influence how the time is spent. If the primary goal is to develop skills in a particular technique, then discussing related articles, role-playing, or inviting experts might be most useful. If expanding theoretical knowledge is the main purpose, then related cases would be presented and relevant articles and books could be read and discussed. If the goal is to provide a source of personal and professional support for members, then cases that provoke countertransference or are personally taxing might be the primary focus along with personal disclosure by members.

Structure and Format

Perhaps the most common format for both supervision and consultation groups is for members to take turns presenting cases. Others ask questions, make suggestions, and offer alternative perspectives about how to conceptualize or manage cases. If a supervisor is running the group, he or she may structure the meetings to accomplish whatever specific objectives have been determined. Despite the commonality of this format, there are many alternatives that can be used exclusively or in combination to enhance the utility of a group.

In consultant-initiated or supervision groups, the leader determines the basic structure of the group and then describes the type of group he or she wants to offer in an advertisement or invites specific participants. Although those who respond are self-selected, the leader can choose those he or she thinks will best fit. The group continues as long as the leader chooses. If particular members do not feel their needs are being met, they as individuals can decide to discontinue.

Peer groups without a designated leader, however, may decide that they would benefit from consulting an outside expert. The dynamic shifts when an existing group makes this decision and then searches for someone to meet the identified need. Members determine a group structure, decide whether they want to suggest a one-time meeting, an extended but time-limited contract, or an indefinite open-ended schedule. Members also determine whether they want someone to instruct, facilitate, or consult as well as where meetings occur. The outside person may be asked to travel to meetings. A selected member is appointed to contact the prospective consultant and to negotiate an agreement regarding time, fee, and other logistical matters. Of course, the prospective consultant may decline to participate or may discontinue, but the group retains the power to invite someone else and, once the consultation commences, to decide to end it.

A consultant working under either of these models must be aware of the potential for impaired objectivity. If hired by the group, a consultant may be inclined to avoid conflict, withhold challenging feedback, or be too accommodating to ensure continuation of the arrangement. The group is clearly hiring the consultant and holds the power. Conversely, consultants who host the group can make the rules, but are also invested in the general satisfaction of members, which is required to sustain the group. So, they could be vulnerable to some of the same influencing forces as those who are selected by the group.

The obligation to obtain and document the informed consent of members applies to any psychologist who is providing a psychological service; this includes both consultation and supervision (APA, 2002; Association of State and Provincial Psychology Boards, 2001; CPA, 2000). The ethics codes of other mental health professionals have similar requirements (American Association for Marriage and Family Therapy [AAMFT], 2001; American Association of Pastoral Counselors [AAPC], 1994; American Counseling Association, 2005; American Psychiatric Association, 2009 National Association of Alcohol and Drug Abuse Counselors, 2008; National Association of Social Workers, 2008). The informed consent for the supervisor or "host-consultant" would likely be more comprehensive in that it would include all of the rules and policies. When the group hires a consultant, the limits to confidentiality, reporting obligations, availability, and so on should still be discussed. The hired consultant, however, may suspend some of his or her routine policies in favor of arranging a novel agreement regarding fees, meeting times, and other matters.

Methods for Critiquing Group Members' Work

Several professional associations and credentialing bodies recommend or suggest supervisors review actual work samples (AAMFT, 2001; AAPC, 2009; ACES, 1993). Live supervision, cotherapy, and review of automated recordings and clinical records are mentioned as possible strategies for accessing work samples. Although there are no such requirements for voluntary, consultant-initiated, or peer consultation, use of these methods can enhance learning opportunities. Commonly, members present cases or pose questions and solicit feedback. Other methods, however, are possible.

Automated Recordings

Audio or video recordings of therapy and testing sessions are often created (with the informed consent of clients, documented in their records) by students and other trainees for review by their supervisors or by members of their supervision groups. Similarly, psychologists engaged in board-mandated supervision may be required to submit recordings of their clinical work. Practicing psychologists, however, also can use this technique. Beyond training, psychologists rarely have opportunities to have their work examined and evaluated so directly by colleagues. Although such scrutiny is likely to provoke anxiety, it can provide a valuable opportunity for feedback.

Clinical Records

Another strategy for critiquing work samples involves clinical records and reports. Unless these records are reviewed only by employees of the same agency or institution and clients are informed at the outset that other staff may access their records for consultation purposes, these documents should be redacted to protect client privacy. When such reviews occur in an employment setting, there is the added advantage of random selection. If redaction is required, clinicians must select a file or files in advance, and they may be more inclined to choose one of their better records. An alternative is to have another group member randomly choose a file without looking at the name and then have the therapist read the record to other group members.

Role-Play Techniques

When therapists are feeling stuck or frustrated with a client, they may find themselves repeating the same ineffective interventions and getting the same responses. Role-playing a typical interaction with other group members in these cases helps the psychologist gain another perspective. When the therapist plays the role of the client, empathy may be enhanced. Hearing group members respond with different interventions can also be a source of creative ideas for the therapist. This technique can also be useful when there is a therapeutic impasse or conflict with the client or when the therapist is preparing to deliver some difficult feedback or information.

Formal Case Presentations

Similar to the standard turn-taking strategy, group members can make formal case presentations. These presentations can be more comprehensive and follow a formal outline (see Appendix F, this volume). Although the objective of such a presentation may be for the therapist to obtain assistance, it can also be primarily educational. Cases can be chosen, for example, to illustrate particular concepts, the application of a theoretical tenet, or a technique. Similarly, group members can alternate responsibility for presenting on particular topics. They can research a subject or attend a seminar and present the material. Such presentations can be scheduled regularly or occasionally. One possible format is to allocate the first hour for a formal presentation and the second hour for members to raise their own questions, issues, and cases.

Academic Learning

Another focus for a consultation group can be professional development and education. Members decide to read professional books or articles and prepare to discuss them. The group can decide to read a breadth of materials or focus on a particular topic. Eating disorders, substance abuse, multicultural counseling, anxiety disorders, and group therapy are some examples. Ethical issues such as therapeutic boundaries, confidentiality, and reporting obligations can provide fodder for lively discussion. Such a format can be used to study a new assessment instrument or treatment technique.

In rural or other more remote areas where professional development seminars are not readily accessible, this method can provide a valuable and creative learning opportunity. This study group format can be used in combination with consultation with an expert. The group might travel to attend a training seminar and then arrange a consultation with the presenter. The expert might agree to meet with the group periodically (in person, by phone, or by teleconference) to make recommendations for reading and answer questions as needed. In some states, continuing education credits might be available for such endeavors.

Professional and Personal Support

Finally, professional support groups might focus more on personal issues that might impact clinical work. Psychotherapists differ in terms of their need and desire for personal support. Some prefer that their consultation groups focus exclusively on client cases and professional literature. Others are looking for a personal support group and only secondarily for professional resources. Most prefer some combination of the two.

Some groups use a "check-in" model in which each member has an opportunity to share some personal information at the start of the group before shifting to more clinical business. Others designate periodic meetings for personal connections; these meetings might include a meal or some other less formal activity, and clinical work is not discussed. Still other groups use their meetings to talk about personal experiences and issues that have the potential to compromise their objectivity and effectiveness, and they seek the judgment and support of colleagues to help ensure that they are insulating their work appropriately. Of course such issues can and should be addressed in any consultation group when they are significant. The focus of these discussions should always be determined with some consideration for the potential to impact work. Sharing vacation pictures and stories, for example, would be more of a purely social activity and would not likely have a place in a professional consultation group.

STRATEGIES FOR FORMING A CONSULTATION GROUP

The potential benefits of participating in a voluntary consultation group are great, but doing so requires time, effort, and commitment. Therefore, those wanting to establish or retool such a group will benefit if the initial formation, or later the reformation, of a group reflects a thoughtful, deliberate process designed to help members anticipate and mitigate future problems.

Identifying Potential Members

The goals of the group will determine the composition and, to some extent, the best strategies for determining membership. Because the utility of a group depends in large measure on the compatibility of its members, careful selection is crucial. For psychotherapists who are new to the profession or area or who are not well connected with their professional communities, the first step is finding colleagues who share their interests. The following are suggestions for identifying potential members for a consultation group.

- Consult a specialty directory, sometimes published by professional associations, to find the names of people who claim expertise in a particular area of practice.
- Examine publications wherever therapists advertise (e.g., free papers, telephone directories, professional newsletters, websites) and identify those providing similar types of clinical services.
- Volunteer to serve on a committee or plan a conference on a topic of interest.
- Join and participate in a professional association whose mission reflects individual professional interests.
- Invite known colleagues who share professional interests to a meeting.
- Invite colleagues to collaborate on a conference program proposal reflecting shared interests.
- Assemble a group for a one-time meeting to discuss a professional book or article written by a local author; invite the author to participate.
- Attend training on a particular topic. Announce your interest in starting a consultation group with that focus, and encourage others who might be interested to contact you during the conference. Or leave an informational flyer at the registration table.
- Advertise or put a notice in a professional newsletter or on a list serve soliciting interested colleagues to contact you.
- Design a study group and apply to the licensing board for continuing education credits. Invite colleagues to participate.

Identifying even one colleague with whom to collaborate can provide the seeds of a consultation group. One individual can host an initial meeting to discuss the possibility of forming a group. Clearly, establishing such a group requires effort. Sharing the task with a colleague can help diminish the work and risk of rejection and can enhance the rewards.

INITIATING A CONSULTATION OR SUPERVISION GROUP

Organizing a new consultation or supervision group should be a thoughtful process that encompasses opportunities for reflection at the outset and throughout. Decisions about every aspect of the group's membership and functioning should be carefully considered. When a supervisor or consultant is offering the group, that individual will make many of these decisions. Even so, they should be communicated to prospective group members and discussed in detail at the outset. Peer consultation groups differ in that the responsibility for structuring the group is shared by all members.

When group members are involved in these discussions to whatever degree possible and appropriate, a precedent for communicating about process issues is established. At this point, a commitment can be made to revisit these issues as the group develops and as members have opportunities to experience the impact of their initial decisions. As members' needs evolve, flexibility will be necessary to allow modifications in various aspects of the structure.

Composition of Consultation Groups

Authors have argued both for (Allen, 1976; Chaiklin & Munson, 1983; Parihar, 1983) and against (Getzel & Salmon, 1985; Schreiber & Frank, 1983; Wendorf, Wendorf, & Bond, 1985) designing homogeneous groups. Consultation groups can be designed to be homogeneous in terms of some variables and heterogeneous relative to others. If the primary goal of the group is to improve skills in using a particular therapeutic technique, then including colleagues who use that technique will be most useful. Such a group can focus on biofeedback, forensic assessment, hypnosis, or projective testing, for example. Similarly, a group of clinicians who provide supervision may form a consultation group. Theoretical orientation can also provide a common ground for organizing. Psychoanalytic or family systems therapists might prefer to consult with colleagues who share that perspective. Similarly, clinicians working with particular diagnostic groups may benefit from a homogeneous membership (e.g., eating disorders, substance abuse). Most authors support homogeneity with regard to experience level (Bernard & Goodyear, 2009; Carroll, 1996).

Although similarity may be desired in some areas, differences can also enhance the experience. If the goal of the group is to increase knowledge of professional ethics, for example, assembling a group with broad representation may be useful. Such a group may include members serving various populations as well as academics, researchers, and those doing assessment. Members may be generalists and more interested in broadening their knowledge rather than deepening specializations. In this case, a heterogeneous group may be advantageous.

Beyond considerations involving client needs and characteristics, a group can be designed to be homogeneous or heterogeneous with regard to member characteristics. Some psychologists may prefer similarity or diversity with regard to sexual orientation, ethnicity, race, gender, religion, years of experience, age, and so on. Groups may also consist of members of the same profession or may include individuals from different professions such as psychology, social work, family therapy, substance abuse counseling, and psychiatry.

Factors to Consider in Beginning a Group

The following are lists of questions and issues that should be considered by supervisors, consultants, and peers when planning for a new group.

Membership

- How many members will the group have?
- How can new members join?
- What steps will be taken to ensure a good fit when new members are added?
- What will the group do if it becomes clear that one member is not fitting in?
- What is the procedure for leaving the group? How much notice should members give when they decide to discontinue?
- Will members be expected to discuss with other participants a decision to discontinue?

Location

- Where will meetings be held?
- Will they occur in the supervisor or consultant's office?
- Will meeting locations alternate among members to distribute the inconvenience of travel?
- Will meetings occur in a private room in a library, restaurant, or other community location?

Schedule

- At what time of day and week will meetings be scheduled?
- How frequently will the group meet?
- For how long will the group meet each time?

Duration

- Will this be a time-limited group?
- What will determine whether and when the group will stop meeting?

A time-limited commitment, particularly for a new group, may be the most reasonable strategy. The limited duration may encourage members' commitment to attendance, offer a built-in opportunity to assess effectiveness, and provide a relatively uncomplicated opportunity to discontinue participation if the group is not a good fit for them.

Time Allocation

- How will the group time be allocated? Will time be divided equally among members or will the discussion format be open, allowing members to share freely, trusting the members with the responsibility of getting their needs met?
- Will members alternate responsibility for making presentations about cases or topics?
- How much if any time will be allocated for discussion of personal issues?

Conflicts and Problems

- Will regularly scheduled opportunities to voice concerns be built into the schedule?
- Will members be asked to make a commitment to sharing their concerns about the group with other members?

Other Commitments

Group members might be asked to commit to one or more of the following:

- disclose personal information whenever they are experiencing stressful (positive or negative) life events that could compromise clinical objectivity or effectiveness;
- inform one another when they have concerns about a member's objectivity, effectiveness, boundaries, or other aspects of their professional behavior;
- directly address problems they have with other group members, the group's structure, or with other aspects of their participation; and
- attend meetings regularly, arriving on time, and stay for the entire meeting.

PROBLEMS THAT DIMINISH THE VALUE OF CONSULTATION AND SUPERVISION GROUPS

The potential benefits of participation in group consultation and supervision are numerous, but so are the factors that could compromise the value and result in emotional harm to members, thwarted professional development, and premature attrition. Often, the problems that develop in the context of a group could, theoretically, be addressed if the group members were comfortable or at least willing to discuss process issues. When members can voice their dissatisfaction directly, the possibility of making modifications to address the problems is certainly increased.

Dissatisfaction related to the group structure may be less emotion laden, easier to raise, and more amenable to correction. Examples include concern about the amount of time spent on cases versus personal issues and a desire to change the meeting time, location, or frequency. A particular arrangement may have worked well for a long time, but changes in personal and professional circumstances result in evolving needs. One member may be seeing a greater number of clients and so have less time available. Another may be seeing increasingly complex cases and feel the need for more frequent consultation or may prefer a group that focuses on a particular population.

Another category of issues that may result in dissatisfaction with a consultation or supervision group involves changing preferences. Members may determine that more or less diversity in terms of particular variables (gender, ethnicity, types of clients, years of experience) among members is desirable. They may prefer more personal connections and find the group to be too business oriented. Others may think that the group focuses too much on personal connection. Clearly, there is no right or wrong in terms of these issues; they are only a matter of preference, which will likely evolve throughout an individual's career.

Unlike structural issues, personality conflicts and dissatisfaction related to more personal characteristics of members are more challenging to address. Precipitating real change may seem hopeless and the potential for hurt feelings great. A member may feel annoyed, for example, about another person who he or she believes dominates discussions or is a "know-it-all." One member may perceive another as professionally incompetent or as having poor boundaries with clients. Although challenging, these issues can be addressed tactfully with careful attention to the impact on those being asked to hear and manage this feedback.

Because these sources of dissatisfaction are so personal, it is likely that some individuals will withdraw from a group without disclosing their actual reasons for doing so. They may be more likely to decrease the frequency of their attendance and/or just stop attending. This might be done without explanation, or more likely, they may offer another more palatable reason for leaving—one that may be partially accurate, although secondary.

Several authors have discussed the developmental stages of groups (M. S. Corey & Corey, 2002; Tuckman, 1965; Tuckman & Jensen, 1977). Any psychologist trained since the mid-1960s is likely familiar with Tuckman's (1965) five stages of a group's development: forming, storming, norming, performing, and adjourning. More recently, M. S. Corey and Corey (2002) described four stages. The Initial Stage is a time for orientation regarding structure, ground rules, fears, and goals. Group members in the Transition Stage, perhaps the corollary to Tuckman's "storming," commonly experience resistance, conflicts, and performance anxiety. They may feel more vulnerable as they begin to take risks to state their preferences and needs. The third, the Working Stage, is a time when initial conflicts are resolved and the group becomes more cohesive. When conflict occurs, it is readily addressed. Finally, the Ending Stage involves consolidating gains and preparing for termination. These stages are readily applicable to supervision and consultation groups (Bernard & Goodyear, 2009; Haynes et al., 2003).

CONCLUSION

As mental health professionals, accepting the challenge of finding ways to address difficult issues in consultation and supervision groups is imperative. Particularly when there is a supervisor or consultant-led group, the responsibility to teach and model strategies for addressing conflicts in groups is significant. A parallel process often occurs in which dynamics in a consultation or supervision group are replayed in the members' own therapy groups (Bernard & Goodyear, 2009; Bradley & Ladany, 2001). Avoiding these issues or allowing them to be addressed in ways that are harmful to individual members is likely to have a far-reaching detrimental impact. Conversely, the potential value of effectively navigating through the stages of the group's development can extend not only to members of that group but to the clients served by each of them.

8

MANDATED SUPERVISION: ETHICAL CHALLENGES FOR SUPERVISORS AND SUPERVISEES

Most supervision of psychologists and other mental health profession-als occurs in the context of their training. Practicums, internships, and post-doctoral training experiences all include clinical supervision. Most but certainly not all supervisees in these circumstances are early in their profes-sional development. However, professionals at any point in their careers may commit ethical violations or exhibit other behavior that results in discipli-nary action by employers, professional association ethics committees, or licensing boards. Clinical supervision is sometimes required as part of the plan to rehabilitate the clinician or remediate the problems that led to the errors (Celenza, 2007; Juhnke, Kelly, & Cooper, 2008; Robinson, 2006) or as a prac-tice safeguard when the individual's ability to practice safely and effectively is questioned.

Supervisors who agree to provide mandated supervision in these cases must be cognizant of the unique clinical and ethical challenges inherent in this work. Helping individuals who have been disciplined by employers, pro-fessional association ethics committees, or licensing boards has been likened to supervising those on "probation or parole" (Adams, 2001, p. 316). This type of supervision requires particular expertise and specialized competency

(Walzer & Miltimore, 1993). Those who provide such supervision should certainly be competent in supervision. Additionally, they must have knowledge and understanding of the clinical and ethical challenges inherent in supervising colleagues who have committed some ethical violation and are required to participate as part of a rehabilitative or disciplinary action.

This chapter is focused primarily on board-ordered supervision, but many of the concepts and techniques will be applicable to supervision required by employers and ethics committees as well. The issues addressed in this chapter include

- the role and function of licensing boards and supervisors,
- the importance of initial and ongoing assessment,
- goals and objectives of mandated supervision,
- the potential impact of transference and countertransference on the supervisory process, and
- supervision methods and strategies.

Although supervision is a more likely intervention than consultation, the possible role of a consultant is also considered.

THE ROLE AND FUNCTION OF LICENSING BOARDS

Employers and professional ethics committees may require specialized supervision. Licensing boards, however, represent a more common source of mandated supervision. To understand the requirements of licensing boards, it is important to recognize that boards are not professional associations, and they do not exist to further the interests of licensees. Instead, the mission of licensing boards is to protect the public (Bricklin, Bennett, & Carroll, 2003; Cobia & Pipes, 2002; Plaut, 2000). To this end, they establish minimum qualifications needed to practice, ensure that prospective licensees meet these standards, and monitor licensees to ensure that these standards are not violated. When licensees violate established standards, licensing boards may revoke a license or, more commonly, limit the scope of the individual's practice or require some corrective action (Van Horne, 2004) such as remedial education, psychotherapy (particularly when impairment is a factor), or clinical supervision.

Before a licensee is mandated to participate in any rehabilitation plan, including supervision, some assessment is necessary to ensure that supervision is indeed an appropriate strategy, one that is likely to address or ameliorate at least some of the problems that contributed to the violations (Cobia & Pipes, 2002; Schoener, 1989; Schoener & Gonsiorek, 1988). If the primary problem is addiction, depression, bipolar disorder, or sociopathy, for example, and that problem has not been adequately addressed, supervision is unlikely to be successful. Further, such an assessment should not be conducted by a prospective or current supervisor, psychotherapist, or consultant whose objectivity and effectiveness is likely to be compromised by performing this dual role relative to the subject of the evaluation (Kaslow et al., 2007).

Ideally, a thorough assessment will have been conducted, and supervision will have been deemed an appropriate intervention. A skilled evaluator will have obtained and studied all relevant documents and materials necessary to establish the facts of the case. Materials might include a description of the allegations; the subject's responses to these allegations; transcripts or recordings of interviews conducted by board staff, board members, and investigators; and any related depositions or testimony (Schoener & Gonsiorek, 1989). Further, relevant medical and mental health records should also be examined. Evaluators may also interview individuals who might provide collateral information about the subject, including past and current psychotherapists, employers, supervisors, family members, and colleagues. Psychological testing and extensive interviews with the subject are often a part of such an evaluation. The report of such an evaluation should be made available to the supervisor (Schoener & Gonsiorek, 1989).

When such an extensive assessment is not conducted, as sometimes occurs, the supervisor should carefully consider whether to accept the case. As discussed, an unidentified mental health problem or severe character disorder, for example, may make supervision ineffective at best and, at worst, may provide cover for a potentially dangerous practitioner who is at risk for further harming clients. Even when an assessment was conducted and used to develop a supervision plan, the supervisor must continually evaluate the individual's ability to make use of the supervision.

VIOLATIONS THAT RESULT IN MANDATED SUPERVISION

Mandated supervision may be ordered in cases involving various violations. When sexual exploitation of a client does not result in revocation of licensure, for example, supervision may be required. Other boundary problems that may result in an order for supervision are inappropriate touch, excessive self-disclosure, and transgressing the limits of one's role. The latter category involves offering services to clients that do not fall under the rubric of practice of psychology or other mental health profession. Examples include providing clothing to the client, helping the client clean his or her house, advocating for the client by becoming involved in his or her life and relationships (e.g., with his or her spouse or partner, boss, friends, or relatives), lending money, traveling with the client, or arranging dates for clients. One such action does not typically lead to a complaint. Rather, a constellation of similar behaviors without theoretical foundation or therapeutic justification might suggest impaired objectivity.

In addition to addressing boundary problems, supervision may require the remediation of incompetence or of skill deficiencies in specific areas of practice such as report writing; record keeping; administration, scoring, and interpretation of particular psychological tests; or forensic work. In other cases, the individual's practice style, policies, and procedures may underlie the ethics complaint. Examples include inadequate informed consent procedures and written materials, loose confidentiality practices, failure to clarify the nature of the therapeutic relationship, and informality or lack of professionalism in the practice setting.

GOALS AND OBJECTIVES OF BOARD-ORDERED SUPERVISION

Board-ordered supervision requires consideration of several general goals and objectives.

Supervisory Goals

Various supervisory goals have been addressed in the literature (Bernard & Goodyear, 2004). Opinions vary as to the relative importance of the supervisee's needs (such as training, education, and professional development; Eisenberg, 1956) versus those of the client. But, when supervision is mandated in response to a finding of ethical violations, the primary goal must be client welfare and more generally, the protection of the public. Although the welfare of the supervisee is important, when the best interests of the client conflict with those of the supervisee, the supervisor must ensure that client's interests take precedence.

Nevertheless, supervisors in mandated cases are responsible for working toward the rehabilitation of the licensee. Although the supervisee will likely develop professionally throughout the supervision, the more fundamental goal is rehabilitation or the remediation of identified problems. Supervisors must teach the skills, concepts, and practices necessary to remediate or "treat" the deficits and problems contributing to the individual's ethical errors.

Finally, those providing board-ordered supervision, like other supervisors, must serve as a gatekeepers for the profession (Bernard & Goodyear, 2004; Falvey, 2002). They are responsible for making judgments and recommendations about the supervisee's fitness to practice. If the supervisee is not fit or if the supervisor has reservations about fitness, this opinion must be reported to the licensing board. Even though such action may compromise the supervisee's capacity to make a living, the supervisee's mental health, or the supervisory relationship, the welfare of clients is paramount. Such decisions and their implementation can represent a significant challenge for supervisors who may identify with their supervisees and feel a sense of loyalty to them. Consultation with colleagues can help supervisors maintain objectivity and obtain the support needed to take whatever action they deem appropriate.

Supervisory Objectives

These three general goals of mandated supervision—ensuring client welfare, facilitating the supervisee's rehabilitation, and serving as a gatekeeper for the profession—generate objectives that inform the work of supervisors. Although similar in some ways to other types of supervision, especially that of students and new professionals, board-ordered supervision involves unique skills, commitment, and a willingness to assume all of the commensurate responsibilities and liabilities.

First, supervisors must help their supervisees to formulate a realistic and comprehensive conceptualization of the personal and professional factors that set the stage for errors. Review of documents related to the complaint is important in this regard (Robinson, 2006). Often the problems that preceded the violations began long before any unethical behavior occurred. In addition to clarifying major violations, supervisors can help supervisees to identify the many subtle and in-and-of-themselves-insignificant decisions that set them on a trajectory of error. A plane can fly a few degrees off course for brief periods and still arrive at its destination if the errors are promptly recognized and corrected. If they go unnoticed, however, the plane will be significantly off course within hours. Similarly, psychologists and other mental health professionals may diverge from standards in small ways that over time result in significant mistakes that harm clients and become the subject of complaints, lawsuits, and disciplinary actions.

Second, violations should be examined in terms of the actual and potential impact on the involved clients, students, employees, and others who may have been affected. Such exploration should include helping supervisees recognize that avoiding future complaints is only a secondary objective, less important than ensuring that their future clients receive competent, beneficial services that do not cause harm. Some licensees who have been disciplined maintain that the rules governing their professional behavior are too rigid, that they only tried to "go the extra mile" to be helpful, and that it was only the unreasonable rules that made their altruistic behavior problematic. Even when the client is the complainant, the licensee may believe that someone has influenced the client to alter his or her recognition of their behavior as helpful to a belief that it has been harmful. Careful examination of both the actual and potential impact and the reasons for the existence of these rules is a necessary component of rehabilitative supervision.

A third objective is to help supervisees generalize their learning to novel situations and cases, thereby diminishing the likelihood of future ethical errors. Requiring supervisees to present all of their cases or, at a minimum, to apply specific criteria for determining which cases to present is necessary to achieve this objective. Supervisors must be alert for themes and issues that resonate with those evident in the complaint case. When such themes are noted, the supervisor must determine how best to capitalize on the learning opportunity. Careful judgment is required to determine whether and when to raise the issue of the similarity to behavior contributing to the complaint. Neither defensiveness nor shame facilitate learning; when, in the judgment of the supervisor, directly identifying the similarity would exacerbate either, it may be preferable to address only the current issue without directly naming the connection. When client welfare is at stake, however, the need for action takes precedence over the need for insight. When, in the supervisor's judgment, the supervisee seems able to psychologically manage defensiveness and benefit from insight, making the connection or allowing the supervisee to do so is the better strategy. The desired outcome is for the supervisee to be able to explain how he or she would avoid and, if necessary, respond to a similar set of circumstances in the future. Further, evidence of this understanding should be apparent in the individual's ongoing clinical work.

Throughout the course of supervision, supervisees must learn to identify the events, circumstances, and subjective experiences signaling that they may be at risk for impaired objectivity and effectiveness. Supervisors may address this objective in the context of discussions related both to the complaint case and to current cases. If a client presents with a particular therapeutic issue (e.g., suicidal thoughts) or life circumstance similar to the complaint case or that of the supervisee's own experience (e.g., divorce), these parallels may be illuminated in supervision and considered in terms of their potential impact on the supervisee's conceptualizations of and decisions in the complaint case. Ideally, the supervisee will take steps to ensure that such circumstances do not result in further problems. Delineated steps allow supervisees to recognize situations with increased potential for impaired objectivity, to carefully filter decisions and responses through this awareness, and to routinely raise these cases in supervision. These steps provide the foundation of a comprehensive prevention plan.

Supervisors must keep these goals and objectives in mind throughout the process of mandated supervision. They are likely, however, to encounter obstacles to achieving these goals and objectives, particularly if they are unaware of what these obstacles might be. Unexamined supervisee transference and supervisor countertransference constitute two potential obstacles that, if undetected, can seriously compromise if not sabotage the supervisory relationship and therefore the efficacy of supervision.

SUPERVISEE TRANSFERENCE

Licensees ordered to participate in supervision likely will have been engaged in a long, arduous process. The stress involved in facing a board complaint has been well documented (Adams, 2001; Bass et al., 1996; Chauvin & Remley, 1996; Fleer, 2000; V. W. Hilton, 1997; Montgomery, Cupit, & Wimberley, 1999; M. B. Peterson, 2001; Remley, 1992; Schoenfeld, Hatch, Gonzalez, 2001; J. T. Thomas, 2001, 2002, 2005; Van Horne, 2004; Williams, 2001). Respondents to board complaints must assume significant expense for legal and clinical consultation (Hedges, 2000; Lewis, 2004; M. B. Peterson, 2001; Welch, 2001). If they have lost a job, been removed from insurance provider panels, or required by colleagues to leave a group practice, they will probably have diminished financial resources. Psychologically, emotionally, and financially, facing a complaint can have a significant impact.

By the time a licensee arrives in the supervisor's office, the cumulative impact of these stresses is evident and may manifest in the supervisory relationship. Although transference can occur in any supervisory relationship (Driver & Martin, 2005; Frawley-O'Dea & Sarnat, 2001; Gill, 2001; Jacobs, David, & Meyer, 1995), when the supervision occurs as the result of a board action, there is great potential for supervisees to develop strong responses to supervisors. Licensees generally lack any legitimate way to communicate with the complainant, particularly when that individual is a former client. They also are unlikely to be in contact with the colleagues who were involved in reporting them. Further, they are not able to directly express their unedited thoughts and feelings to and about board members without serious consequence. In short, the individuals associated with the genesis of the stress are not available to be the recipients of the licensee's responses, but the supervisor is. This reality may imbue the supervision with an emotional intensity. The supervisory relationship, then, may provide fertile ground for experiencing and expressing a backlog of suppressed or repressed feelings. These feelings, in combination with any generated directly, may be felt and expressed in the context of the supervisory relationship. To the extent that supervisors are aware of the common responses of supervisees, they may understand, accurately interpret, and effectively use these responses in the supervision (J. T. Thomas, 2005). Caution should be maintained, however, to ensure that the boundary between supervision and therapy is appropriately maintained throughout this process.

Manifestations of Complaint-Related Feelings in Supervision

Supervisees may feel anger toward board members, employers, or ethics committee members whose decisions they have experienced as unjust, unreasonable, or hostile (Juhnke et al., 2008; J. T. Thomas, 2005). This anger may sensitize them to any inaccuracies in the official description or characterization of the case. Even when the inaccuracies involve peripheral details, when one's work is scrutinized and the stakes are so high, accuracy becomes critical. When supervisors inaccurately recall details of the complaint case or other cases presented, supervisees may not only correct them but also may feel misunderstood, mischaracterized, or unfairly scrutinized. Trust and confidence in the supervisor may be shaken.

Supervisees also may feel angry about what they perceive, accurately or inaccurately, as board members' lack of understanding of their theoretical approaches, techniques, or professional perspectives. Had board members understood these things, the thinking goes, perhaps they would have come to different conclusions about the allegations. Later, when the perspectives of the supervisor and supervisee diverge, the supervisee may attribute this divergence to the supervisor's lack of training and education in the supervisee's area of practice and so may dismiss or passively resist an intervention or directive.

Another source of distress involves the supervisee's colleagues. When other mental health professionals have been involved in filing a complaint, the supervisee may feel hurt, angry, betrayed, and shocked. Conversely, the supervisee may recognize and acknowledge his or her own errors. But, if colleagues were aware of the problematic behavior and did nothing to intervene and preempt the violation, ironically, the supervisee may experience similar feelings of betrayal. Either of these themes may echo in the supervisory relationship. Supervisees may feel angry or resentful toward their supervisors when a clinical decision is challenged or a behavior is identified as problematic. These feelings will be intensified if this identification occurs for the first time in a report to the board. When the supervisee becomes aware of a problem in his or her clinical work, perhaps in response to a client's anger, and that problem was not identified and prevented by the supervisor, the supervisee may similarly experience anger and betrayal.

Feelings about client-complainants are typically complex and may include guilt and shame as well as anger and frustration. When the case was particularly challenging and required an inordinate amount of effort, the supervisee's anger may focus on what may feel like a lack of gratitude on the part of the client. When the supervisee is required to work hard in the supervision, (e.g., complete assigned readings, rewrite reports, submit audio tapes, or develop and revise practice forms) and the supervisor is critical of these efforts in a report to the board, the supervisee may feel that the hard work he or she has done has not been adequately appreciated. Further, the supervisee may expect, consciously or unconsciously, that the supervisor will factor in this hard work as a way to offset mistakes in other areas.

Supervisees may express guilt about the impact of their unethical behavior or about the impact on their other clients. They may report remorse about errors leading to the complaint or about abandoning the client and/or other clients, particularly if they were suddenly fired. This theme is reflected in supervision when, for example, the supervisor requires the supervisee to set limits with clients regarding previously tolerated behavior (e.g., accepting late-night calls).

Supervisees may, in fact, disappoint clients as they alter previously established protocols or fail to meet the expectations that they have cultivated in their clients. They may also project feelings of responsibility for their clients' disappointment onto the supervisor, who then becomes the perceived culprit, thus relieving the supervisee of the burden of that guilt. Supervisors must monitor the supervisee's clinical work to ensure that such anger is not acted out with clients. Supervisees are at risk, for example, for attributing responsibility for unpopular therapeutic decisions to the supervisor, subtly enlisting their clients in commiserating about and acting out the supervisee's resentments toward the supervisor, the board, or perhaps other authority figures.

Supervisees might also feel embarrassed, humiliated, and ashamed of their behavior, particularly if it has been publicized in a newspaper, professional newsletter, on the Internet, or informally through the grapevine. These feelings potentially create fear of further exposure to judgment and criticism. Supervisees may become guarded in case presentations, volunteering only sanitized, innocuous information about their interventions. They may avoid raising questions or discussing doubts, anxieties, and regrets related to their clinical work. Such an approach can limit the potency of supervision to prevent further errors and, more generally, to enhance supervisee effectiveness.

Supervisees may, as a compensatory response to feelings of interiority, challenge the boundaries of the supervisory relationship in overt or subtle ways. A covert attempt at reversing the roles, one characteristic of a boundary violation (M. R. Peterson, 1992), may occur with the supervisee essentially trying to supervise the supervisor. The following case illustrates one way in which this role reversal may occur.

Late Cancellation

James, a supervisee, cancels an appointment 1 hour before the scheduled time. He is aware of the supervisor's policy of charging for appointments not canceled at least 24 hours in advance. Because he had a flat tire, he points out to his supervisor, it was not his fault, and he doesn't feel he should have to pay for the time. When the supervisor indicates he will be charged, James says, "In my practice, I would never charge when the cancellation is unavoidable and particularly when it occurs for the first time. I give people the benefit of the doubt." He adds that none of his colleagues would have charged under such circumstances either.

In this example, James attempts to educate his supervisor about what policies she should have and how they should be enforced. The supervisor may feel intimidated by such a response, particularly if she is not confident in her own policy. The supervisor may even want to rethink or revise her policy. She must be careful, however, to consider that as a separate decision to be made in the context of her own supervision or consultation, not in response to the supervisee's recommendation. Doing otherwise reinforces the boundary crossing and communicates the supervisor's lack of confidence and inability to ensure that the supervisory relationship has clear boundaries of which she is in charge. The supervisor has a policy in place; she must reassure the supervisee that she means what she says and can be counted on to follow through.

The issue becomes more complex if the supervisor does not have or has not communicated a clear policy regarding late cancellations. This scenario illustrates the importance of modeling ethical behavior. Supervisees, whose behaviors have been so thoroughly examined by the board and now by the supervisor, will probably be exquisitely attuned to the supervisor's mistakes. If a policy has not been established in advance, the supervisor must consider that in her deliberations about whether to charge the full fee for the missed appointment, to reduce or waive the fee, or whether to alter the policy in any way. Telling the supervisee that she will reconsider her decision may be helpful, but she must do so in a way that clarifies that the decision is hers and not the supervisee's. If she decides that she is in error, she might tell the supervisee:

> My policy is to charge for appointments not canceled 24 hours in advance. I realize, however, that I may not have made that clear to you at the outset. I have therefore decided not to charge you for that appointment. Now that this is clear, I will charge you for late cancellations that occur in the future.

Such a response is respectful of the supervisee, demonstrates that his concerns will be considered, and conveys that the supervisor is still in charge of her practice policies.

Decisions about the most appropriate response to such a boundary transgression depend on the supervisor's interpretation or understanding of its meaning. Supervisory interventions must be only as firm as necessary.

Although increased firmness may result in a clearer message, it also increases the possibility that the supervisee will feel hurt, embarrassed, ashamed, offended, or defensive. A too-soft response may come across as weak and unclear. The supervisee may hear what is intended to be a directive as an "option" offered for consideration. The most effective response will reflect an appropriate balance as well as an empathic understanding of the likely impact on the individual supervisee.

The effectiveness of any supervisory intervention is ultimately determined by evaluating its impact. If the supervisee's subsequent comments or behaviors reflect a pervasive pattern of boundary transgression in both clinical work and the supervisory relationship and he or she has not been amenable to more gentle interventions, then the supervisor's response must be recalibrated to ensure a clearer message is conveyed. The supervisor in the preceding example might say, "It sounds as if you want to educate me about practice standards and to make recommendations about my policies. This feels like a shift in the boundaries of the relationship, in which it is my job to supervise you." If appropriate, the supervisor might add a supervisory (not therapeutic) interpretation, such as, "This shift is reminiscent of some of the difficulties you have had in delineating the boundaries in relationships with your clients." In other cases, the boundary transgression may represent an isolated instance. The supervisor should not ignore it, of course, but a simple observation may be sufficient.

Another way in which a supervisee might attempt to alter the boundaries is to cast the supervisor in the role of his or her client. This may occur in the form of an offhand comment about the supervisor (e.g., "Your move to the new office must be stressful for you"). It might also occur in the context of the supervisee's presentation of a case example. The supervisee may offer an example in which the supervisor is assigned the role of the client. An example involving an intimate issue intensifies the boundary challenge. The supervisee might say, "Let's say you came to me for help with a sexual dysfunction."

When such a boundary shift occurs, the supervisor must address the issue directly and immediately or as soon as is feasible. The supervisor must not respond with a therapeutic interpretation, which could be a knee-jerk countertransferential response to the anxiety generated by the transgression into the supervisor's personal life. As with the preceding example, the supervisor must titrate his or her response to reflect the perceived seriousness of the current transgression and the degree to which the behavior is part of a pattern. A relatively gentle response acknowledges the transgression and recommends another approach: "In that example, you have assigned me the role of your client and attributed to me a very personal presenting problem. I'd like you to reformulate your question using another example and a different cast of characters." A more poignant response specifically highlights the intimate nature of the example and identifies its use as inappropriate.

> I am aware of the fact that you chose to cast me, your supervisor, in the role of your patient/client and that you have chosen to use a very personal presenting issue. Each of these choices represents a challenge to the boundaries of this relationship. What is your hypothesis about what led you to make these particular choices?

The latter response likely will garner more attention and make it clear that the supervisor is dissatisfied with the supervisee's choices. It more clearly delineates the boundary but is also likely to generate more anxiety in the supervisee. Ideally, such anxiety will precipitate self-reflection and vigilance. The risk of its prompting shame and defensiveness is not, in and of itself, a reason to avoid such a direct response. Yet, supervisors must be aware of the potential risks and benefits of specific interventions and use their best professional judgment about when and how to intervene. The supervisor's errors in this regard can result in confusion about the boundaries on the part of the supervisee and precipitate further challenges.

Supervisees' feelings of inadequacy might also manifest in self-deprecating statements and tentative case presentations. In lieu of facing the challenges endemic to supervision, they may convey neediness as a plea for therapy or for a more supportive, rather than confrontational response, as in this example. Following a supervision session, the supervisee writes this note:

> I've enclosed the check that I forgot to bring to our session. I'm really sorry about being so absentminded, and I really appreciate your understanding and flexibility with me. After I left this afternoon, I realized that I may have come across as lacking confidence. My eye contact wasn't very good, and I didn't want you to think this was typical for me or that I was being disrespectful. I think I'm afraid of your judgment and that I fear being seen as a failure. This is probably related to my wife's recent decision to leave me and to having been fired from my job. We can explore this further on Thursday. I'll be interested in hearing your always wise perspective. Thanks again for all of your help. I feel very lucky that you are willing to work with me.

The supervisee in this case may not only be insecure but also may be confused about the nature of the relationship. When such confusion becomes apparent, regardless of its genesis, the supervisor should not only clarify the boundaries but also use the opportunity to examine his or her own behavior. Both the supervisor and the supervisee may own a part in the confusion, but the supervisor is responsible for recognizing and repairing the problem.

Excessive fear of making mistakes constitutes another possible supervisee transference response. Such anxiety may manifest in various ways. Supervisees may, for example, become apologetic and self-denigrating as a way to preempt their supervisors' criticism. Anxiety may also make it difficult for them to accurately assess their errors. Supervisees may be so anxious about making a mistake that they assume they are being accused or that they have actually made an error even when presented with a neutral question. In response to a supervisor asking, "How often are you seeing this client?" the supervisee might say, "You're right. I'm sorry. I should have known that was too often" (or "not often enough").

Similarly, supervisees may readily acknowledge missteps although they lack a clear understanding of the issues underlying those mistakes or of precisely what was wrong with what they did. The supervisory conversation may go something like this:

Supervisee: I know I've made mistakes.

Supervisor: Tell me about one of the mistakes you think you made in this case.

Supervisee: A boundaries problem?

Supervisor: Can you be more specific?

Supervisee: Well, maybe because I accepted the plant from the client, right? [*Failing to perceive the larger context, the supervisee focuses instead on a detail that does not in and of itself reflect the problem.*]

Supervisor: What do you see as problematic about accepting the plant? What do you see as the potential negative impact of that decision on your client?

Supervisee: It was against the rules, maybe, about dual relationships?

Supervisor: How do you see this rule applying to these circumstances? [*or*] Why do you think such a rule was established?

Supervisee: I don't know. I just know I made mistakes. You are absolutely right.

If the supervisor takes the supervisee's admission of errors as evidence of understanding, a learning opportunity is missed, and the supervisee will likely continue to feel anxious about being found out. This interchange illuminates the limitations of the supervisee's insight and creates an opportunity to ameliorate the confusion.

Finally, supervisees who are burdened emotionally and financially are vulnerable to feeling overwhelmed by requests or directives from their supervisors and may respond negatively. Acknowledging these feelings may diffuse them or at least allow the supervisee to recognize them as related to their total experience rather than to their inability to meet a particular requirements. The supervisor might say, for example, "I recognize that this requirement is difficult and that it may feel overwhelming. Let's consider one part of it at a time."

Of course, when supervisees complain, overtly or covertly, supervisors must examine their demands, perhaps in consultation with another supervisor, to ensure that they are indeed reasonable. They might also adjust the requirements, taking into account the supervisee's capacity, needs, and other obligations. Again, when such adjustments are made, it must be made clear that the supervisor is responsible for the decision.

If supervisors recognize or suspect any of these transference responses in their supervisees, they can use the experience as an opportunity to inform their work and thus help the supervisee. Supervisors can, in summary, identify the themes and potential connections to the complaint experience, share their insights when appropriate, and avoid overreacting or overcorrecting to avoid unpleasant feelings—either the supervisee's or their own. Such acknowledgment helps supervisees to feel understood and may diffuse the intensity of their responses to their supervisors.

SUPERVISOR'S COUNTERTRANSFERENCE AND RELATED ERRORS

When psychologists or other mental health professionals learn that a colleague has been accused of or disciplined for ethical violations, they experience a range of feelings, which may include anger at the colleague, the complainant, or the licensing board; anxiety about their own vulnerability to a complaint; and sympathy for any of the involved parties (Gabbard, 1995). Supervising a colleague under these circumstances—assuming responsibility for his or her professional behavior and for the welfare of his or her clients—can intensify these feelings. Overidentification with supervisees, fear of their anger, concerns about their mental health, and feeling overwhelmed with the responsibilities associated with such supervision all have the potential to inform and enhance or to contaminate the supervisory relationship. In and of themselves, such responses are understandable and not problematic. Unrecognized, misinterpreted, and unchecked, however, they can become dangerous.

Awareness of these possible countertransference responses allows supervisors to recognize and accurately interpret them, and decreases the likelihood that they will negatively affect the efficacy of the supervision and the quality of the supervisory relationship.

Anger

The supervisee is not the only member of the supervisory dyad likely to experience anger in the wake of a complaint. Depending on the nature of the violations and the degree of publicity, supervisors may feel angry with supervisees for compromising the public trust in the profession. Cases of sexual exploitation typically generate criticism of the profession and may result in embarrassment, outrage, and resentment among other professionals. When supervisors experience such feelings, particularly to the degree that these responses remain unconscious, they are at risk for acting them out in the supervision. Supervisors may become, for example, punitive and demanding with their supervisees. Supervisory directives and assignments may become unnecessarily onerous, and otherwise legitimate feedback about the supervisee's work may develop a critical, hostile, or shaming tone, diluting or rendering useless its helpful aspects.

Embarrassment and Overfunctioning

Supervisors have reason to be concerned about their vicarious liability for the errors of their supervisees (Falvey, 2002; Harrar, VandeCreek, & Knapp, 1990). This concern can, however, become exaggerated and cause the supervisor to become excessively controlling, intrusive, and authoritarian. Similarly, excessive concern about how a supervisee's behavior reflects on the supervisor's reputation may also contaminate the supervision.

Supervisees may have to write reports to the licensing board or others responsible for mandating the supervision. These reports provide supervisees with an opportunity to offer their independent perspectives about the supervision. Reviewing a supervisee's report is not in and of itself problematic. Doing so can, in fact, enhance the effectiveness of the supervision by providing information about the supervisee's progress, which can help supervisors identify issues requiring additional attention. Supervisors demanding the final word on what is and is not included in a supervisee's report, however, compromises the recipient's ability to observe the individual's progress, robs the supervisee of a vehicle for communication with the board, and detracts from the time available for reviewing clinical cases. When supervisors interject themselves in this way, they transgress the boundaries of their role.

Supervisors may have an urge to edit when a supervisee writes something in a report that directly criticizes them. A supervisee may also describe his or her interpretation of something the supervisor said in a way that, although perhaps not intended to be critical, leaves the supervisor feeling misrepresented. The supervisee in the following example wrote to the board about two events that occurred in the supervision:

> Dr. Smith was extremely helpful to me. I felt understood when he was willing to eat his lunch during our session, displaying his humanity. His self-disclosure about his own marital difficulties also helped me to realize that I am not the only psychologist who uses self-disclosure.

Dr. Smith likely would not address these incidents in his report. If asked, he might say that he ate the last bite of his lunch as the supervisee walked through his door. Regarding the "self-disclosure," Dr. Smith might indicate that, in the context of a case presentation about a couple, he said, "I understand that. Almost every couple struggles with finances at times."

Such misrepresentation could precipitate anger and embarrassment in the supervisor. The supervisee may have written this innocently in an honest attempt to describe what was helpful in the supervision. She may, on the other hand, have been acting out her anger at the supervisor or the board, with a full understanding that this was likely to reflect poorly on the supervisor or that it would support her contention that her behavior was consistent with a standard of practice. Possible interpretations range along a continuum and must be considered in context.

Dr. Smith must, in any case, think carefully about whether and how to respond to such comments in a report. A defensive explanation to the board could confirm that the supervisee's shot was a direct hit. Further, if the inclusion of these comments in the report is consciously or unconsciously malicious, such a response might enhance the gratification experienced by the supervisee, thereby reinforcing the behavior. An angry confrontation conveys that message as well. The supervisor may be vulnerable to responding in an overly controlling way (e.g., insisting that the supervisee get advanced approval of all future reports). In some cases, a decision not to directly address the comments, at least not at that time, is the most appropriate response. Yet, the risks of electing not to address it should also be considered. Ignoring it will likely reinforce the supervisee's distorted sense of the supervisor's intended message. Clearly, decisions are complex and must be carefully thought through.

Another situation in which supervisors might experience embarrassment occurs when a supervisee indicates that he plans to "go public" about perceived mistreatment by the board. The supervisee may consider making a presentation at a conference, writing an article for a state or national newsletter, providing an interview to a reporter, or speaking out at some other public forum, and possibly identifying the supervisor. The supervisor may be concerned about how he or she will be represented by the supervisee in such a forum or that the supervisee may undermine his or her own professional credibility.

Should supervision time be allocated to discuss or plan such actions? If so, how much time, and what exactly is the supervisor's role in such discussions? These questions must be considered in consultation with an informed colleague to ensure that the supervisor's motives are consistent with the goals and objectives of the supervision. These goals and objectives serve as a compass to guide the supervisor's decisions. Questions for consideration include the following:

- Does what the supervisee is contemplating impact his or her clients?
- Does the amount of time spent contemplating these ancillary professional decisions in supervision significantly detract from time available to examine clinical and ethical issues in the supervisee's work?
- Does the situation parallel or reflect the context of the violations?
- Does the situation present an opportunity for learning to think through professional decisions, anticipate consequences, and develop strategies with broader applicability?
- In what ways do these discussions positively impact the supervisee's professional development and, more specifically, his or her clinical effectiveness?
- Is the supervisor overprotective of the supervisee?
- To what extent is the supervisor using these discussions as a strategy to ensure that the board and colleagues have a positive impression of his or her skills?

These and related questions can help the supervisor decide whether to allocate time and how to address the issues in the context of the supervision. Supervisors must recognize that although they maintain ultimate authority over supervisees' clinical decisions, that authority does not extend to all of their professional decisions.

Overidentification With the Supervisee

When clients accuse colleagues of some ethical violation, particularly when transference may have contributed to distorted perceptions, others often think about their own challenging clients, impasses, and conflicts and about the "dormant" complaints that could come to life. Such thoughts are understandable and can help supervisors develop empathy for their supervisees. They can also lead supervisors to become overly supportive and uncritical and to ignore signs of problems. Supervisors may collude with supervisees in vilifying board members, the complainant, colleagues, and others who may be involved. Supervisors' identification with supervisees may also generate anxiety about their own imperfections and past mistakes. Defenses used to cope with anxiety can lead to exaggerating or minimizing the seriousness of supervisee errors. Such countertransference has the potential to distract both supervisors and supervisees and to inhibit learning that might otherwise result from self-reflection.

Fear and Avoidance of Supervisees' Anger

As discussed, it is not unusual for supervisees to feel anger and resentment about mandated supervision. Although supervisees may be successful in containing their anger in meetings with board members and investigators, doing so on a continuing basis in the context of regular scrutiny and demands is more difficult. Supervisors, hearing of their supervisees' anger about others, may fear becoming the target of that anger. Not wanting to be perceived as a part of the oppressive torment that supervisees complain about, they may unconsciously assume a laissez-faire stance with supervisees, overlooking errors and carefully modulating feedback to avoid provocation. None of these approaches serves supervisees or their clients.

Supervisors also may find themselves feeling superior to others involved in the case, such as the supervisee's employer or board members. The supervisor may wish to rescue the supervisee so as to be perceived as a good guy in a sea of villains. When this agenda supersedes the goals and objectives of the supervision, the work is ethically compromised.

Impotence

The task of supervising a colleague who has had ethical or legal problems can be challenging in many respects. When the individual is overtly or covertly resistant, supervisors may feel helpless, ineffectual, or overwhelmed. Supervisors may, in response, make weak requests rather than requiring compliance with supervisory directives. Such feelings may result in supervisors ignoring subtle boundary challenges in supervision. A supervisee may consistently arrive late, not follow through with supervisory plans, or fail to keep the supervisor informed about important aspects of their work. Or he may request that he be supervised on an "as-needed" rather than regular basis or that the supervisor unofficially decrease the frequency of meetings. The supervisee might say, "There is nothing to present." Supervisors who are feeling helpless are at risk for tolerating departures from the contract, for example, by allowing a phone session because "traffic is bad" or agreeing to cancel or end a meeting early when the supervisee reports that all is going well.

Default to the Role of Therapist

Decisions about when and how to address supervisees' personal problems in the context of supervision are challenging for any supervisor but particularly for those in mandated cases. Identifying and maintaining appropriate balance—respecting the boundary between personal and professional matters—is difficult, and errors can be made in either direction. Supervisors may become concerned about supervisees' mental health, but they fear diverging into the role of therapist and so avoid comment and ignore problems. The converse of this error is responding therapeutically to signs of mental health problems or even subtle requests for treatment from the supervisee. Discomfort with the role and responsibilities of supervision and feeling more competent as a psychotherapist put the supervisor at risk for sliding into the role of therapist. Doing so represents a transgression of the boundaries of the relationship, which can create an inappropriate model and result in the neglect of supervisory goals.

Supervisors who recognize indications of their own countertransference can take steps to identify and correct for errors that might result. Intense feelings of anger or sympathy, uncharacteristic behaviors, avoidance of conflict, and authoritarian demands are some examples. The responsibilities of a supervisor in a board discipline case can be daunting, and consultation with colleagues is often necessary.

SUPERVISION STRATEGIES FOR MANDATED CASES

Methods and strategies for other types of supervision certainly have applicability in mandated supervision. Building a working alliance (Beck, Sarnat, & Barenstein, 2008; Bordin, 1983; Follette & Callaghan, 1995), learning alliance (Dewald, 1997; Fleming & Benedek, 1964), or a supervisory alliance (Clemens, 2006; Teitelbaum, 2001) is critical for successful supervision. Similarly, supervisees in any context are helped by supervisors clarifying expectations regarding the supervisee's clinical work and their work in the context of supervision (Fall & Sutton, 2004; Guest & Dooley, 1999; Knapp & Vandecreek, 2006; Osborn & Davis, 1996). Other techniques associated with various theoretical models of supervision are also applicable (see Chapter 3, this volume). Teaching concepts, assigning reading, and providing both formative and summative evaluative feedback are examples (Falender & Shafranske, 2004).

Examination of Supervisee Strengths

Other generally useful supervision strategies are especially important in mandated supervision. Observing and highlighting the supervisee's strengths is one example. The fears and vulnerability experienced by psychologists who have faced licensing board complaints has been documented (Van Horne, 2004; Williams, 2001). They are likely to feel ashamed and embarrassed when they have to face a colleague whose job it is to conduct a detailed examination of their work and in particular their mistakes. It is not uncommon for supervisees to feel that the supervisor's perception of them is incomplete, distorted, or wholly inaccurate. Some may respond by seizing opportunities to note their accomplishments, which may be perceived by supervisors as evasive maneuvers to avoid facing mistakes. These conflicting agendas could result in a dynamic of covert efforts on the part of both parties to persuade the other to see the picture from their vantage point. In reality, both perspectives are valid and deserve attention.

One technique for avoiding these pitfalls is to review the supervisee's curriculum vitae or resume and other documents that highlight their strengths. The supervisee might be invited to submit positive evaluations or letters of recommendation for the supervisor's review. Supervisors might make a point of commenting when they believe the supervisee has handled something well or made a particularly astute clinical decision. Deliberately noting good work can help diffuse or serve as an antidote to shame and help rebuild a sense of professional identity and integrity. If the supervisor can accurately recognize the supervisee's strengths and convey that recognition, the supervisor's feedback may be perceived as more credible. Related techniques for assisting Level 1 trainees (Stoltenberg & McNeill, 2009; Stoltenberg, McNeill, & Delworth, 1998) may be applicable as these supervisees work to reestablish themselves and to resume whatever levels of professional development they had previously achieved (see Chapter 4, this volume).

When the supervisor invites and highlights evidence of the supervisee's strengths, the supervisee's need to do so in response to challenges may be preempted. Beyond decreasing supervisee defensiveness, focus on strengths affords opportunities to build on them. Further, supervisee's professional self-esteem typically suffers in the wake of a board complaint. Rebuilding and fortifying strengths through providing positive feedback will likely reduce anxiety and help supervisees to reestablish their sense of professional self-efficacy and effectiveness (Daniels & Larson, 2001).

Complaint Case as a Learning Tool

Supervisees present with varying degrees of insight regarding the cases on which complaints have been based and, more importantly, about their errors in those cases. Assume, for these purposes, that complaints are not based on false reports and that supervisees have indeed made mistakes constituting violations of ethical standards. Some maintain their conduct has been reasonable and appropriate, if not exceptional. They may contend that complainants were severely disturbed and misinterpreted the supervisee's behavior and that licensing boards have acted unreasonably. Others acknowledge that they have made mistakes and express remorse but are unclear about the exact nature of those mistakes and the impact or potential impact on clients. Depending on the violation, a supervisee may have been misinformed about or unaware of the rule and, after being educated, recognized the violation. Some supervisees admit their mistakes but are confused about why they acted in the ways they did. Of course, some aspects of this question are more appropriately examined in psychotherapy, but other aspects are best addressed in supervision.

Whatever the level of supervisee insight at the start of supervision, the supervisor may be wise to use the case as a learning tool. Each case is unique and particularly useful because the supervisor is likely to have substantial collateral information about it. The board may be able to provide copies of redacted case notes or reports, a summary of the complainant's allegations, supporting documents (e.g., copies of correspondence between the supervisee and the client), and tapes or transcripts from the investigation or hearing that offer the supervisee's relatively candid responses to allegations. Supervisees can benefit from reflecting on their earlier perspectives and the recorded impressions and conclusions of others.

The supervisor may begin by asking a supervisee to describe his behavior and decisions in the complaint case. The supervisee should identify the preceding decisions that set him on a trajectory to the errors leading to the complaint. Typically, supervisees in such circumstances have made a series of choices that alone may not represent ethical violations. Disclosing benign personal information in an informal exchange at the end of a therapy session, for example, may be inconsequential. A pattern of such disclosure that more closely resembles a social conversation than a therapeutic interaction may be misleading or confusing to a client and may plant seeds for unrealistic expectations for the relationship. Months later, when the psychotherapist recognizes the confusion and suddenly becomes very formal, the client is likely to feel disappointed, angry, and confused. Guiding a supervisee in identifying these early transgressions can be useful in avoiding future errors. Doing so may be empowering, particularly when the supervisee believes the complaint was unforeseeable. At this point, the supervisee may begin to identify more significant errors and violations. The supervisor may encourage the supervisee to take the next step by explaining exactly what made that decision or action an error.

Supervisees can be encouraged, in conjunction with discussing their mistakes, to describe the actual and potential repercussions for the client or other individuals (e.g., student, employee, colleague). How was the person harmed or how might he or she have been harmed? The next step is to consider what rules or codes of ethics are applicable and exactly how might they apply. Supervisees may initially say something vague and general such as "confidentiality." They must be encouraged to be specific and clear and to consider the reasons for the rules.

Those found in violation of an ethics code or rule and who have acknowledged their mistakes have considered what factors may have contributed to these mistakes. To further refine their thinking, they may be asked to describe their beliefs about why they behaved as they did, that is, what factors (personal, professional) may have played a role. These might include

- inadequate education or training,
- inappropriate role models (previous supervisors, professors, their own psychotherapists),
- poor boundaries in the work setting,
- personal distress related to situational stressors,
- past or concurrent personal experiences that increased the therapist's vulnerability, and
- the intersection of the client's issues with the therapist's personal needs or acute mental health problems (e.g., bipolar disorder, depression, chemical dependency).

Most ethical violations are complex and multidetermined. Certain types of cases and situations are likely to provoke anxiety in most psychotherapists. Clients with character disorders, particularly those with a diagnosis of borderline personality disorder, commonly experience dissatisfaction and disillusionment in relationships (Welch, 2001). The complaints and boundary challenges that typify these cases may challenge the psychotherapist's professional self-confidence, generate anxiety, and result in errors that combine to pose a significant liability risk (Hedges, 2000; Welch, 2001). Clients who are chronically or acutely suicidal or threaten violence, for example, are unsettling for most.

In addition to these more generic issues, there are idiosyncratic differences among individuals. Psychotherapists who are new to the field and who feel insecure may be vulnerable to clients who are flattering or who frequently tell them how well they are doing. Other vulnerabilities are related to individual history and may elicit strong feelings of anger, sympathy, or fear. Feelings of hostility may come out in a critical tone of voice, and excessive identification with the client may result in impulses to be helpful in ways that go beyond the boundaries of the psychologist's role. A woman trying to make it on her own in business, a young adolescent who has been abused or abandoned, a child caught in the middle of a custody dispute, or a man who does not assert himself with his partner are examples of cases that might stir significant countertransference in a therapist with a related personal experience.

Supervisors may help supervisees by asking about how their thinking has evolved since their initial decisions and what has contributed to those changes. Each component is important.

- What were the critical decision points in the case?
- If faced with the same set of circumstances today, how would the supervisee behave?

- What types of individual clients, diagnoses, therapeutic issues, and life circumstances might trigger similar challenges in the future?
- What are the generic and idiosyncratic red flags that would alert the supervisee to his or her vulnerability?

This process of intensive self-reflection is important for several reasons. The experience of dealing with a board complaint is exceedingly stressful and at times may feel pointless. When supervisees are able to view supervision as a way to broaden their professional skills and deepen their knowledge, the potential value of the experience may become more apparent, and supervisees may be more inclined to invest themselves in it. Clarifying what they have learned increases the likelihood that they will be able to internalize and ultimately generalize their learning to novel cases. Perhaps most important, the habit of continual professional self-reflection and analysis can be cultivated and integrated into the individual's professional life.

Providing board-mandated supervision to psychologists and other mental health professionals carries with it unique challenges for supervisors. The amorphous apprehension associated with these challenges may deter some capable supervisors. Illuminating potential pitfalls may diffuse the anxiety associated with them. Breaking down the underlying, contributing elements may allow prospective supervisors to make informed decisions about accepting such work.

MODELING ETHICAL BEHAVIOR FOR MANDATED SUPERVISEES

Supervisors who offer this type of specialized supervision must be aware of the significant responsibility they have relative to their supervisees and supervisees' clients. Among them, the responsibility to model ethical behavior is critical (Cobia & Pipes, 2002). As discussed, an individual who has weathered an ethics complaint watches the supervisor closely. Therefore, supervisors must not cut corners with informed consent, assuming that this individual, a colleague, understands the limits of confidentiality, for example (see Chapter 6, this volume). This assumption may or may not be accurate, but that is irrelevant. Every consumer of psychological or other mental health services is entitled to make decisions about participation in light of relevant information. Further, supervisees probably do not understand exactly what types of communication will occur between the supervisor and the board, their site supervisor, psychotherapist, psychiatrist, or attorney. They may not know whether they will receive copies of reports about them, what recourse they have if they disagree with something in a report, or what types of records will be kept.

In addition to communicating about what information will be given to the licensing board, psychologists providing mandated supervision must obtain informed consent regarding potential risks and benefits of participation. These include the supervisor's reporting obligations; the possible inclusion of supervision records or reports in future lawsuits; the potential impact of the supervisor's reports on the individual's status with a licensing board, professional association, insurance panels, and employers; possible consequences of the supervisee's dishonesty about, misrepresentation of, or failure to inform the supervisor about critical aspects of clinical work; and the supervisee's financial obligations, including charges for missed appointments and an estimate of other costs such as charges for report preparation, document review, phone calls, listening to electronic recordings of the supervisee's clinical work, and consultations with the supervisee's attorney and others concerned with the case. Supervisors must also explain the circumstances under which they may suspend or terminate the supervision. In addition to criteria listed earlier (see Chapter 6, this volume), these may include

- failure to meet financial obligations,
- failure to follow supervisory directives,
- supervisor's belief that the supervision is ineffective,
- emergence of clinical issues that the supervisor believes he or she lacks the expertise to supervise effectively, and
- changes in the supervisor's professional circumstances.

Supervisors owe it to their supervisees to address these issues clearly, not only because supervisees are consumers but also because doing so models respect for the clients these supervisees serve.

Another opportunity to model ethical behavior involves report writing and documentation of the supervision. Supervisors must be aware of ethical standards, board rules, state laws, and professional guidelines relevant to the reports they write. Any report should include, for example, data adequate to substantiate the findings and a clear description of the foundation for recommendations as well as limitations, qualifications, or reservations about observations and conclusions (American Psychological Association [APA], 2002).

A significant number of ethics violations involve boundary transgressions and multiple relationships (APA, 2007). Supervisors must therefore be vigilant about their boundaries with supervisees. Some behaviors that may occur in the context of supervision are specifically prohibited by professional ethics codes (APA, 2002) and by state board rules. Sexual contact with supervisees is one example. Other less egregious boundary transgressions, however, can also be harmful. Self-disclosures about unrelated or personal matters as well as eating or making phone calls during supervisory sessions might convey to the supervisee that the supervision is not that important.

Such informality may not only detract from the supervisory relationship but also model a lack of professionalism. Similarly, the supervisor must be vigilant about boundary crossings on the part of the supervisee. When they occur, the supervisor must challenge the supervisee about the transgression and attempt to restore the professional relationship.

Developing a clear contract that specifies all of the aforementioned goes a long way toward obviating confusion, inaccurate expectations, and misunderstanding. As with any type of supervision, both parties sign the contract, and the supervisee is provided with a copy.

Another strategy for cultivating appropriate boundaries in supervisees is ensuring that they have opportunities to acknowledge and discuss their responses to their own clients. Noting the likelihood that they will experience strong feelings or countertransference toward clients (Hayes et al., 1998) will encourage them to discuss—in supervision—feelings of attraction, irritation, love, or frustration in response to clients when those feelings occur (Robinson, 2006). Supervisors should emphasize the difference between feelings and actions and should further encourage analysis of these feelings in a manner that is consistent with their theoretical approach. In addition to encouraging supervisees to raise these issues, the supervisor should be aware of more subtle indicators of countertransference. A supervisee's uncharacteristic comments, resistance to discussing certain clients, or nonverbal reactions may suggest responses in need of attention (Ladany, Constantine, Miller, Erickson, & Muse-Burke, 2000)

TECHNIQUES FOR MANDATED SUPERVISION

Board-mandated supervision is by design and necessity more intrusive and intensive than many other types of supervision. To whatever extent the clients are at increased risk because of the supervisee's past difficulties, supervisors assume a greater responsibility for ensuring their welfare. Strategies for close monitoring of the supervisee's work must be used.

Guidelines and specific criteria regarding which cases are presented help to ensure that higher risk cases and situations are monitored. Many such criteria are useful with any supervisee, but others are unique to board-mandated supervision. Depending on the supervisee's work setting, the size and makeup of his or her caseload, and the nature of the violations, the supervisor may identify the types of cases and circumstances to be presented. Members of the supervisory dyad may collaborate to establish, refine, and revise their agreements about criteria for case selection. Any supervisee should be required, for example, to present cases involving clients who are suicidal, potentially violent, angry about or challenging the boundaries of the psychotherapist, or who raise allegations of unethical behavior. Similarly, client disclosures that may require mandated reports must be discussed. Supervisees under disciplinary order, however, should also identify the types of clients, therapeutic issues, and life circumstances likely to stimulate countertransference and reawaken personal issues that might impair their objectivity and effectiveness. Further, boundary challenges on the part of clients (e.g., requests for contact outside of sessions, unusual appointment hours, or personal information about the therapist) must be processed during supervision.

Relying exclusively on supervisees' self-reports about their work is inadequate in any supervision but particularly problematic when the supervisee has a history of ethical difficulties. Review of recordings of psychotherapy or assessment sessions, case notes, and reports; live observation; role-playing therapeutic interactions; and cotherapy (Bernard & Goodyear, 2004; Schoener & Conroe, 1989) will provide the supervisor with another window into the individual's professional behavior and compliance with board rules, ethics codes, stipulations in the order, and supervisory directives. The value and necessity of those techniques that intrude into the therapist–client relationship should, of course, be carefully considered in terms of the risks and benefits to both the supervisee and the client. The informed consent of the client is required. If the supervisor is offsite, periodic visits to the work setting will allow access to information not otherwise readily available. Observing and assessing how the office is arranged, the appropriateness of the lighting, and where files and other confidential materials are kept are examples. Authorization allowing ongoing communication between the on- and off-site supervisors is essential.

POWER IN THE SUPERVISORY RELATIONSHIP

Any supervisory relationship presumes an inherent and inevitable power difference (M. R. Peterson, 1992). These power differentials may be enhanced to the extent that they reflect power differences in the cultural context in which the supervision occurs. Factors such as race, ethnicity, gender, and sexual orientation may affect the relative power of both members of the supervisory dyad. This is particularly evident when the supervisor is a member of the majority culture in terms of one or more of these factors and the supervisee is a member of the minority culture (Toldson & Utsey, 2008). When a supervisee is required to participate as a condition for maintaining licensure, employment, or membership in a professional association, the supervisor holds additional power (Cobia & Pipes, 2002), the misuse of which could be personally and professionally devastating to the supervisee as well as to his or her current and future clients. Awareness of this power difference typically results in some degree of inhibition on the part of supervisees. Fears about making another error or eliciting the anger of the supervisors thus putting supervisees' careers at risk may result in editing disclosures about themselves, their cases, mistakes, misgivings, and uncertainties. The effectiveness of the supervision likely will be diminished if the supervisee cannot candidly discuss and seek help for these vulnerabilities.

Dynamics created by these power differences can ignite the countertransference of a supervisor who is insecure, threatened, or overly gratified by this power. Conversely, a supervisor who experiences significant discomfort with this degree of power may be at risk for minimizing it by behaving in informal ways with the supervisee, consulting the supervisee about his or her own clinical work, or in some other way acting out their countertransference by shifting the boundaries. Obtaining regular consultation from a colleague with appropriate expertise will mitigate the potential for acting out this countertransference in harmful ways.

MAINTAINING THE SUPERVISORY RELATIONSHIP

Supervision involves a significant relationship component. Supervisors must, therefore, be willing to directly address problems that arise in the supervisory relationship. The inherent challenges (power, limits to confidentiality, evaluative nature of the relationship) should be discussed at the outset and revisited as necessary. Supervisees must be encouraged to address difficulties directly with the supervisor as soon as they become aware of them.

Supervisors must convey, throughout the process, empathy and respect for their supervisees. As challenging as this work might be for supervisors, it is exceedingly humbling and difficult for a supervisee required to undergo this degree of professional exposure and scrutiny. Supervisors who are continuously mindful of this dynamic are more likely to communicate their understanding and thereby create an atmosphere of safety.

CONCLUSION: WHY PROVIDE MANDATED SUPERVISION?

Providing board-mandated supervision to psychologists and other mental health professionals carries unique and significant challenges for supervisors. The vague apprehension that many feel when contemplating whether to offer this service reflects these challenges. They need not deter capable psychologists from considering offering such supervision. Use of the suggested strategies will diffuse the anxiety associated with such supervision. Breaking down the underlying contributing elements allows prospective supervisors to address them directly and make a more informed decision about accepting such a job.

Mandated supervisees benefit from working with a colleague who understands the unique nuances of this type of supervision. Providing such supervision reflects a commitment to improving the profession and affords supervisors an opportunity to inform their own work by examining the errors of others. It also provides an impetus for ensuring that their own clinical practice is up to date with regard to evolving professional standards, laws, and ethics codes. Supervisors have a built-in incentive for reading related publications and ensuring that forms, policies, and procedures reflect current standards. Moreover, providing supervision to colleagues under board order is professionally challenging and stimulating, and watching colleagues recover from this significant interruption in their professional lives is but one of the gifts of engaging in this work.

9

DOCUMENTATION OF SUPERVISION AND CONSULTATION

The necessity for documentation of clinical supervision and consultation has become increasingly evident. Some of the authors who have addressed these two topics have not directly discussed the need for keeping records of the supervision and consultation (Bradley & Ladany, 2001; Brown, Pryzwansky, & Schulte, 2001; Fall & Sutton, 2004; Gill, 2001; Jacobs, David, & Meyer, 1995; Kaiser, 1997; Neufeldt, 2007; Powell, 2004; Stoltenberg, McNeill, & Delworth, 1998). Others have offered compelling reasons and methods for recording various aspects of supervision and consultation (Bernard & Goodyear, 2009; Celenza, 2007; Disney & Stephens, 1994; Falender & Shafranske, 2004; Falvey, 2002; Falvey Caldwell, & Cohen, 2002; Falvey & Cohen, 2003; Guest & Dooley, 1999; Harrar, VandeCreek & Knapp, 1990; Haynes, Corey, & Moulton, 2003; Knapp & VandeCreek, 1997; Luepker, 2003; Storm & Todd, 1997a; Stromberg, et al., 1988; Walker & Jacobs, 2004).

Falvey (2002) has described the documentation of supervision as an essential risk management strategy; she has stated that "documentation is no longer an option in supervision" (p. 117). Unlike consultation, supervision is typically a requirement of some outside entity, such as a graduate program, insurance company, employer, licensing board, or other credentialing body. Therefore, evidence that the supervision requirement has been met is needed. Further, supervisors assume responsibility, to varying degrees, for the work of the supervisee and for the welfare of their supervisees' clients. To that end, supervisors must keep records that both demonstrate and facilitate this level of accountability. Consultation, on the other hand, can take various forms and generally involves less responsibility on the part of the consultant for the work of recipients of consulting services. Requirements for records, therefore, are different.

In this chapter, the following issues are addressed:

- ethical standards and standards of practice for record keeping in supervision and consultation,
- purposes of supervision records created by supervisors and supervisees,
- purposes of consultation records created by consultants and consultees, and
- content of and formats for supervision records.

STANDARDS OF PRACTICE REGARDING RECORDS OF SUPERVISION AND CONSULTATION

Documentation of clinical work is addressed by the ethical standards and practice guidelines of most mental health professional associations (American Association for Marriage and Family Therapy [AAMFT], 2001; American Counseling Association, 2005; American Psychological Association [APA], 2002, 2007; Association of State and Provincial Psychology Boards [ASPPB], 2003; Canadian Psychological Association [CPA], 2000; National Association of Social Workers [NASW], 2008) and by some credentialing bodies (AAPC, 1994; ASPPB, 2005). Requirements for record keeping in supervision and consultation, however, are sometimes absent from these documents. Some organizations and credentialing bodies have developed specialty guidelines that offer more specific direction for supervisors, but they either do not address consultation or do so only indirectly (AAMFT, 2007; American Association of Pastoral Counselors [AAPC], 1997, 2009; Association for Counselor Education and Supervision [ACES], 1993; NASW, 1994).

These specialty codes and guidelines for supervision are helpful in that they specifically discuss many ethical and practice issues neglected in general ethics codes. Unfortunately, record keeping is rarely addressed directly. Many note the need for written evaluations and contracts for supervision, which implies the need for some type of record. For example, the AAPC *Supervision Standards of Practice* (1997) includes a section on record keeping that requires supervisors to maintain up-to-date supervision records. The content of those records is not specified, but the expectation that supervision records be kept is clear. Several organizations have published guidelines that discuss documentation only in limited ways. The ACES (1993), ASPPB (2003), and AAMFT (2007) address record keeping as it pertains to supervision contracts and evaluations.

Some sets of guidelines and ethics codes for supervision have specifically considered the issue of record keeping. The AAPC *Supervision Standards of Practice* (1997), for example, includes a brief section on record keeping that states: "Supervisors maintain up-to-date records of supervision" (p. 3). The NASW's *Guidelines for Clinical Social Work Supervision* (1994) suggests that supervisors document dates of contact, progress toward goals, and provide recommendations. Similarly, *The Approved Clinical Supervisor (ACS) Code of Ethics* (Center for Credentialing & Education, 2008) simply states that supervisors must "keep and secure supervision records" (p. 1). The CPA supervision guidelines recommend that supervisors "maintain records to a standard required by the nature of the psychological activity and setting, and to the extent needed to maintain an effective supervisory relationship" (2009, p. 6).

Although APA has not published specialty guidelines for supervisors or consultants, the Ethics Code (APA, 2002), unlike some other associations' codes that pertain only to treatment, provides ethical standards applicable to "psychologists' activities that are part of their scientific, educational, or professional roles" (p. 2). The APA Ethics Code further specifies the "supervision of trainees" (p. 2) as a covered area of practice. Therefore, supervisors and consultants can find guidance regarding the content of consultation and supervision records. APA requires that psychologists document their work with five objectives in mind:

1. facilitate provision of services later by them or by other professionals,
2. allow for replication of research design and analyses,
3. meet institutional requirements,
4. ensure accuracy of billing and payments, and
5. ensure compliance with law (APA, p. 8).

The APA *Record Keeping Guidelines* (2007) reflect these objectives: "Psychologists strive to maintain accurate, current, and pertinent records of professional services as appropriate to circumstances" (p. 4). Although ASPPB (2005) defines *client* in a general way, information pertaining to the "maintenance and retention of records" (p. 4) is clearly intended to address client records rather than supervisory records.

PURPOSES OF RECORD KEEPING OF SUPERVISION

Many authors have asserted the need for the documentation of supervision (Adams, 2001; Bridge & Bascue, 1990; Falvey, 2002; Falvey & Cohen, 2003; Knapp & VandeCreek, 1997; Luepker, 2003; Storm & Todd, 1997a; Walker & Jacobs, 2004). Luepker (2003) stated, "Just as psychotherapists need to document what transpires during treatment, so should supervisors document what transpires during clinical supervision" (p. 109). Records of supervision are maintained for several purposes.

Client Welfare

One of the primary goals of supervision is to ensure the welfare of the supervisee's clients (Bernard & Goodyear, 2009; Loganbill, Hardy & Delworth, 1982), and records of supervision support this goal. Documentation allows supervisors to recall particular cases and provide continuity in their feedback. Supervisors can also use records to monitor caseload size and composition (Falvey & Cohen, 2003), treatment plans, clients' progress, and the status of the therapeutic relationship. In the absence of a contract specifying that a supervisor is responsible for only a circumscribed portion of a supervisee's work (e.g., assessments, work with particular types of clients), supervisors are generally accountable for all of the supervisees' clients. This is especially evident with trainees and students. Supervisors must, therefore, have a method for tracking all cases, ensuring that they are informed about the status of each client, and following up on more critical cases.

Supervisee Professional Development

Another purpose of supervision is to facilitate the professional development of the supervisee. Records allow supervisors to track supervisees' progress toward professional goals. A supervisee may be working on establishing clearer boundaries, for example, or on a more technical issue, such as attending more to feelings and less to content. Another individual's goal may be learning more about a particular theoretical orientation, cultural group, mental disorder, or client population. Noting times when the individual is successful or is struggling in a particular area allows supervisors to recall specific examples. Further, such records allow supervisors to document demonstrations of general strengths and weaknesses. Such information is helpful in providing both specificity and continuity in their feedback to the supervisee and in preparing useful evaluations and letters of recommendation in the future. Similarly, records help supervisors to recall particular challenges in specific cases, follow up on earlier clinical concerns, and monitor compliance with supervisory recommendations and directives.

Conflicts and Impasses

Records of conflicts or disagreements between supervisor and supervisee should be created for future reference. In these circumstances, supervisors benefit from seeking supervision or consultation themselves to effectively and objectively assess their blind spots and possible errors that may be contributing to the impasse with the supervisee (Storm & Todd, 1997b; Taibbi, 1993). Records of the content of supervision sessions can augment supervisors' memories and assist them in accurately representing the conflict to a more objective consultant. When there is a difference of opinion about a case, records can be reviewed with the supervisee to ensure that each individual's perceptions of what was decided comport with one another.

Risk Management

The supervisor's records represent a risk management strategy in that they can offer legal protection for both the supervisor and supervisee (Adams, 2001; Bridge & Bascue, 1990; Falvey & Cohen, 2003; Haynes et al., 2003; Luepker, 2003; NASW, 1994). Supervisors can use records to substantiate their defense in the event of a lawsuit from either the supervisee or, in cases in which vicarious liability is alleged, from the supervisee's client. In the event of a lawsuit filed against the supervisee, the supervisor's records can substantiate the individual's effort to seek help with complex cases, such as those involving suicidal behavior, threats of violence, and conflicts with clients. Such records can demonstrate that their decisions were reached in collaboration with another professional. Similarly, records can augment a defense for either party in a licensing board complaint.

Compliance

Agencies, institutions, professional associations, licensing boards, and legal jurisdictions may have policies, ethics codes, rules, or laws with implications for supervision. If supervision is provided to graduate students, for example, educational institutions may require documentation by the supervisor verifying that the student has met program requirements (Storm & Todd, 1997a). Similarly, when a licensing board or employer mandates supervision, supervisors are likely to be required to write reports describing the content of supervisory sessions. Notes kept throughout the supervision allow supervisors to compile accurate reports throughout and at the conclusion of supervision (Celenza, 2007). Further, psychologists and other mental health professionals may be required to keep records of their professional financial transactions. When supervisees pay for supervision, records of financial transactions must be maintained.

PURPOSES OF SUPERVISEES' RECORDS

Supervisees benefit from creating their own records of their supervisory sessions. The preparation of such records enhances the value of the supervision in several ways.

Development of Clinical Skills

Supervisees' records of supervisory sessions can assist them in recalling suggestions or directives received as they prepare for their next sessions with the client. Reviewing notes just before a session can help them focus on their own professional development goals as well as the therapeutic goals of the client.

Preparation for Supervision

Supervisors may require their supervisees to prepare a case summary in advance of a supervisory session to focus the presentation of the case (Walker & Jacobs, 2004). Students, trainees, and other novice supervisees are likely to benefit most from such deliberate and thorough preparation. In addition to the implications for treatment, such preparation may help them learn how to prepare and present clinical cases (see Appendix F, this volume). More experienced supervisees are not as likely to need such specific instructions regarding the content of a case presentation.

Risk Management

Like supervisors, supervisees can use supervisory records as a risk management strategy. Records of supervisory sessions can provide evidence that they sought collaboration and support for difficult clinical decisions and judgment calls in treatment. Particularly in the event of an undesired outcome, such records can be advantageous. Some record of relevant supervisory recommendations should be included in the client's file (Glenn & Serovich, 1994). Minimally, the client record should include a dated entry indicating that consultation or supervision was obtained about the case. A notation summarizing the recommendations generated would be more helpful. This information may be recorded on a separate sheet allowing easy access (see Appendix G, this volume). Supervision pertaining only to the supervisee should be recorded separately.

Optimizing Utility of Supervision

Perhaps most important, creating a record of what transpired in supervision forces the supervisee to reflect on, synthesize, and restate the input received and then to integrate it into an action plan. Having a supervisee read back what he or she has recorded can be helpful in ensuring that supervisor and supervisee are in agreement about what has been decided. Another alternative is to have the supervisee write a summary of the supervision and have the supervisor review and approve it. Both procedures afford opportunities for clarification.

PURPOSES OF CONSULTANTS' RECORDS

The role of the clinical consultant involves a lesser degree of responsibility and liability. Further, the consultant's responsibilities vary according to the contract, setting, and purpose of the consultation. Some consultation looks very much like clinical supervision. A credentialed professional may elect to meet with a colleague who possesses particular expertise on a regular basis to develop new competency, enhance the quality of his or her work, or as a risk management strategy. Cases may be presented in the form of written reports, case notes, audio or video recordings, or oral summaries, just as is done in supervision. Keeping some record of the cases presented and feedback provided will augment the consultant's memory of particular cases and provide continuity. Unlike supervision, however, in consultation there is generally no requirement that all of the consultee's cases be monitored. The consultee determines which cases are presented.

A consultant hired by an agency, program, or by clinicians in a group practice may be asked to provide input about particular policies and procedures, crisis management or clinical record keeping, for example. The consultant's task may involve reviewing written material, interviewing staff, and/or designing and providing relevant training. A report may or may not be prepared, and records of the content of the training may not be maintained. Financial records, perhaps in the form of an invoice, will likely be needed. Another type of consultation may involve a one-time meeting with a group of clinicians focused on a specific topic. A psychologist or other mental health clinician may meet with an existing peer consultation or practice group to address a topic of interest to the group. The consultant in this case may elect to keep a record of financial transactions as well as documents on which he or she relied or may decide not to keep any record of the content of the consultation.

PURPOSES OF CONSULTEES' RECORDS

Again, decisions about the type of record, if any, will depend on the nature of the service provided. When consultation is focused on a particular clinical case or cases, notes regarding that case will be helpful in the same ways as are notes from clinical supervision: to augment recall, provide evidence of collaboration, synthesize the feedback, and make a plan for implementation. Records of other types of consultation, particularly educationally focused consultation, are optional and may be useful in much the same way as notes taken at a workshop or professional seminar.

CONTENT AND FORMAT OF SUPERVISION AND CONSULTATION RECORDS

Most relevant literature pertains to records of supervision rather than consultation, but some has implications for both. As stated, the format and type of information recorded will vary. Supervisors of students and mandated supervisees may need to keep more detailed records of both their own and supervisees' activities to verify that all requirements have been met. In any case, supervisors and consultants should maintain a file for each supervisee or consultee.

Supervision and consultation files will likely contain both clinical and administrative materials. Clinical records are those pertaining primarily to the treatment of the supervisee's clients, whereas administrative records focus primarily on the supervisee.

Clinical Material

The clinical portion of a record would likely contain the following:

- caseload-monitoring log;
- progress notes reflecting the content of supervisory or consultation sessions; and
- work samples submitted for review, if appropriate (e.g., case notes and reports, with identifying information redacted or client informed consent documented).

Caseload-Monitoring Log

As discussed, supervisors maintain responsibility for both supervisees and supervisees' clients and therefore need a system for monitoring all of their supervisees' cases or all of the cases for which they have responsibility. A *caseload-monitoring log*, sometimes referred to as a *supervision log* (Falvey et al., 2002; Storm & Todd, 1997b) serves this purpose. A caseload-monitoring log is a form on which brief information about each client (e.g. name, age, diagnosis) is recorded along with the dates on which the case was discussed. The supervisor can determine at a glance what cases were reviewed during the last and previous sessions and can readily identify cases that need to be examined. Clients are numbered for easy reference. These numbers may be recorded in the supervisor's record in more detailed corresponding notes about the content of each supervision session. An entry might look like this:

> 1. John D. (42) 296.33—divorced, 2 adol. children; alcoholic, 3 years sober; anger 5/24/09; 12/11/09

Other authors and professional associations have suggested similar formats for supervision records. Falvey et al. (2002) proposed a form that includes columns in which to record eight informational items: date, duration of supervision session, number of cases in the supervisee's caseload, new cases added, closed cases, cases reviewed, estimated time for the next case review, and a place to check when the "next review" is completed. This form is designed primarily for student-supervisees. Schoener (1989) designed a form for recording supervision with psychotherapists who have sexually exploited their clients. It contains four categories: case presented, notes or tape used, description, and recommendations or direction. The AAMFT (2007) handbook suggested a six-category log: supervisor's initials, date, hours, setting, whether the supervision was "live" (i.e., observation of a therapy session), and how much time was spent reviewing audio- or videotapes.

If the supervisee is beginning an internship or practicum and accepts his or her first clients while under supervision, then the supervisor and supervisee could record clients simultaneously on identical forms when a case is opened. Alternatively, if the supervision involves an already existing caseload, the supervisee should complete the list of clients, retain a copy, and submit a copy to the supervisor. Each can modify the list as new clients are added and others terminate.

Supervision or Consultation Progress Notes

As discussed, records of supervision are generally more detailed than those of consultation. Therefore, each date recorded on the client-monitoring log must correspond to a detailed note recorded elsewhere in the supervision file. Such notes are similar to psychotherapy case notes in that they describe the content of the session. The specific format will vary by setting. In general, supervision progress notes might be recorded on a form that lists the date, number of session, and a summary of the topics and cases discussed. Some supervisors will find it useful to record all discussions about particular clients in one place, thus requiring a separate file or page for each case. Others will find it more useful to record content by date, the client's name and number or some other identifiers that will enable later reference. In the case of group supervision, the record should also include the names of colleagues present in the group. Finally, the context of supervision should be clarified (e.g., phone, e-mail, individual or group meeting, video or audio).

A supervision progress note also might contain an overview of significant or relevant aspects of the case, particularly if this is the first presentation of the client. This may include age, ethnicity, race, relationship status, occupation, and significant relationships. The note should also reflect questions or issues raised, clients' presenting issues, observations, evaluative comments, plans, recommendations, and supervisory directives.

Consultation requires a different order of priority: The consultee's needs generally are considered more prominently than the needs of clients. Session content, then, might be most effectively recorded by date, with a focus on the consultee's goals and progress. Information about clients might be included as well but only as it relates to the objectives of the consultation. Any recommendations made by the consultant should of course be reflected in the record.

Work Samples

Supervisees may be required to submit work samples, such as recordings of psychotherapy sessions or test administrations, case notes, intake assessments, and testing reports. Supervisors may review, discuss, and sometimes cosign these documents, which would be retained in the client's file. If a case note or report is redacted and reviewed primarily for educational purposes, the supervisor might record his or her feedback directly on the document and retain a copy in the supervision file as a record of both the supervisee's performance and the supervisory feedback provided. Additionally, a supervisor might use a checklist to evaluate client files to ensure that they contain all required materials (see Appendix H, this volume) and to assess the quality of the record (see Appendix I, this volume). Clinical consultants may also request work samples to assist them in providing the requested feedback.

Nonclinical Material

In addition to clinical material, a supervision or consultation record must include documentation of the nonclinical aspects of the case. The following is a list of some such items that may be included in a supervision or consultation file. It is not designed to be exhaustive, nor is it intended to suggest that every file must include all of these items. Rather, this list provides a menu of options from which items can be selected to reflect particular needs and preferences. A supervisor or consultant's administrative records may include the following types of information.

Administrative Records

- dates of service, including communication with or pertaining to the supervisee;
- contract for supervision or consultation and other informed consent documents;
- authorizations for release of information pertaining to the supervisee or consultee;
- copies of all correspondence with and about the supervisee or consultee; and
- supplemental documents illustrating reasons for consultation or supervision (e.g., licensing board orders, human resources documents).

Materials Submitted by the Supervisee or Consultee

- application materials (application forms, letters of recommendation, transcripts, resume or curriculum vitae);
- supervisee or consultee questionnaire (e.g., background information);
- self-evaluations completed by the supervisee, evaluations completed by the supervisor or others, supervisor evaluations completed by the supervisee;
- records of hours worked, hours spent in various professional activities such as client contact, individual and group supervision, and record keeping;
- work samples, such as reports and case notes; and
- reports written by the supervisee or consultee about the supervision or consultation (e.g., as might be required by a licensing board or employer).

Materials Created by the Supervisor or Consultant

- supervisee evaluations and
- reports written by the supervisor or consultant regarding the recipient.

Financial Records

- fee agreement;
- balance sheet listing charges, payments, and account information; and
- copies of bills or statements of account provided to the supervisee or consultee.

RETENTION OF RECORDS OF CONSULTATION AND SUPERVISION

According to Falvey (2002), records of supervision should be retained as long as the records of the clinical work they reflect. Requirements for record retention are sometimes established by agencies or institutions, federal, state and provincial law, licensing board rules, and sometimes by insurance companies who pay for the treatment. The Health Insurance Portability and Accountability Act of 1996, for example, states that health care records must be retained for 6 years. Generally, the most conservative of the applicable regulations should be followed. In the absence of such regulations, professional guidelines should be considered. The APA *Record Keeping Guidelines* (2007) suggest that clinical records be retained for 7 years.

CONCLUSION

Supervisors and consultants provide services in a broad range of contexts and do so with a similar breadth of purposes and objectives. The need for specific components of a supervision or consultation record will shift depending on these variables. There is no single format, system, or form that will be effective in all situations. Supervisors and consultants must consider their own needs and preferences, the needs of those they serve, institutional and legal mandates, and ethics codes and guidelines promulgated by their professional associations and licensing boards. With due consideration for each of these factors, supervisors and consultants can design effective systems for record keeping.

APPENDIX A:
ETHICAL ISSUES—DEFINITIONS

advertising and competency: Presenting information to clients and prospective clients and the general public regarding the skills and services that can be provided by a particular clinician (supervisor or supervisee).

boundaries, multiple relationships: Limitations on the dimensions of relationships between supervisors and supervisees, multiple and dual relationships, multiple roles, relationships outside of supervision.

competency, delegation: Assignment of responsibilities commensurate with supervisees' ability to execute them safely and effectively with available supervision.

competency (supervisee or consultee): Training, education, skills, professional experience, and personal characteristics needed to establish professional competency.

competency (supervisor or consultant): Training, education, skills, and professional experience needed to qualify as a clinical supervisor or consultant.

consultation, peer review: Provision of feedback, commentary, and/or suggestions regarding clinical issues made by one mental health professional or a colleague, trainee, or student for whom the consultant has no official responsibility.

crisis procedures: Directives for supervisees regarding how to proceed in the event of a client's mental health crisis.

diversity: Policies regarding antidiscrimination and fair treatment of supervisees.

documentation of supervision: Records of supervision (including session content and performance appraisals) and related procedures (such as record retention and maintenance).

due process: Procedures for supervisees to follow when they have a grievance regarding their supervision and for supervisors to follow in responding to supervisee grievances.

endorsement: Supervisors' statements verifying supervisees' completion of requirements, their competency, and ability to practice safely and effectively.

evaluation (supervisees'): Methods, timing, content, and procedures related to supervisees' performance evaluation.

exploitation of supervisees: Policies regarding the protection of supervisees from abuse or other treatment that takes unfair advantage of their vulnerable positions relative to supervisors and other professional staff.

fees: Financial compensation for supervision paid by supervisees or others.

impairment (supervisees'): Compromised ability to safely and effectively provide mental health assessment or treatment as the result of a mental or physical condition.

informed consent (clients'): Clients' agreement to engage in treatment or assessment with a full understanding of factors that might reasonably affect their willingness to participate.

informed consent (supervisees'): Supervisees' agreement to engage in clinical supervision with a full understanding of factors that might reasonably affect their willingness to participate.

interruption or termination of supervision: A situation in the supervisor's life that interrupts supervision, such as the supervisor's illness, death, job change, or other circumstances necessitating a temporary or permanent absence.

methods and responsibilities: Strategies and techniques used in the practice of clinical supervision.

personal development: Requirements involving supervisees' personal growth, self-disclosure, or mental health treatment.

privacy (clients'): Limitations to clients' privacy related to the disclosure of information about them in the context of supervision.

privacy (supervisees'): Extent of and limitations to supervisees' privacy in the context of supervision.

recording and observation: Electronic recording or observation by supervisors of psychotherapy, assessment, or other professional services rendered by supervisees.

reporting obligations: Supervisors' responsibility to protect the public by reporting supervisees (as well as other professionals) to appropriate authorities for specified violations of law or ethics codes.

sexual contact, harassment: Sexual relationships between supervisors and supervisees; exploitation of supervisees by supervisors; unwanted sexual attention to supervisees by supervisors.

APPENDIX B: PSYCHOLOGY PROFESSIONAL ASSOCIATIONS— ETHICS CODES

	Professional association		
Ethical issue	APA (2002)	ASPPB (2005)	CPA (2000)
Advertising and competency	5.01 (b, c)	III. A3, G2, J2, K1	III.2, 5
Boundaries, multiple relationships	3.05, 3.06, 7.04, 7.05, 7.07	III. B1, 2a, b	I.26; II.28; III.31, 33, 34, 35
Competency (delegation)	2.05	III. A10, K2	I.6; II.7
Competency (supervisee or consultee)	2.05	—	II.6, 8, 9, 10, 11, 12
Competency (supervisor or consultant)	2.01 (a, b, c, e), 2.03	III. A1, 2	II.6, 8, 9, 10, 11, 12; III.4
Consultation, peer review	3.10, 4.06	III. A2, 4, F9	II.8, 9, 20, 25; III.38; IV.18, 21, 24
Crisis procedures	—	—	—
Diversity	2.01 (b), 3.01, 3.03	—	I.2, 9, 10, 11, 38; II.14, 21
Documentation of supervision	6.01, 6.02	III. A7	II.19
Due process	—	—	I.13
Endorsement	—	—	—
Evaluation	7.06	—	II.25
Exploitation of supervisees	3.04, 3.05 (a, b), 3.06, 3.08	III. E1	I.26; III.31
Fees for supervision	6.04	—	I.15; III.14
Impairment	2.06, 7.04	III. C1	II.11, 12
Informed consent (clients)	3.10 (a), 4.02 (a, b), 6.04, 10.01 (a, c)	—	I.17, 22, 23, 24, 25, 26, 27, 29, 30, 36
Informed consent (supervisees)	3.10, 4.02, 7.02, 7.04, 7.06 (a)	—	I.17, 22, 23, 24, 25, 26, 27, 28, 29, 30, 36; III.14
Interruption or termination of supervision	3.12	—	I.30, 41
Methods and responsibilities	—	III. A9	I.27; II.1, 2, 3, 4, 18, 19, 25; III.40, 41
Personal development	7.04	—	II.12
Privacy (client or patient)	4.01, 4.02, 4.04 (a, b), 4.06	III. F1, 9	I.37, 40, 43

(*continues*)

Ethical issue	Professional association		
	APA (2002)	ASPPB (2005)	CPA (2000)
Privacy (supervisee)	4.01, 4.02, 4.04 (a, b), 4.06	—	I.37, 40, 43
Recording and observation	4.03	III. F11	—
Reporting obligations	1.05, 4.05 (b)	III. L1	I.45; II.40
Sexual contact, harassment	3.02, 7.07	III. E1	I.4; II.28

Note. A dash indicates that no section of a code addresses a given issue. APA = American Psychological Association; ASPPB = Association of State and Provincial Psychology Boards; and CPA = Canadian Psychological Association.

APPENDIX C: COUNSELING PROFESSIONAL ASSOCIATIONS— ETHICS CODES

	Professional association		
Ethical issue	AAPC (1994)	ACA (2005)	NAADAC (2008)
Advertising and competency	V. D, I. G, V. A	C3 a; C4 a, b, c, d, f ; F3 a, d, e; F5 c; F6 e	4, 7
Boundaries, multiple relationships	I. G, III. E, V. A	F3 a, d, e; F5c; F6e	7
Client or patient privacy	IV. C, D	A2 b; B3 a, b; B6 b, c; F1 c	2, 6
Competency, delegation	V. D	—	—
Competency (supervisee or consultee)	I. C, F	C2 c; F5 b; F7 b; F9 a, b; F11 c	—
Competency (supervisor or consultant)	V. D	C2 a, c; D 2a; F2 a	9
Consultation, peer review	I. D, IV. D	C2 e; D2 a, b, c, d	—
Crisis procedures	—	F4 b	—
Diversity	I. B	F2 b; F11 a, c	1
Documentation of supervision	—	F5 a, b	—
Due process	—	F4 a, d; F9 b3	—
Endorsement	—	F5 d	—
Evaluation	—	F5 a, b; F9 a, b	—
Exploitation of supervisees	II. A, V. B	C3 d, f; C6 d; F3 a, b, c, d	6, 7
Fees for supervision	II. C	—	—
Impairment	I. D, E	C2 g, h; F5 b, d; F8 b; F9 b, c	4
Informed consent (clients)	IV. E	A2 a, b, d; B3 b; B6 b, c; F1 b	2, 3
Informed consent (supervisees)	—	F4 a; F7 b; F9 a	—
Interruption or termination of supervision	—	A 2b; C2 h; F4 b	—
Methods and responsibilities	—	F1 a	—
Personal development	—	F7 b; F9 c	—
Privacy (supervisee or consultee)	—	—	—
Recording and observation	IV. E	B6 c	3
Reporting obligations	IV. D, F	H2 c	6, 8
Sexual contact, harassment	V. B, C	C6 a; F3 b, c, d	—

Note. A dash indicates that no section of a code addresses a given issue. AAPC = American Association of Pastoral Counselors; ACA = American Counseling Association; NAADAC = National Association of Alcohol and Drug Abuse Counselors.

APPENDIX D: OTHER MENTAL HEALTH PROFESSIONAL ASSOCIATIONS— ETHICS CODES

	Professional association			
Ethical issue	AAMFT (2001)	ApA (2009)	NASW (2008)	NASW (2005)
Advertising and competency	4.4, 8.1, 8.2, 8.4, 8.5, 8.6, 8.7	—	1.04 a; 4.06 c; 4.07 b	—
Boundaries, multiple relationships, exploitation	4.1, 4.2, 4.3, 4.6, 7.5	—	1.06 b; 3.01 b, c; 3.02 d	—
Client or patient privacy	1.12, 2.3, 2.6	2	1.07 a, b, c, e, i, q; 2.02	3, 5
Competency, delegation	4.4	5 (2), (3), (4)	—	—C
Competency (supervisee or consultee)	3.7, 4.4, 4.5	5 (3)	1.04 a, b, c; 1.05 a, b, c; 2.10 a, b; 4.01 a, b, c,	2, 6, 10, 11
Competency (supervisor or consultant)	3.1, 3.11, 3.7, 8.7	2 (3); 3 (2); 5 (1)	1.04 a, b, c; 1.05 a, b, c; 2.10 a, b, 3.01 a; 4.01 a,b, c; 4.05 b; 5.01 c	2, 6, 10, 11
Consultation, peer review	2.3, 2.6	1 (3); 4 (4); 5 (2), (3)	1.04 a, b, c; 1.06 b; 1.07 c, q; 2.02; 2.05 a, b, c; 2.07 b; 2.09 a; 2.10 a	6
Crisis procedures	—	—	—	—
Diversity	1.1	1 (2)	1.05 a, b, c; 3.01 b; 4.02	10
Documentation of supervision	3.6	—	—	—
Due process	—	—	3.01 d; 3.02 b; 3.09f	—
Endorsement	—	—	—	—
Evaluation	—	—	3.01; 3.02 b; 3.03	—
Exploitation of supervisees	3.8, 3.9, 4.1, 7.5	4 (14)	1.06 b; 3.01 c; 3.02 d	—
Fees for supervision	3.6, 7.2	2 (7)	—	—
Impairment	3.3, 4.1	2 (4)	2.09 a, b; 4.05 a, b	—
Informed consent (clients)	2.1, 2.3, 2.6, 7.2, 7.4	—	1.03 f; 1.07 e; 3.02 c	5
Informed consent (supervisees)	2.6, 3.5, 7.2, 7.4	—	1.07 e	—
Interruption or termination of supervision	—	—	1.07 o; 1.15	—

(continues)

	Professional association			
Ethical issue	AAMFT (2001)	ApA (2009)	NASW (2008)	NASW (2005)
Methods and responsibilities	—	—	—	—
Personal development	3.3	—	—	—
Privacy (supervisee)	2.6, 4.7	2	1.07 c; 2.02	—
Recording and observation	1.12	—	1.02 f	—
Reporting obligations	1.6	—	1.01; 2.09 b; 2.10 b; 2.11 d	—
Sexual contact, harassment	3.8, 3.9, 4.3, 4.6	4 (14)	2.07 a; 2.08	—

Note. Dash indicates that no section of a code addresses a given issue. AAMFT = American Association for Marriage and Family Therapy; APA = American Psychiatric Association; NASW = National Association of Social Workers.

APPENDIX E: MENTAL HEALTH PROFESSIONAL ASSOCIATIONS— ETHICAL AND SPECIALTY GUIDELINES

Professional association

Ethical issue	AAMFT (2007)	AAPC (1997)	ACES (1993)	ASPPB[a] (2003)	CCE (2008)	CPA (2009)
Advertising and competency	p. 15	—	1.02	I. C (1), D (2, 3), E (2)	—	—
Boundaries, multiple relationships, exploitation	pp. 11, 12, 15	3.2, 3.2.1, 3.2.2, 3.2.3, 3.3	2.09; 2.10; 2.11; 3.12; 3.17; 3.18; 3.19	II. D (1, 2, 3)	5	III. 2, 4, 7, 8
Client or patient privacy		—	1.03; 1.04	III. F1, F9	2	—
Competency, delegation	p. 13	—	3.09	I. B (1, 2, 3), E (2, 3), II. A (1, 2), B (3)	8	p. 5; III. 5
Competency (supervisee or consultee)	pp. 13, 15	2.1, 2.1.1, 2.1.2	3.09	I. B (1), E (3), II. A (1), B (1), IV. A (1)	8	p. 3; II. 2, 3, 4
Competency (supervisor or consultant)	pp. 12, 13, 16	1.1, 2.2, 2.3	2.01; 2.02	II. A (1, 2, 3), B (2, 3), IV. B (1), V. A (1, 2, 3)	11	p. 2; II. 2, 3, 4
Consultation, peer review	p. 12	2.2, 2.3, 4.4	3.03	—	6	p. 2
Crisis procedures	p. 16	—	2.05	II. C (1, 2, 3)	5, 14	II. 8, 9
Diversity		—	—	III. B (2, 3), D (1)	4	I. 2; II.
Documentation of supervision	pp. 12, 14, 15	2.1.2, 5.1	—	III. A7, V. B (1)		II. 7
Due process		—	2.14; 3.16	V. B (2), C (1, 3)	13	—
Endorsement	pp. 12, 14	—	2.d; 2.13	V. C (1)	10	—
Evaluation	pp. 12, 14, 16	2.1.1, 2.1.2	2.d; 2.08; 2.12; 3.09; 3.15; 3.16	I. B (1), II. B (1, 2, 3), IV. A (1, 2, 3), IV. B (2, 3)	7	III. 10
Exploitation of supervisees	pp. 12, 13	3.2.1	—	II. D (1, 2, 3)	5	III. 4
Fees for supervision	p. 12	2.1.3	2.12; 2.13	III. A (2, 3), C (1)	—	—
Impairment		1.3	1.01; 1.02; 1.03; 1.04	—	9	—
Informed consent (clients)			2.09; 2.12; 2.14; 3.05; 3.07; 3.12; 3.15	I. C (1)	1, 2	III. 9
Informed consent (supervisees)		1.2		I. B (1, 2, 3), IV. A (1), B (2, 3)	3	I. 6; II. 1

Interruption or termination of supervision	—	1.4, 3.2.2	—	I. A, C (1, 2, 3)	—	—
Methods and responsibilities	pp. 1, 11, 12, 14, 16	1.4, 2.1.1, 2.1.2, 4.1, 5.2, 5.3	2.a, b, c, d; 2.03; 2.06; 2.07; 2.08; 2.12; 3.04; 3.08; 3.11; 3.13; 3.15	I. A (1, 2, 3), B, II. A, C (1, 2, 3), E (1, 2, 3), III. A (1), B (1), V. A (1, 2, 3)	1	p. 4; I. 3, 4, 5
Personal development	—	—	3.17; 3.18; 3.19	—	—	—
Privacy (supervisee)	pp. 12, 13, 14, 15	—	3.13; 3.14	—	—	—
Recording and observation	p. 14	2.1.1	1.01; 1.04, 2.06	—	—	—
Reporting obligations	p. 12	1.4, 4.3	—	—	—	—
Sexual contact, harassment	—	—	2.10	II. D (1, 2, 3)	5	— III. 8

Note. Dash indicates that no section of a code addresses a given issue. AAMFT = American Association for Marriage and Family Therapy; AAPC = American Association of Pastoral Counselors; ACES = Association for Counselor Education and Supervision; ASPPB = Association of State and Provincial Psychology Boards; CCE = Center for Credentialing & Education; and CPA = Canadian Psychology Association.
aThe ASPPB *Supervision Guidelines* includes three sections, each focusing on a different type of supervisee. Although not numbered in the document, for clarification, the parenthetical numbers refer to each of these sections: (1) doctoral level candidates; (2) credentialed nondoctoral personnel; and (3) uncredentialed personnel providing psychological services.

APPENDIX F: CLINICAL CASE PRESENTATION FORMAT

- Client description: In most cases, include the client's age, race, ethnic background, gender, and relationship or marital status. Include other information if relevant (e.g., occupation, education, religious affiliation, family constellation, medical issues, and previous treatment).

- Presenting problems, clinical impressions, diagnosis: Include both the client's conceptualization of his or her concerns as well as that of the psychotherapist. Interpretations and dynamics might also be presented.

- Background and history: Provide a brief summary of the client's significant life experiences and his or her feelings about and responses to them. This section might include information about abuse or other traumatic experiences, chemical use or abuse, social history and support system, and family history.

- Summary of treatment to date: Describe issues that have been addressed with this client, interventions made, and assessment of their effectiveness.

- Goals, objectives, and strategies: List the general agreed-upon goals, related objectives, and strategies developed to achieve them.

- Psychotherapist's goals for this consultation or supervision: Identify specific questions or issues about which feedback is being sought.

- Other: Include other pertinent information that does not fit into these categories. Examples include the psychotherapist's personal responses to the client, transference and countertransference dynamics, and the client's strengths and limitations.

APPENDIX G: SUMMARY OF CASE CONSULTATION OR SUPERVISION

Date: _____

Clinician: _____

Consultant(s) or Supervisor: _____

_____

Focus of Consultation or Supervision or Questions:

Recommendations:

APPENDIX H: CLINICAL RECORD CHECKLIST

Included	Missing	
_____	_____	Intake summary and assessment
_____	_____	Diagnosis (five axis)
_____	_____	Treatment plan
_____	_____	HIPAA consent, signed and dated
_____	_____	Informed consent to treatment or assessment, signed and dated
_____	_____	Fee agreement, signed and dated
_____	_____	Client data form (contact information, etc.)
_____	_____	Case log with dates of service and service provided
_____	_____	Billing records including dates, types, and length of service; fees; and payments
_____	_____	Authorization for release of information forms, signed and dated
_____	_____	Case progress notes, psychotherapy notes for each session
_____	_____	Record of supervision or consultation
_____	_____	Psychological test data
_____	_____	Discharge summary or notation regarding circumstances of termination
_____	_____	Other: _____

Comments:

APPENDIX I: CLINICAL RECORD QUALITY ASSESSMENT

	Below standards	Meets standards	Exceeds standards
Intake assessment	_____	_____	_____
Diagnosis supported	_____	_____	_____
Treatment plan	_____	_____	_____
Psychotherapy notes	_____	_____	_____
Case log	_____	_____	_____
Current	_____	_____	_____
Legible, accessible	_____	_____	_____
Documentation of supervision or consultation	_____	_____	_____
Psychological reports	_____	_____	_____
Discharge summary	_____	_____	_____

Comments:

REFERENCES

Adams, J. M. (2001). *On your side: Protecting your mental health practice from litigation*. East Hampton, NY: Mimesis.

Allen, J. (1976). Peer group supervision in family therapy. *Child Welfare, 55*, 183–189.

Allphin, D. (2005). Supervision as an alchemical process. In C. Driver & E. Martin (Eds.), *Supervision and the analytic attitude* (pp. 115–130). London, England: Whurr Publishers.

Alonso, A. (1983). A developmental theory of psychodynamic supervision. *The Clinical Supervisor, 1*(3), 23–26.

Alonso, A., & Rutan, J. S. (1988). Shame and guilt in psychotherapy supervision. *Psychotherapy, 25*, 576–581.

Altfeld, D. A., & Bernard, H. S. (1997). An experiential group model for group psychotherapy supervision. In C. E. Watkins Jr. (Ed.), *Handbook of psychotherapy supervision* (pp. 381–399). New York, NY: Wiley.

American Association for Marriage and Family Therapy. (2001). *AAMFT code of ethics*. Retrieved June 24, 2009, from http://www.aamft.org/resources/lrm_plan/Ethics/ethicscode2001.asp

American Association for Marriage and Family Therapy. (2007). *Approved supervisor designation standards and responsibilities handbook*. Alexandria, VA: Author.

American Association of Pastoral Counselors. (1994). *Code of ethics*. Retrieved June 25, 2009, from https://aapc.org/content/ethics

American Association of Pastoral Counselors. (1997). *Supervision standards of practice*. Fairfax, VA: Author.

American Association of Pastoral Counselors. (2009). Supervision standards. In *Membership standards and certification manual* (pp. 32–33). Fairfax, VA: Author.

American Counseling Association. (2005). *ACA code of ethics*. Retrieved June 25, 2009, from http://www.counseling.org/Resources/CodeOfEthics/TP/Home/CT2.aspx

American Medical Association. (2001). *Principles of medical ethics*. Retrieved June 25, 2009, from http://www.cirp.org/library/statements/ama/

American Psychiatric Association. (2009). *The principles of medical ethics with annotations especially applicable to psychiatry*. Retrieved June 29, 2009, from http://www.psych.org/MainMenu/PsychiatricPractice/Ethics/ResourcesStandards.aspx

American Psychological Association. (1993). Guidelines for providers of psychological services to ethnic, linguistic, and culturally diverse populations. *American Psychologist, 48*, 45–48.

American Psychological Association. (2002). *Ethical principles of psychologists and code of conduct*. Retrieved June 24, 2009, from http://www.apa.org/ethics/code2002.html

American Psychological Association. (2007). Record keeping guidelines. *American Psychologist, 62,* 993–1004.

American Psychological Association Ethics Committee. (2008). Report of the Ethics Committee, 2007. *American Psychologist, 63,* 452–459.

Anderson, S. K., & Kitchener, K. S. (1996). Nonromantic, nonsexual posttherapy relationships between psychologists and former clients: An exploratory study of critical incidents. *Professional Psychology: Research and Practice, 27,* 59–66.

Archer, R. P., & Peake, T. H. (Eds.). (1984). *Clinical training in psychotherapy.* New York, NY: Haworth Press.

Association for Counselor Education and Supervision. (1993). *Ethical guidelines for counseling supervisors.* Retrieved June 25, 2009, from http://www.acesonline.net/ethical_guidelines.asp

Association of State and Provincial Psychology Boards. (2003). *Supervision guidelines.* Montgomery, AL: Author.

Association of State and Provincial Psychology Boards. (2005). *ASPPB code of conduct.* Retrieved June 25, 2009, from http://www.ok.gov/OSBEP/documents/ASPPB_Code_of_Conduct_2005%5B1%5D.pdf

Ault-Richie, M. (1988). Teaching an integrated model of family therapy: Women and students, women as supervisors. *Journal of Psychotherapy and the Family, 3,* 175–192.

Barnett, J. E. (2000, September/October). The supervisee's checklist: Ethical, legal, and clinical issues. *The Maryland Psychologist, 4,* 18–20.

Barnett, J. E. (2005). Important ethical, legal issues surround supervision roles. *National Psychologist, 14,* 9.

Barnett, J. E. (2008). Mentoring, boundaries, and multiple relationships: Opportunities and challenges. *Journal Mentoring, 16,* 3–16.

Barnett, J. E., & Hillard, D. (2001). Psychologist distress and impairment: The availability, nature, and use of colleague assistance programs for psychologists. *Professional Psychology: Research and Practice, 32,* 205–210.

Barnett, J. E., Lazarus, A. A., Vasquez, M. J. T., Moorehead-Slaughter, O., & Johnson, W. B. (2007). Boundary issues and multiple relationships: Fantasy and reality. *Professional Psychology: Research and Practice, 38,* 401–410.

Bartell, P. A., & Rubin, L. J. (1990). Dangerous liaisons: Sexual intimacies in supervision. *Professional Psychology: Research and Practice, 21,* 442–450.

Bass, L. J., De Mers, S. T., Ogloff, J. R. P., Peterson, C., Pettifor, J. L., Reaves, R. P., et al. (1996). *Professional conduct and discipline in psychology.* Washington, DC: American Psychological Association.

Beck, J. S., Sarnat, J. E., & Barenstein, V. (2008). Psychotherapy-based approaches to supervision. In C. A. Falender & E. P. Shafranske (Eds.), *Casebook for clinical supervision: A competency-based approach* (pp. 57–96). Washington, DC: American Psychological Association.

Bellman, (2002). *The consultant's calling: Bringing who you are to what you do.* San Francisco, CA: Jossey-Bass.

Benowitz, M. S. (1991). *Sexual exploitation of female clients by female psychotherapists: Interviews with clients and a comparison to women exploited by male psychotherapists.* Unpublished doctoral dissertation, University of Minnesota, Minneapolis.

Berman, E. (1997). Psychoanalytic supervision as the crossroads of a relational matrix. In M. H. Rock (Ed.), *Psychodynamic supervision: Perspectives of the supervisor and the supervisee* (pp. 161–186). Northvale, NJ: Jason Aronson.

Bernard, J. M. (1992). The challenge of psychotherapy-based supervision: Making the pieces fit. *Counselor Education and Supervision, 31,* 232–237.

Bernard, J. M., & Goodyear, R. K. (2004). *Fundamentals of clinical supervision* (3rd ed.). Boston, MA: Pearson.

Bernard, J. M., & Goodyear, R. K. (2009). *Fundamentals of clinical supervision* (4th ed.). Upper Saddle River, NJ: Pearson.

Bersoff, D. (2003). *Ethical conflicts in psychology* (3rd ed.). Washington, DC: American Psychological Association.

Biaggio, M., Paget, T. L., & Chenoweth, M. S. (1997). A model for ethical management of faculty–student dual relationships. *Professional Psychology: Research and Practice, 28,* 184–198.

Bob, S. (1999). Narrative approaches to supervision and case formulation. *Psychotherapy: Theory, Research, Practice, Training, 36,* 146–153.

Bonosky, N. (1995). Boundary violations in social work supervision: Clinical, educational, and legal implications. *The Clinical Supervisor, 13*(2), 79–95.

Borders, L. D. (1990). Developmental changes during supervisees' first practicum. *The Clinical Supervisor, 8*(2), 157–167.

Borders, L. D., & Brown, L. L. (2005). *The new handbook of counseling supervision.* Mahwah, NJ: Erlbaum.

Bordin, E. S. (1983). A working alliance model of supervision. *Counseling Psychologist, 11,* 35–42.

Borys, D. S., & Pope, K. S. (1989). Dual relationships between therapist and client: A national study of psychologists, psychiatrists, and social workers. *Professional Psychology: Research and Practice, 20,* 283–293.

Boscolo, L., Cecchin, G., Hoffman, L., & Penn, P. (1987). *Milan systemic family therapy.* New York, NY: Basic Books.

Boszormenyi-Nagy, I. (1976). Behavior change through family change. In A. Burton (Ed.), *What makes behavior change possible?* (pp. 227–258). New York, NY: Brunner/Mazel.

Boszormenyi-Nagy, I., & Krasner, B. (1986). *Between give and take: A critical guide to contextual therapy.* New York, NY: Brunner/Mazel.

Boszormenyi-Nagy, I., & Ulrich, D. (1981). Contextual family therapy. In A. Gurman & D. Kniskern (Eds.), *Handbook of family therapy* (pp. 159–186). New York, NY: Brunner/Mazel.

Bowen, M. (1978). *Family therapy in clinical practice.* New York, NY: Jason Aronson.

Bowen, M. (1980). The key to the use of the genogram. In E. A. Carter & M. McGoldrick (Eds.), *The family life cycle: A framework for family therapy.* New York, NY: Gardner Press.

Bowen, M. (1988). *Family therapy in clinical practice* (4th ed.). Northvale, NJ: Jason Aronson.

Bowman, V. E., Hatley, L. D., & Bowman, R. L. (1995). Faculty–student relationships: The dual role controversy. *Counselor Education and Supervision 34,* 232–242.

Boyd, J. (1978). *Counselor supervision: Approaches, preparation, practices.* Muncie, IN: Accelerated Development.

Bradley, L. J., & Gould, L. J. (2001). Psychotherapy-based models of counselor supervision. In L. J. Bradley & N. Ladany (Eds.), *Counselor supervision: Principles, process, and practice* (3rd ed., pp. 147–175). Philadelphia, PA: Brunner-Routledge.

Bradley, L. J., & Ladany, N. (2001). *Counselor supervision: Principles, process, and practice* (3rd ed.). Philadelphia, PA: Brunner-Routledge.

Braverman, S. (1997). The use of genograms in supervision. In T. C. Todd & C. L. Storm (Eds.), *The complete systemic supervisor: Context, philosophy, and pragmatics.* (pp. 349–362). Boston, MA: Allyn & Bacon.

Bricklin, P., Bennett, B., & Carroll, W. (2003). *Understanding licensing board disciplinary procedures.* Washington, DC: American Psychological Association.

Bridge, P., & Bascue, L. O. (1990). Documentation of psychotherapy supervision. *Psychotherapy in Private Practice, 8,* 79–86.

Brightman, B. (1984–1985). Narcissistic issues in the training experience of the psychotherapist. *International Journal of Psychoanalytic Psychotherapy, 10,* 293–317.

Brown, D., Pryzwansky, W. B., & Schulte, A. C. (2001). *Psychological consultation: Introduction to theory and practice* (5th ed.). Boston, MA: Allyn & Bacon.

Burian, B. K., & Slimp, A. O. (2000). Social dual-role relationships during internship: A decision-making model. *Professional Psychology: Research and Practice, 31,* 332–338.

Burkard, A. W., Johnson, A. J., Madson, M. B., Pruitt, N. T., Contreras-Tadych, Kozlowski, J. M., et al. (2006). Supervisor cultural responsiveness and unresponsiveness in cross-cultural supervision. *Journal of Counseling Psychology, 53,* 288–301.

California Board of Psychology. (2008). *Laws and regulations booklet.* Sacramento, CA: Author

Campbell, C. D., & Gordon, M. C. (2003). Acknowledging the inevitable: Understanding multiple relationship in rural practice. *Professional psychology: Research and Practice, 34,* 430–434.

Campbell, J. M. (2000). *Becoming an effective supervisor: A workbook for counselors and psychotherapists.* Philadelphia, PA: Accelerated Development.

Canadian Psychological Association. (2000). *Canadian code of ethics for psychologists* (3rd ed.). Retrieved June 25, 2009, from http://www.cpa.ca/cpasite/userfiles/Documents/Canadian%20Code%20of%20Ethics%20for%20Psycho.pdf

Canadian Psychological Association. (2001). Companion manual to the *Canadian code of ethics for psychologists*. Ottawa, Ontario, Canada: Author.

Canadian Psychological Association. (2009). *Ethical guidelines for supervision in psychology: Teaching, research, practice, and administration*. Retrieved June 25, 2009, from http://www.cpa.ca/cpasite/userfiles/Documents/COESupGuideRevApproved7Feb09revisedfinal.pdf

Caplan, G. (1970). *The theory and practice of mental health consultation*. New York, NY: Basic Books.

Carroll, M. (1996). *Counseling supervision: Theory, skills, and practice*. London, England: Cassell.

Caruth, E. G. (1990). Interpersonal and intrapsychic complexities and vulnerabilities in the psychoanalytic supervisory process. In R. C. Lane (Ed.), *Psychoanalytic approaches to supervision* (pp. 181–193). New York, NY: Brunner/Mazel.

Cashwell, C. S., Looby, E. J., & Housley, W. F. (1997). Appreciating cultural diversity through clinical supervision. *The Clinical Supervisor, 15*(1), 75–85.

Caudill, O. B., Jr. (1996). Can therapists be vicariously liable for sexual misconduct? In L. E. Hedges, R. Hilton, V. W. Hilton, & O. B. Caudill Jr. (Eds.), *Therapists at risk: Perils of the intimacy of the therapeutic relationship* (pp. 269–273). Northvale, NJ: Jason Aronson.

Cecchin, G., Lane, G., & Ray, W. (1993). Form strategizing to nonintervention: Toward irreverence in systemic practice. *Journal of Marital and Family Therapy, 19*, 125–136.

Celenza, A. (2007). *Sexual boundary violations: Therapeutic, supervisory, and academic contexts*. Lanham, MD: Jason Aronson.

Center for Credentialing & Education. (2008). *The approved clinical supervisor (ACS) code of ethics*. Retrieved July 13, 2009, from http://www.cce-global.org/extras/cce-global/pdfs/acs_codeofethics.pdf

Chaiklin, H., & Munson, C. E. (1983). Peer consultation in social work. *The Clinical Supervisor, 1*(2), 21–34.

Chauvin, J. C., & Remley, T. P. (1996). Responding to allegations of unethical conduct. *Journal of Counseling and Development, 74*, 563–568.

Clemens, N. A. (2006). Dealing with the therapist's emotional responses. In J. H. Gold (Ed.), *Psychotherapy supervision and consultation in clinical practice* (pp. 35–58). Lanham, MD: Jason Aronson.

Cobia, D. C., & Boes, S. R. (2000). Professional disclosure statements and formal plans for supervision: Two strategies for minimizing the risk of ethical conflicts in post-master's supervision. *Journal of Counseling and Development, 78*, 293–296.

Cobia, D. C., & Pipes, R. B. (2002). Mandated supervision: An intervention for disciplined professionals. *Journal of Counseling and Development, 80*, 140–144.

Colapinto, J. (1988). Teaching the structural way. In H. A. Liddle, D. C. Breunlin, & R. C. Schwartz (Eds.), *Handbook of family therapy training and supervision* (pp. 17–37). New York, NY: Guilford Press.

Connell, G. (1984). An approach to supervision of symbolic-experiential psychotherapy. *Journal of Marital and Family Therapy, 10,* 273–280.

Connell, G., Mitten, T., & Whitaker, C. (1993). Reshaping family symbols: A symbolic–experiential perspective. *Journal of Marital and Family Therapy, 19,* 243–251.

Conroe, R. M., & Schank, J. A. (1989). Sexual intimacy in clinical supervision: Unmasking the silence. In G. R. Schoener, J. Milgrom, J. C. Gonsiorek, E. T. Luepker, & R. M. Conroe (Eds.), *Psychotherapists' sexual involvement with clients: Intervention and prevention* (pp. 245–262). Minneapolis, MN: Walk-In Counseling Center.

Constantine, M. G. (2001). Multiculturally-focused counseling supervision: Its relationship to trainees' multicultural counseling self-efficacy. *The Clinical Supervisor, 20*(1), 87.

Constantine, M. G., Fuertes, J. N., Roysircar, G., & Kindaichi, M. M. (2008). Multicultural competence: Clinical practice, training and supervision, and research. In W. B. Walsh (Ed.), *Biennial review of counseling psychology* (Vol. 1, pp. 97–127). New York, NY: Routledge/Taylor & Francis Group.

Constantine, M. G., Warren, A. K., & Miville, M. L. (2005). White racial identity dyadic interactions in supervision: Implications for supervisees' multicultural counseling competence. *Journal of Counseling Psychology, 52,* 490–496.

Cook, D. A., & Helms, J. E. (1988). Visible racial/ethnic group supervisees' satisfaction with cross-cultural supervision as predicted by relationship characteristics. *Journal of Counseling Psychology, 35,* 268–274.

Corey, G., Corey, M. S., & Callanan, P. (2007). *Issues and ethics in the helping professions* (7th ed.). Belmont, CA: Thompson Brooks/Cole.

Corey, M. S., & Corey, G. (2002). Groups: *Process and practice* (6th ed.). Pacific Grove, CA: Brooks/Cole.

Cormier, L. S., & Bernard, J. M. (1982). Ethical and legal responsibilities of clinical supervisors. *The Personnel and Guidance Journal, 60,* 486–491.

Coster, J. S., & Schwebel, M. (1997). Well functioning in professional psychologists. *Professional Psychology: Research and Practice, 28,* 5–13.

Cottone, R. R. (2005). Detrimental therapist–client relationships—Beyond thinking of "dual" or "multiple" roles: Reflections on the 2001 AAMFT Code of Ethics. *American Journal of Family Therapy, 33,* 1–17.

Cottone, R. R., & Tarvydas, V. M. (2003). *Ethical and professional issues in counseling* (2nd ed.). Upper Saddle River, NJ: Merrill Prentice Hall.

Council for Accreditation of Counseling and Related Educational Programs. (2001). *The 2001 standards.* Retrieved June 25, 2009, from http://www.cacrep.org/2001Standards.html

Counselman, E., & Gompert, P. (1993). Psychotherapy supervision in small leader-led groups. *Group, 17,* 25–32.

Crespi, T. D. (1995). Gender sensitive supervision: Exploring feminist perspectives for male and female supervisors. *The Clinical Supervisor, 13*(2), 19–29.

Daniels, J. A., & Larson, L. M. (2001). The impact of performance feedback on counseling self-efficacy and counselor anxiety. *Counselor Education and Supervision, 41,* 120–130.

Davenport, D. S. (1992). Ethical and legal problems with client-centered supervision. *Counselor Education and Supervision, 31,* 227–231.

Delany, D. J. (1972). A behavioral model for the practicum supervision of counselor candidates. *Counselor Education and Supervision, 12,* 46–50.

Dewald, P. A. (1987). *Learning process in psychoanalytic supervision: Complexities and challenges.* Madison, CT: International Universities Press.

Dewald, P. A. (1997). The process of supervision in psychoanalysis. In C. Watkins Jr. (Ed.), *Handbook of psychotherapy supervision* (pp. 31–43). New York, NY: Wiley.

Disney, M. J., & Stephens, A. M. (1994). *Legal issues in clinical supervision.* Alexandria, VA: American Counseling Association.

Doehrman, M. (1976). Parallel processes in supervision and psychotherapy. *Bulletin of the Menninger Clinic, 40,* 3–104.

Downs, L. (2003). A preliminary survey of relationships between counselor educators' ethics education and ensuing pedagogy and responses to attractions with counseling students. *Counseling and Values, 48,* 2–13.

Driver, C., & Martin, E. (Eds.). (2005). *Supervision and the analytic attitude.* London, England: Whurr Publishers.

Ebert, B. W. (2002). Dual-relationship prohibitions: A concept whose time never should have come. In A. A. Lazarus, & O. Zur (Eds.), *Dual relationships in psychotherapy* (pp. 169–209). New York, NY: Springer Publishing Company.

Eisenberg, S. (1956). *Supervision in the changing field of social work.* Philadelphia, PA: Jewish Family Service of Philadelphia.

Ekstein, R., & Wallerstein, R. S. (1958). *The teaching and learning of psychotherapy.* New York, NY: Basic.

Ekstein, R., & Wallerstein, R. S. (1972). *The teaching and learning of psychotherapy* (2nd ed.). New York, NY: International Universities Press.

Elizur, J. (1990). "Stuckness" in live supervision: Expanding the therapist's style. *Journal of Family Therapy, 12,* 267–280.

Ellis, A. (1989). Thoughts on supervising counselors and therapists. *Psychology: A Journal of Human Behavior, 26,* 3–5.

Ellis, M. V., & Ladany, N. (1997). Inferences concerning supervisee and clients in clinical supervision: An integrative review. In C. E. Watkins Jr. (Ed.), *Handbook of psychotherapy supervision* (pp. 447–507). New York, NY: Wiley.

Emerson, S. (1995). A different final exam: Using students' own family genograms. *The Family Journal, 39*, 57–58.

Epstein, L. (2001). Collusive selective inattention to the negative impact of the supervisory interaction. In S. Gill (Ed.), *The supervisory alliance: Facilitating the psychotherapist's learning experience* (pp. 139–163). Northvale, NJ: Jason Aronson.

Estrada, D. (2005). Multicultural conversations in supervision: The impact of the supervisor's racial/ethnic background. *Guidance & Counseling, 21*(1), 14–20.

Falender, C., & Shafranske, E. (2004). *Clinical supervision: A competency-based approach.* Washington, DC: American Psychological Association.

Fall, M., & Sutton, J. M. (2004). Clinical supervision: A *handbook for practitioners.* Boston, MA: Pearson Education.

Falvey, J. E. (1987). *Handbook of administrative supervision.* Alexandria, VA: Association for Counselor Education and Supervision.

Falvey, J. E. (2002). *Managing clinical supervision: Ethical practice and legal risk management.* Pacific Grove, CA: Brooks/Cole.

Falvey, J. E., Caldwell, C. F., & Cohen, C. R. (2002). *Documentation in supervision: The focused risk management supervision system (FoRMSS).* Pacific Grove, CA: Brooks/Cole.

Falvey, J. E., & Cohen, C. R. (2003). The buck stops here: Documenting clinical supervision. *The Clinical Supervisor, 22*(2), 63–80.

Fisher, B. L. (1989). Differences between supervision of beginning and advanced therapists: Hogan's hypothesis empirically revisited. *The Clinical Supervisor, 7*(1), 57–74.

Fisher, C. B. (2003). *Decoding the ethics code: A practical guide for psychologists.* Thousand Oaks, CA: Sage.

Fleer, J. (2000, Summer). When the state licensing board comes to call. *The Independent Practitioner,* 212–213.

Fleming, J. (1953). The role of supervision in psychiatric training. *Bulletin of the Menninger Clinic, 17*, 157–159.

Fleming, J., & Benedek, T. (1964). Supervision: A method of teaching psychoanalysis. *Psychoanalytic Quarterly, 33*, 71–96.

Follette, W. C., & Callaghan, G. M. (1995). Do as I do, not as I say: A behavior-analytic approach to supervision. *Professional Psychology: Research and Practice, 26*, 413–421.

Frame, M. W., & Williams, C. B. (2005). A model of ethical decision making from a multicultural perspective. *Counseling and Values, 49*, 165–179.

Frawley-O'Dea, M. G., & Sarnat, J. E. (2001). *The supervisory relationship: A contemporary psychodynamic approach.* New York, NY: Guilford Press.

Freeman, S. C. (1993a). Reiterations on client-centered supervision. *Counselor Education and Supervision, 21*, 213–215.

Freeman, S. C. (1993b). Structure in counseling supervision. *The Clinical Supervisor,* *11*(1), 245–252.

French, J. R. P., Jr., & Raven, B. (1959). Bases of social power. In D. Cartwright (Ed.), *Studies in social power*. Ann Arbor: University of Michigan.

Freud, S. (1973). Analysis of a phobia in a five-year-old boy. In J. Strachey (Ed. & Trans.), *The standard edition of the complete psychological works of Sigmund Freud* (Vol. 10). London, England: Hogarth Press. (Original work published 1909)

Freud, S. (1986). On the history of the psychoanalytic movement. In J. Strachey (Ed.) & J. Riviere (Trans.), *The standard edition of the complete psychological works of Sigmund Freud* (Vol. 14). London, England: Hogarth Press. (Original work published 1914)

Friedlander, M. L., Siegel, S., & Brenock, K. (1989). Parallel process in counseling and supervision: A case study. *Journal of Counseling Psychology, 36,* 149–157.

Fruzzetti, A. E., Waltz, J. A., & Linehan, M. M. (1997). Supervision in dialectical behavior therapy. In C. Watkins Jr. (Ed.), *Handbook of psychotherapy supervision* (pp. 84–100). New York, NY: Wiley.

Fukuyama, M. A. (1994). Critical incidents in multicultural counseling supervision: A phenomenological approach to supervision research. *Counselor Education and Supervision, 34,* 142–151.

Gabbard, G. O. (1994). Teetering on the precipice: A commentary on Lazarus's "How certain boundaries and ethics diminish therapeutic effectiveness." *Ethics & Behavior, 4,* 283–286.

Gabbard, G. O. (1995). Transference and countertransference in the psychotherapy of therapists charged with sexual misconduct. *Psychiatric Annals, 25,* 100–105.

Gabbard, G. O., & Lester, E. P. (1995). *Boundaries and boundary violations in psychoanalysis*. Washington, DC: American Psychiatric Publishing.

Gaoni, B., & Newmann, M. (1974). Supervision from the point of view of the supervisee. *American Journal of Psychotherapy, 23,* 108–114.

Garcia, J. G., Cartwright, B. Winston, S. M., & Borzuchowska, B. (2003). A transcultural integrative model for ethical decision making in counseling. *Journal of Counseling & Development, 81,* 268–277.

Gatmon, D., Jackson, D., Koshkarian, L., Martos-Perry, N., Molina, A., Patel, N., et al. (2001). Exploring ethnic, gender, and sexual orientation variables in supervision: Do they really matter? *Journal of Multicultural Counseling and Development, 29,* 102–112.

Getz, H. G., & Protinsky, H. O. (1994). Training marriage and family counselors: A family of origin approach. *Counselor Education and Supervision, 33,* 183–190.

Getzel, G. S., & Salmon, R. (1985). Group supervision: An organizational approach. *The Clinical Supervisor, 3*(1), 27–43.

Gibson, P. A. (2008). Teaching ethical decision making: Designing a personal value portrait to ignite creativity and promote personal engagement in case method analysis. *Ethics & Behavior, 18,* 340–352.

Gill, S. (Ed.). (2001). *The supervisory alliance: Facilitating the psychotherapist's learning experience*. Northvale, NJ: Jason Aronson.

Glasser, R. D., & Thorp, J. S. (1986). Unethical intimacy: A survey of sexual contact between psychology educators and female graduate students. *American Psychologist, 41*, 43–51.

Glenn, E., & Serovich, J. M. (1994). Documentation of family therapy supervision: A rationale and method. *American Journal of Family Therapy, 22*, 345–355.

Gloria, A. M., Hird, J. S., & Tao, K. W. (2008). Self-reported multicultural supervision competence of white predoctoral intern supervisors. *Training and Education in Professional Psychology, 2*, 129–136.

Gonsalvez, C. J., Oades, L. G., & Freestone, J. (2002). The objectives approach to clinical supervision: Towards integration and empirical evaluation. *Australian Psychologist, 37*, 68–77.

Gonsiorek, J. C. (Ed.). (1995). *Breach of trust: Sexual exploitation by health care professionals and clergy*. Thousand Oaks, CA: Sage.

Goodman, R. W., & Carpenter-White, A. (1996). The family autobiography assignment: Some ethical considerations. *Counselor Education and Supervision, 35*, 230–238.

Goodyear, R. K., & Guzzard, C. R. (2000). Psychotherapy supervision and training. In S. D. Brown & R. W. Lent (Eds.) *Handbook of counseling psychology* (3rd ed., pp. 83–108). New York, NY: Wiley.

Goodyear, R. K., & Nelson, M. L. (1997). The major formats of psychotherapy supervision. In C. E. Watkins, *Handbook of psychotherapy supervision* (pp. 328–344). New York, NY: Wiley.

Gordon, R. (2005, September). The ethics of supervising a family member. *The Pennsylvania Psychologist*, 5–6.

Gottlieb, M. C. (1993). Avoiding dual relationships: A decision-making model. *Psychotherapy, 30*, 41–48.

Gottlieb, M. C., Robinson, K., & Younggren, J. N. (2007). Multiple relations in supervision: Guidance for administrators, supervisors, and students. *Professional Psychology: Research and Practice, 38*, 241–247.

Grinberg, L. (1997). On transference and countertransference and the technique of supervision. In B. Martindale, M. Mörner, M. E. C. Rodriguez, & J. P. Vidit (Eds.), *Supervision and its vicissitudes*. London, England: European Federation for Psychoanalytic Psychotherapy in the Public Health Services.

Guest, C. L., & Dooley, K (1999). Supervisor malpractice; Liability to the supervisee in clinical supervision. *Counselor Education and Supervision, 38*, 269–279.

Gutheil, T. G. (1993). The concept of boundaries in clinical practice: Theoretical and risk management dimensions. *American Journal of Psychiatry, 150*, 188–196.

Gutheil, T. G., & Gabbard, G. O. (1993). Obstacles to the dynamic understanding of therapist patient sexual relations. *American Journal of Psychotherapy, 46*, 515–525.

Gutheil, T. G., & Simon, R. I. (2002). Non-sexual boundary crossings and boundary violations: The ethical dimension. *Psychiatric Clinics of North America, 25,* 585–592.

Haas, L. J., & Malouf, J. L. (2005). *Keeping up the good work: A practitioner's guide to mental health ethics* (4th ed.). Sarasota, FL: Professional Resource Exchange.

Hackney, H. L., & Goodyear, R. K. (1984). Carl Rogers' client-centered supervision. In R. F. Levant & J. M. Schlien (Eds.), *Client-centered therapy and the person-centered approach* (pp. 278–296). New York, NY: Praeger Publishers.

Haley, J. (1976). *Problem solving therapy.* San Francisco, CA: Jossey-Bass.

Haley, J. (1980). *Leaving home: Therapy of disturbed young people.* New York, NY: McGraw-Hill.

Haley, J. (1987). *Problem solving therapy* (2nd ed.). San Francisco, CA: Jossey-Bass.

Hammel, G. A., Olkin, R., & Taube, D. O. (1996). Student–educator sex in clinical and counseling psychology doctoral training. *Professional Psychology: Research and Practice, 27,* 93–97.

Handelsman, M. M., Gottlieb, M.C., & Knapp, S. C. (2005). Training ethical psychologists: An acculturation model. *Professional Psychology: Research and Practice, 36,* 59–65.

Harrar, W. R., VandeCreek, L., & Knapp, S. (1990). Ethical and legal aspects of clinical supervision. *Professional Psychology: Research and Practice, 21,* 37–41.

Harris, E. (2003, September). *Legal and ethical risks and risk management in professional practice: Sequence 1.* Symposium conducted at a meeting of the Minnesota Psychological Association, Saint Paul, MN.

Hart, G. (1982). *The process of clinical supervision.* Baltimore, MD: University Park Press.

Harvey, O. J., Hunt, D. E., & Schroder, H. M. (1961). *Conceptual systems and personality organization.* New York, NY: Wiley.

Hawkins, P., & Shohet, R. (2006). *Supervision in the helping professions: An individual, group, and organizational approach* (3rd ed.). Philadelphia, PA: Open University Press.

Hayes, J. A., McCracken, J. E., McClanahan, M. K., Hill, C., Harp, J. S., & Carozzoni, P. (1998). Therapist perspectives on countertransference: Qualitative data in search of a theory. *Journal of Counseling Psychology, 45,* 468–482.

Haynes, R., Corey, G., & Moulton, P. (2003). *Clinical supervision in the helping professions: A practical guide.* Pacific Grove, CA: Brooks/Cole.

Hays, P. A. (2008). *Addressing cultural complexities in practice: Assessment, diagnosis, and therapy* (2nd ed.), Washington, DC: American Psychological Association.

Hedges, L. E. (2000). *Facing the challenge of liability in psychotherapy: Practicing defensively.* Northvale, NJ: Jason Aronson.

Helbok, C. M., Marinelli, R. P., & Walls, R. T. (2006). National survey of ethical practices across rural and urban communities. *Professional Psychology: Research and Practice, 37,* 36–44.

Herlihy, B., & Corey, G. (1996). *ACA ethical standards casebook* (5th ed.). Alexandria, VA: American Counseling Association.

Herlihy, B., & Corey, G. (2006). *Boundary issues in counseling: Multiple roles and responsibilities* (2nd ed.). Alexandria, VA: American Counseling Association.

Hernandez, P. (2008). The cultural context model in clinical supervision. *Training and Education in Professional Psychology, 2*, 10–17.

Heru, A. M., Strong, D. R., Price, M., & Recupero, P. R. (2004). Boundaries in psychotherapy supervision. *American Journal of Psychotherapy, 58*, 76–89.

Hess, A. K. (1987). Psychotherapy supervision: Stages, Buber, and a theory of relationship. *Professional Psychology: Research and Practice, 18*, 251–259.

Hess, A. K. (2008). Legal and ethical considerations in psychotherapy supervision. In A. K. Hess, K. D. Hess, & T. H. Hess (Eds.), *Psychotherapy supervision: Theory, research, and practice* (pp. 521–536). Hoboken, NJ: Wiley.

Hill, M., Glaser, K., & Harden, J. (1995). A feminist model for ethical decision making. In E. J. Rave & C. C. Larsen (Eds.), *Ethical decision making in therapy: Feminist perspectives* (pp. 18–37). New York, NY: Guilford Press.

Hilton, D., Russell, R., & Salmi, S. (1995). The effects of supervisor's race and level of support on perceptions of supervision. *Journal of Counseling and Development, 73*, 559–563.

Hilton, V. W. (1997). The therapist's response to accusations: How to avoid complaints and suits. In L. E. Hedges, R. Hilton, V. W. Hilton, & O. B. Caudill Jr., *Therapists at risk: Perils of the intimacy of the therapeutic relationship* (pp. 99–107). Northvale, NJ: Jason Aronson.

Hipp, J. L., & Munson, C. E. (1995). The partnership model: A feminist supervision/consultation perspective. *The Clinical Supervisor 13*(1), 23–38.

Hogan, R. (1964). Issues and approaches in supervision. *Psychotherapy: Theory, Research and Practice, 1*, 139–141.

Holloway, E. L. (1987). Developmental models of supervision: Is it development? *Professional Psychology: Research and Practice, 18*, 209–216.

Holloway, E. L. (1995). *Clinical supervision: A systems approach.* Thousand Oaks, CA: Sage.

Holloway, E. L., & Carroll, M. (1999). *Training counselling supervisors: Strategies, methods and techniques.* London, England: Sage.

Holloway, E. L., & Johnston, R. (1985). Group supervision: Widely practiced but poorly understood. *Counselor Education and Supervision, 24*, 332–340.

Hopkins, B. R., & Anderson, B. S. (1990). *The counselor and the law* (3rd ed.). Alexandria, VA: American Association for Counseling and Development.

Hoyt, M. F., & Goulding, R. (1989). Resolution of a transference–countertransference impasse: Using Gestalt techniques in supervision. *Transactional Analysis Journal, 19*, 201–211.

Hyman, M. (2008). Psychoanalytic supervision. In A. K. Hess, K. D. Hess, & T. H. Hess (Eds.), *Psychotherapy supervision: Theory, research, and practice* (2nd ed., pp. 97–113). Hoboken, NJ: Wiley.

Inman, A. G., & Ladany, N. (2008). Research: The state of the field. In A. K. Hess, K. D. Hess, & T. H. Hess (Eds.), *Psychotherapy supervision: Theory, research, and practice* (2nd ed., pp. 500–520). Hoboken, NJ: Wiley.

Issacharoff, A. (1984). Countertransference in supervision: Therapeutic consequences for the supervisee. In L. Caligor, P. M. Bromberg, & J. D. Meltzer (Eds.), *Clinical perspectives on the supervision of psychoanalysis and psychotherapy* (pp. 89–105). New York, NY: Plenum Press.

Jacobs, C. (1991). Violations of the supervisory relationship: An ethical and educational blind spot. *Social Work, 36*, 130–135.

Jacobs, D. (2001). Narcissism, eroticism, and envy in the supervisory relationship. *Journal of the American Psychoanalytic Association, 49*, 813–829.

Jacobs, D., David, P., & Meyer, D. J. (1995). *The supervisory encounter: A guide for teachers of psychotherapy and psychoanalysis.* New Haven, CT: Yale University Press.

Jakubowski-Spector, P., Dustin, R., & George, R. L. (1971). Toward developing a behavioral counselor education model. *Counselor Education and Supervision, 11*, 242–250.

Jarmon, H. (1990). The supervisory experience: An object relations perspective. *Psychotherapy, 22*, 195–201.

Johnson, M. T. (1995). Case examines supervisor liability. *Monitor, 26*, 15.

Johnson, W. B., Forrest, L., Rodolfa, E., Elman, N. S., Robiner, W. N., & Schaffer, J. (2008). Addressing professional competence problems in trainees: Some ethical considerations. *Professional Psychology: Research and Practice, 39*, 589–599.

Johnson, W. B., Ralph, J., & Johnson, S. J. (2005). Managing multiple roles in embedded environments: The case of aircraft carrier psychology. *Professional Psychology: Research and Practice, 36*, 73–81.

Jordan, K. (1998). The cultural experiences and identified needs of the ethnic minority supervisee in the context of Caucasian supervision. *Family Therapy, 25*, 181–187.

Juhnke, G. A. (1996). Solution-focused supervision: Promoting supervisee skills and confidence through successful solutions. *Counselor Education and Supervision, 36*, 48–57.

Juhnke, G. A., Kelly, V. A., & Cooper, J. B. (2008). Mandated supervision: Trouble for an external consulting clinical supervisor. In L. E. Tyson, J. R. Culbreth, & J. A. Harrington (Eds.), *Critical incidents in clinical supervision: Addictions, community, and school counseling* (pp. 25–32). Alexandria, VA: American Counseling Association.

Kadushin, A. (1992). *Supervision in social work* (3rd ed.). New York, NY: Columbia University Press.

Kadushin, A., & Harkness, D. (2002). *Supervision in social work* (4th ed.). New York, NY: Columbia University Press.

Kaiser, T. L. (1997). *Supervisory relationships: Exploring the human element.* Pacific Grove, CA: Brooks/Cole.

Kaser-Boyd, N. (2008). Supervising psychotherapy of abuse survivors. In A. K. Hess, K. D. Hess, & T. H. Hess (Eds.), *Psychotherapy supervision: Theory, research, and practice* (2nd ed., pp. 315–339). Hoboken, NJ: Wiley.

Kaslow, N. J., Celano, M. P., & Stanton, M. (2005). Training in family psychology: A competencies-based approach. *Family Process, 44,* 337–353.

Kaslow, N. J., Forrest, L., Van Horne, B. A., Huprich, S. K., Pantesco, V. F., Grus, C. L., et al. (2007). Recognizing, assessing, and intervening with problems of professional competence. *Professional Psychology: Research and Practice, 38,* 479–492.

Keel, L. P., & Brown, S. P. (1999, July). Professional disclosure statements. *Counseling Today, 42,* 14, 33.

Keith-Spiegel, P., & Koocher, G. P. (1998). *Ethics in psychology: Professional standards and cases* (2nd ed.) New York, NY: Oxford University Press.

Kenfield, J. A. (1993). *Clinical supervision of licensed psychologists: Nature of and satisfaction with the supervisory relationship.* Unpublished doctoral dissertation, University of Minnesota, Minneapolis.

Knapp, S. J., & Slattery, J. M. (2004). Professional boundaries in nontraditional settings. *Professional Psychology: Research and Practice, 35,* 553–558.

Knapp, S. J., & VandeCreek, L. (1997). Ethical and legal aspects of clinical supervision. In C. E. Watkins (Ed.), *Handbook of psychotherapy supervision* (pp. 589–599). New York, NY: Wiley.

Knapp, S. J., & VandeCreek, L. (2003). *A guide to the 2002 revision of the American Psychological Association's ethics code.* Sarasota, FL: Professional Resource Press.

Knapp, S. J., & VandeCreek, L. (2006). *Practical ethics for psychologists: A positive approach.* Washington: DC: American Psychological Association.

Knudson-Martin, C. (1994). The female voice: Applications to Bowen's family systems theory. *Journal of Marital and Family Therapy, 20,* 35–46.

Kolbert, J. B., Morgan, B., & Brendel, J. M. (2002). Faculty and student perceptions of dual relationships within counselor education: A qualitative analysis. *Counselor Education and Supervision, 41,* 193–206.

Koocher, G. P., & Keith-Spiegel, P. (1998). *Ethics in psychology: Professional standards and cases* (2nd ed.). New York, NY: Oxford University Press.

Koocher, G. P., & Keith-Spiegel, P. (2006). *Ethics in psychology: Professional standards and cases* (3rd ed.). New York, NY: Oxford University Press.

Kopp, R. R., & Robles, L. (1989). A single-session, therapist-focused model of supervision of resistance based on Adlerian psychology. *Individual Psychology, 45,* 212–219.

Kramer, J. (1985). Family interfaces: Transgenerational patterns. New York, NY: Brunner/Mazel.

Krause, A. A., & Allen, G. J. (1988). Perceptions of counselor supervision: An examination of Stoltenberg's model from the perspectives of supervisor and supervisee. *Journal of Counseling Psychology, 35,* 77–80.

Kugler, P. (1995). *Jungian perspectives on clinical supervision.* Einsiedeln, Switzerland: Daimon.

Kurpius, D., Gibson, G., Lewis, J., & Corbet, M. (1991). Ethical issues in supervision counseling practitioners. *Counselor Education and Supervision, 31,* 48–57.

Ladany, N., Brittan-Powell, & Pannu, R. K. (1997). The influence of supervisory racial identity interaction and racial matching on the supervisory working alliance and supervisee multicultural competence. *Counselor Education and Supervision, 34,* 284–304.

Ladany, N., Constantine, M. G., Miller, K., Erickson, C. D., & Muse-Burke, J. L. (2000). Supervisor countertransference: A qualitative investigation into its identification and description. *Journal of Counseling Psychology, 47,* 102–115.

Ladany, N., Friedlander, M. L., & Nelson, M. L. (2005). *Critical events in psychotherapy supervision: An interpersonal approach.* Washington, DC: American Psychological Association.

Ladany, N., Inman, A. G., Constantine, M. G., & Hofheinz, E. W. (1997). Supervisee multicultural case conceptualization ability and self-reported multicultural competence as functions of supervisee racial identity and supervisor focus. *Journal of Counseling Psychology, 44,* 284–293.

Lamb, D. H., & Catanzaro, S. L. (1998). Sexual and nonsexual boundary violations involving psychologists, clients, supervisees, and students: Implications for professional practice. *Professional Psychology: Research and Practice, 29,* 498–503.

Lamb, D. H., Catanzaro, S. J., & Moorman, A. S. (2003). Psychologists reflect on their sexual relationships with clients, supervisees, and students: Occurrence, impact, rationales, and collegial intervention. *Professional Psychology: Research and Practice, 34,* 102–207.

Landis, L. L., & Young, M. E. (1994). The reflecting team in counselor education: Special section: Marriage and family training methods. *Counselor Education and Supervision 33,* 210–218.

Lazarus, A. A., & Zur, O. (Eds.). (2002). *Dual relationships and psychotherapy.* New York, NY: Springer Publishing Company.

Leong, F. T. L. (1994). Emergence of the cultural dimension: The roles and impact of culture on counseling supervision. *Counselor Education and Supervision, 34,* 114–116.

Levine, F. M., & Tilker, H. A. (1974). A behavior modification approach to supervision and psychotherapy. *Psychotherapy: Theory, Research and Practice, 11,* 182–188.

Lewis, B. J. (2004, Spring). When the licensing board comes a' calling: Managing the stress of licensing board investigations. *The Independent Practitioner, 24,* 121–124.

Liddle, H. A. (1991). Training and supervision in family therapy: A comprehensive and critical analysis. In A. S. Gurman & D. P. Kniskern (Eds.), *Handbook of family therapy* (Vol. 2, pp. 638–697). New York, NY: Burnner/Mazel.

Liddle, H. A., Becker, D., & Diamond, G. M. (1997). Family therapy supervision. In C. E. Watkins Jr. (Ed.), *Handbook of psychotherapy supervision* (pp. 400–421). New York, NY: Wiley.

Liddle, H. A., Breunlin, D. C., & Schwartz, R. C. (1988). *Handbook of family therapy training and supervision.* New York, NY: Guilford Press.

Liddle, H. A., Breunlin, D. C., Schwartz, R. C., & Constantine, J. A. (1984). Training family therapy supervisors: Issues of content, form, and context. *Journal of Marital and Family Therapy, 10,* 139–150.

Liddle, H. A., & Saba, G. W. (1982). Teaching family therapy at the introductory level: A conceptual model emphasizing a pattern which connects training and therapy. *Journal of Marital and Family Therapy, 8,* 63–72.

Liese, B. S., & Alford, B. A. (1998). Recent advances in cognitive therapy supervision. *Journal of Cognitive Psychotherapy, 12,* 91–94.

Liese, B. S., & Beck, J. S. (1997). Cognitive therapy supervision. In C. Watkins Jr. (Ed.), *Handbook of psychotherapy supervision* (pp. 114–133). New York, NY: Wiley.

Littrell, J. M., Lee-Borden, N., & Lorenz, J. (1979). A developmental framework for counseling supervision. *Counselor Education and Supervision. 19,* 129–136.

Loganbill, C., Hardy, E., & Delworth, U. (1982). Supervision: A conceptual model. *The Counseling Psychologist, 10,* 3–42.

Lopez, S. R. (1997). Cultural competence in psychotherapy: A guide for clinicians and their supervisors. In C. E. Watkins Jr. (Ed.), *Handbook of psychotherapy supervision* (pp. 570–588). New York, NY: Wiley.

Love, P. (2001). *The truth about love: The highs, the lows, and how you can make love last forever.* New York, NY: Simon & Schuster.

Lovell, C. (1999). Supervisee cognitive complexity and the integrated developmental model. *The Clinical Supervisor, 18*(1), 191–201.

Luepker, E. T. (2003). *Record keeping in psychotherapy and counseling: Protecting confidentiality and the professional relationship.* New York, NY: Brunner-Routledge.

Madanes, C. (1981). *Strategic family therapy.* San Francisco, CA: Jossey-Bass.

Madanes, C. (1984). *Behind the one-way mirror.* San Francisco, CA: Jossey-Bass.

Mahoney, M. J. (1991). *Human change process: The scientific foundations of psychotherapy.* New York, NY: Guilford Press.

Maslow, A. H. (1998). *Toward a psychology of being* (3rd ed.) New York, NY: Wiley.

Masters, M. A. (1992). The use of positive reframing in the context of supervision. *Journal of Counseling and Development, 70,* 387–390.

McCarthy, P., DeBell, C., Kanuha, V., & McLeod, J. (1988). Myths of supervision: Identifying the gaps between theory and practice. *Counselor Education and Supervision, 28,* 22–28.

McCarthy, P., Sugden, S., Koker, M., Lamendola, F., Mauer, S., & Renninger, S. (1995). A practical guide to informed consent in clinical supervision. *Counselor Education and Supervision, 35,* 130–138.

McCutcheon, S. R. (2008). Addressing problems of insufficient competence during the internship year. *Training and Education in Professional Psychology, 2,* 210–214.

McDaniel, S., Weber, T., & McKeever, J. (1983). Multiple theoretical approaches to supervision: Choices in family therapy training. *Family Process, 22,* 491–500.

McGoldrick, M., & Gerson, R. (1985). *Genograms in family assessment.* New York, NY: Norton.

Miller, G. M., & Larrabee, M. J. (1995). Sexual intimacy in counselor education and supervision: A national survey. *Counselor Education and Supervision, 34,* 332–343.

Milne, D. L., & James, I. A. (2000). A systematic review of effective cognitive-behavioural supervision. *British Journal of Clinical Psychology, 39,* 111–129.

Milne, D. L., & James, I. A. (2002). The observed impact of training on competence in clinical supervision. *British Journal of Clinical Psychology, 41,* 55–72.

Minuchin, S. (1974). *Families and family therapy.* Cambridge, MA: Harvard University Press.

Minuchin, S., & Fishman, H. (1981). Family therapy techniques. Cambridge, MA: Harvard University Press.

Minuchin, S., Lee, W., & Simon, G. M. (1996). *Mastering family therapy: Journeys of growth and transformation.* New York, NY: Wiley.

Miville, M. L., Rosa, D., & Constantine, M. G. (2005). Building multicultural competence in clinical supervision. In M. G. Constantine & D. W. Sue (Eds.), *Strategies for building multicultural competence in mental health and educational settings* (pp. 192–211). Hoboken, NJ: Wiley.

Moleski, S. M., & Kiselica, M. S. (2005). Dual relationships: A continuum ranging from the destructive to the therapeutic. *Journal of Counseling and Development, 83,* 3–11.

Monk, G., Winslade, J., Crocket, K., & Epston, D. (Eds.). (1997). *Narrative therapy in practice: The archeology of hope.* San Francisco, CA: Jossey-Bass.

Montalvo, B. (1973). Aspects of live supervision. *Family Process, 12,* 343–359.

Montgomery, J. J., Hendricks, C. B., & Bradley, L. J. (2001). Using systems perspectives in supervision. *Family Journal: Counseling and Therapy for Couples and Families, 9,* 305–313.

Montgomery, L. M., Cupit, B. E., & Wimberley, T. K. (1999). Complaints, malpractice, and risk management: Professional issues and personal experiences. *Professional Psychology: Research and Practice, 30,* 402–410.

Moore, B. E., & Fine, B. D. (Eds.) (1990). *Psychoanalytic terms and concepts*. New Haven, CT: American Psychoanalytic Association and Yale University Press.

Morgan, M. M., & Sprenkle, D. H. (2007). Toward a common-factors approach to supervision. *Journal of Marital and Family Therapy, 33,* 1–17.

Mueller, W. J. (1982). Issues in the application of "Supervision: A conceptual model" to dynamically oriented supervision: A reaction paper. *Counseling Psychologist, 10,* 43–46.

Muesser, K. T., & Liberman, R. P. (1995). Behavior therapy in practice. In B. M. Bongar & L. E. Beutler (Eds.), *Comprehensive textbook of psychotherapy: Theory and practice* (pp. 84–110). New York, NY: Oxford University Press.

Nagy, T. F. (2005). *Ethics in plain English: An illustrative casebook for psychologists* (2nd ed.). Washington, DC: American Psychological Association.

National Association of Alcohol and Drug Abuse Counselors. (2008). *Code of ethics*. Retrieved Jun 25, 2009, from http://www.naadac.org/index.php?option=com_content&view=article&id=185&Itemid=115

National Association of Social Workers. (1994). *Guidelines for clinical social work supervision*. Washington, DC: Author.

National Association of Social Workers. (2005). *Standards for clinical social work in social work practice*. Retrieved June 25, 2009, from http://www.socialworkers.org/practice/standards/NASWClinicalSWStandards.pdf

National Association of Social Workers. (2008). *Code of ethics*. Retrieved June 25, 2009, from http://www.socialworkers.org/pubs/code/code.asp

Neufeldt, S. A. (2007). *Supervision strategies for the first practicum* (3rd ed.). Alexandria, VA: American Counseling Association.

Neufeldt, S. A., Karno, M. P., & Nelson, M. L. (1996). A qualitative study of experts' conceptualizations of supervisee reflectivity. *Journal of Counseling Psychology, 43,* 3–9.

Nevels, R., & Maar, J. (1985). A supervision for teaching structural/strategic therapy in a limited setting. *Journal of Psychology, 199,* 347–353.

Newirth, J. (1990). The mastery of countertransferential anxiety: An object relations view of the supervisory process. In R. Lane (Ed.), *Psychodynamic approaches to supervision* (pp. 157–174). New York, NY: Brunner/Mazel.

Nigro, T. (2004). Counselors' experiences with problematic dual relationships. *Ethics & Behavior, 14,* 51–64.

Norcross, J. C., & Halgin, R. P. (1997). Integrative approaches to psychotherapy supervision. In C. E. Watkins Jr. (Ed.), *Handbook of psychotherapy supervision* (pp. 203–222). New York, NY: Wiley.

Norcross, J. C., Prochaska, J. O., & Farber, J. (1993). Psychologists conducting psychotherapy: New findings and historical comparisons of the psychotherapy division membership. *Psychotherapy, 30,* 692–697.

Ogren, M. L., Jonsson, C. O., & Sundin, E. (2005). Group supervision in psychotherapy. The relationship between focus, group climate and perceived attained skill. *Journal of Clinical Psychology, 61,* 373–389.

Osborn, C. J., & Davis, T. E. (1996). The supervision contract. Making it perfectly clear. *The Clinical Supervisor, 14*(2), 121–134.

Osipow, S., & Fitzgerald, I. (1986). An occupational analysis of counseling psychology: How special is the specialty? *American Psychologist, 41,* 535–545.

Pack-Brown, S. P., & Williams, C. B. (2003). *Ethics in a multicultural context.* Thousand Oaks, CA: Sage.

Parihar, B. (1983). Group supervision: A naturalistic field study in a specialty unit. *The Clinical Supervisor, 1*(4), 3–14.

Parry, A., & Doan, R. E. (1994). *Story re-visions: Narrative therapy in the postmodern world.* New York, NY: Guilford Press.

Patterson, C. H. (1964). Supervising students in the counseling practicum. *Journal of Counseling Psychology, 11,* 47–53.

Patterson, C. H. (1983). Client-centered approach to supervision. *Counseling Psychologist, 11,* 21–26.

Patterson, C. H. (1986). *Theories of counseling and psychotherapy* (4th ed.). New York, NY: Harper & Row.

Patterson, C. H. (1997). Client-centered supervision. In C. Watkins Jr. (Ed.), *Handbook of psychotherapy supervision* (pp. 134–146). New York, NY: Wiley.

Patton, M. J., & Kivlighan, D. M. J. (1997). Relevance of the supervisor alliance to the counseling alliance and to treatment adherence in counselor training. *Journal of Counseling Psychology, 44,* 108–111.

Perris, C. (1994). Supervising cognitive psychotherapy and training supervisors. *Journal of Cognitive Psychotherapy: An International Quarterly, 8,* 83–103.

Peterson, M. B. (2001). Recognizing concerns about how some licensing boards are treating psychologists. *Professional Psychology: Research and Practice, 32,* 339–340.

Peterson, M. R. (1992). *At personal risk: Boundary violations in professional-client relationships.* New York, NY: Norton.

Piercy, F., Sprenkle, D., & Constantine, J. (1986). Family members' perceptions of live observation/supervision. *Contemporary Family Therapy, 8,* 171–187.

Pirrotta, S., & Cecchin, G. (1988). The Milan training program. In H. Liddle, D. D. Breunlin, & R. C. Schwartz (Eds.), *Handbook of family therapy training and supervision* (pp. 38–61). New York, NY: Guilford Press.

Plaut, S. M. (2000, May/June). Licensing boards have many functions, but ensuring public trust is ultimate mission. *The National Psychologist, 9,* 15.

Polkinghorne, D. (1988). *Narrative knowing and the human sciences.* Albany: State University of New York Press.

Pope, K. S., Keith-Spiegel, P., & Tabachnick, B. G. (1986). Sexual attraction to clients: The human therapist and the (sometimes) inhuman training system. *American Psychologist, 41,* 147–158.

Pope, K. S., & Vasquez, M. J. T. (1998). *Ethics in psychotherapy and counseling: A practical guide* (2nd ed.). San Francisco, CA: Jossey-Bass.

Pope, K. S., & Vasquez, M. J. T. (2007). *Ethics in psychology and counseling: A practical guide* (3rd ed.). San Francisco, CA: Wiley.

Pope-Davis, D. B., Reynolds, A. L., Dings, J. G., & Nielson, D. (1995). Examining multicultural competencies of graduate students in psychology. *Professional Psychology: Research and Practice, 26, 322–329.*

Pope-Davis, D. B., Reynolds, A. L., Dings, J. G., & Ottavi, T. M. (1994). Multicultural competencies of doctoral interns at university counseling centers: An exploratory investigation. *Professional Psychology: Research and Practice, 25, 466–470.*

Porter, N., & Vasquez, M. (1997). Co-vision: Feminist supervision, process, and collaboration. In J. Worell & N. G. Johnson (Eds.), *Shaping the future of feminist psychology: Education, research and practice* (pp. 155–171). Washington, DC: American Psychological Association.

Powell, D. J. (2004). *Clinical supervision in alcohol and drug abuse counseling: Principles, models, methods* (Rev. ed.). San Francisco, CA: Jossey-Bass.

Presbury, J., Echterling, L. G., & McKee, J. E. (1999). Supervision for inner-vision: Solution-focused strategies. *Counselor Education and Supervision, 39, 146–155.*

Prest, L. A., Darden, E. C., & Keller, J. F. (1990). "The fly on the wall" reflecting team supervision. *Journal of Marital and Family Therapy, 16, 265–273.*

Prest, L. A., Schindler-Zimmerman, T., & Sporakowski, M. J. (1992). The initial supervision session checklist (ISSC): A guide for the MFT supervision process. *The Clinical Supervisor, 10*(2), 117–133.

Prieto, L. R. (1996). Group supervision: Still widely practiced but poorly understood. *Counselor Education and Supervision, 35, 295–307.*

Proctor, B., & Inskipp, F. (2001). Group supervision. In J. Scaife (Ed.), *Supervision in the mental health professions: A practitioner's guide* (pp. 99–121). London, England: Routledge.

Protinsky, H. (1997). Dismounting the tiger: Using tape in supervision. In T. C. Todd & C. L. Storm (Eds.), *The complete systemic supervision: Context, philosophy, and pragmatics* (pp. 298–307). Boston, MA: Allyn & Bacon.

Protinsky, H., & Preli, R. (1987). Interventions in strategic supervision. *Journal of Strategic and Systemic Therapies, 6*(3), 18–23.

Prouty, A. M. (2001). Experiencing feminist family therapy supervision. *Journal of Feminist Family Therapy, 12, 171–203.*

Prouty, A. M., Thomas, V., Johnson, S., & Long, J. K. (2001). Methods of feminist family therapy supervision. *Journal of Marital and Family Therapy, 27, 85–97.*

Recupero, P. R., & Rainey, S. E. (2007). Liability and risk management in outpatient psychotherapy supervision. *Journal of Academic Psychiatry and Law, 35, 188–197.*

Reid, W. H. (1999). *A clinician's guide to legal issues in psychotherapy or proceed with caution.* Phoenix, AZ: Zeig, Tucker & Theisen.

Remley, T. P. (1992). What should I do about an ethical complaint? *American Counselor, 1,* 33, 35.

Remley, T. P. (1993). Consultation contracts. *Journal of Counseling and Development, 72,* 157–158.

Resnick, R. F., & Estrup, L. (2000). Supervision: A collaborative endeavor. *Gestalt Review, 4,* 121–137.

Rita, E. S. (1998). Solution-focused supervision. *The Clinical Supervisor, 17*(2), 127–139.

Riva, M. T., & Cornish, J. A. (1995). Group supervision practices at a psychology predoctoral internship program: A national survey. *Professional Psychology: Research and Practice, 26,* 523–525.

Roberto, L. G. (1997). Supervision: The transgenerational models. In T. C. Todd & C. L. Storm (Eds.), *The complete systemic supervisor: Context, philosophy, and pragmatics* (pp. 156–172). Boston, MA: Allyn & Bacon.

Robinson, G. E. (2006). Supervision of boundary issues. In J. H. Gold (Ed.), *Psychotherapy supervision and consultation in clinical practice* (pp. 83–108). Lanham, MD: Rowman & Littlefield.

Rock, M. H. (Ed.). (1997). *Psychodynamic supervision: Perspectives of the supervisor and the supervisee.* Northvale, NJ: Jason Aronson.

Rodenhauser, P. (1994). Toward a multidimensional model for psychotherapy supervision based on developmental stages. *Journal of Psychotherapy Practice and Research, 3,* 1–15.

Rodolfa, E., Hall, T., Holms, V., Davena, A., Komatz, D., Antunez, M., et al. (1994). The management of sexual feelings in therapy. *Professional Psychology: Research and Practice 25,* 168–172.

Rogers, C. R. (1942). The use of electrically recorded interviews in improving psychotherapeutic techniques. *American Journal of Orthopsychiatry, 12,* 429–434.

Rogers, C. R. (1951). *Client-centered therapy.* Boston, MA: Houghton Mifflin.

Rogers, C. R. (1958). The characteristics of a helping relationship. *Personnel and Guidance Journal, 37,* 6–16.

Romans, J. S. C., Boswell, D. L., Carlozzi, A. F., & Ferguson, D. B. (1995). Training and supervision practices in clinical, counseling, and school psychology programs. *Professional Psychology: Research and Practice, 26,* 407–412.

Rønnestad, M. H., & Skovholt, T. M. (1993). Supervision of beginning and advanced graduate students in counseling and psychotherapy. *Journal of Counseling and Development, 71,* 396–405.

Rosenbaum, M., & Ronen, T. (1998). Clinical supervision from the standpoint of cognitive–behavior therapy. *Psychotherapy, 35,* 220–230.

Rubin, L. J., Hampton, B. R., & McManus, P. W. (1997). Sexual harassment of students by professional psychology educators: A national survey. *Sex Roles, 37,* 753–771.

Russell, R. K., Crimmings, A. M., & Lent, R, W. (1984). Counselor training and supervision: Theory and research. In S. D. Brown & R. W. Lent (Eds.), *Handbook of counseling psychology* (pp. 625–681). New York, NY: Wiley.

Ryan, A. S., & Hendricks, C. O. (1989). Culture and communication: Supervising the Asian and Hispanic social worker. *The Clinical Supervisor, 7*(1), 27–40.

Saccuzzo, D. (2002). *The Psychologist's Legal Update # 13: Liability for failure to supervise adequately: Let the master beware* (Part 1). National Register of Health Service Providers in Psychology. Retrieved June 26, 2009, from http://www.nationalregister.org/onlinestore.htm

Saccuzzo, D. (2003). *The Psychologist's Legal Update # 13: Liability for failure to supervise adequately: Let the master beware* (Part 2). National Register of Health Service Providers in Psychology. Retrieved June 26, 2009, from http://www.nationalregister.org/onlinestore.htm

Sachs, D. M., & Shapiro, S. H. (1976). On parallel processes in therapy and reaching. *Psychoanalytic Quarterly, 45*, 394–415.

Sansbury, D. L. (1982). Developmental supervision from a skills perspective. *The Counseling Psychologist, 10*, 53–57.

Sarnat, J. (1998). Rethinking the role of regressive experience in psychoanalytic supervision. *Journal of the American Academy of Psychoanalysis, 26*, 529–544.

Schank, J. A., & Skovholt, T. M. (2006). *Ethical practice in small communities: Challenges and rewards for psychologists.* Washington, DC: American Psychological Association.

Schlesinger, H. (1981). On being the supervisor studied: Observations and confessions. In R. Wallerstein (Ed.), *Becoming an analyst: A study of psychoanalytic supervision.* New York, NY: International Universities Press.

Schmidt, J. P. (1979). Psychotherapy supervision: A cognitive–behavioral model. *Professional Psychology, 10*, 278–284.

Schoener, G. R. (1989). Supervision of therapists who have sexually exploited clients. In G. R. Schoener, J. H. Milgrom, J. C. Gonsiorek, E. T. Luepker, & R. M. Conroe (Eds.), *Psychotherapists' sexual involvement with clients: Intervention and prevention* (pp. 435–446). Minneapolis, MN: Walk-In Counseling Center.

Schoener, G. R., & Conroe, R. M. (1989). The role of supervision and case consultation in primary prevention. In G. R. Schoener, J. H. Milgrom, J. C. Gonsiorek, E. T. Luepker, & R. M. Conroe (Eds.), *Psychotherapists' sexual involvement with clients: Intervention and prevention* (pp. 477–493). Minneapolis, MN: Walk-In Counseling Center.

Schoener, G. R., & Gonsiorek, J. (1988). Assessment and development of rehabilitation plans for counselors who have sexually exploited their clients. *Journal of Counseling and Development, 67*, 227–232.

Schoener, G. R., & Gonsiorek, J. (1989). Assessment and development of rehabilitation plans for the therapist. In G. R. Schoener, J. Milgrom., J. Gonsiorek,

E. T. Luepker, & R. M. Conroe (Eds.), *Psychotherapists' sexual involvement with clients: Intervention and prevention* (pp. 401–420). Minneapolis, MN: Walk-In Counseling Center.

Schoener, G. R., Milgrom, J., Gonsiorek, J., Luepker, E. T., & Conroe, R. M. (Eds.). (1989). *Psychotherapists' sexual involvement with clients: Intervention and prevention.* Minneapolis, MN: Walk-In Counseling Center.

Schoenfeld, L. S., Hatch, J. P., & Gonzalez, J. M. (2001). Responses of psychologists to complaints filed against them with the state licensing board. *Professional Psychology: Research and Practice, 32,* 491–494.

Schreiber, P., & Frank, E. (1983). The use of a peer supervision group by social work clinicians. *The Clinical Supervisor, 1* (1), 1–14.

Schroll, J. T., & Walton, R. N. (1991). The interaction of supervision needs with technique and context in the practice of live supervision. *The Clinical Supervisor, 9*(1), 1–14.

Schwartz, R., Liddle, H. A., & Breunlin, D. (1988). Muddles of live supervision. In H. A. Liddle, D. C. Breunlin, & R. C. Schwartz (Eds.), *Handbook of family therapy training and supervision* (pp. 183–193). New York, NY: Guilford Press.

Searles, H. F. (1955). The informational value of supervisor's emotional experience. *Psychiatry, 18,* 135–146.

Selvini-Palazzoli, M., Boscolo, L., Cecchoin, G., & Prata, G. (1980). Hypothesizing—circularity—neutrality. *Family Process, 6,* 3–9.

Sexton, T., Montgomery, D., Goff, K., & Nugent, W. (1993). Ethical, therapeutic, and legal considerations in the use of paradoxical techniques: The emerging debate. *Journal of Mental Health Counseling, 15,* 260–277.

Sherman, M. D. (1996). Distress and professional impairment due to mental health problems among psychotherapists. *Clinical Psychology Review, 16,* 299–315.

Sherman, M. D., & Thelen, M. H. (1998). Distress and professional impairment among psychologists in clinical practice. *Professional Psychology: Research and Practice, 29,* 79–85.

Singer, J. A., Baddeley, J., & Frantsve, L. (2008). Supervision of narrative-based psychotherapy. In A. K., Hess, K. D. Hess, & T. H. Hess (Eds.), *Psychotherapy supervision: Theory, research, and practice* (2nd ed., pp. 114–136). Hoboken, NJ: Wiley.

Skovolt, T. M., & Rønnestad, M. H. (1992). *The evolving professional self: Stages and themes in therapist and counselor development.* Chichester, England: Wiley.

Slimp, P. A. O., & Burian, B. K. (1994). Multiple role relationships during internship: Consequences and recommendations. *Professional Psychology: Research and Practice, 25,* 39–45

Smadi, A. A., & Landreth, G. G. (1988). Reality therapy supervision with a counselor from a different theoretical orientation. *Journal of Reality Therapy, 7*(2), 18–26.

Smith, D., & Fitzpatrick, M. (1995). Patient–therapist boundary issues: An integrative review of theory and research. *Professional Psychology: Research and Practice*, *26*, 499–505.

Sonne, J. L. (2006, Fall) Nonsexual multiple relationships: A practical decision-making model for clinicians. *Independent Practitioner*, *26*, 187–192.

Sperry, L. (2007). *The ethical and professional practice of counseling and psychotherapy.* Boston, MA: Pearson.

Stanton, M. (1981). Strategic approaches to family therapy. In A. Gurman & D. Kniskern (Eds.), *Handbook of family therapy* (pp. 361–401). New York, NY: Brunner/Mazel.

Stimmel, B. (1995). Resistance to awareness of the supervisor's transferences with special reference to the parallel process. *International Journal of Psychoanalysis*, *76*, 609–618

Stoltenberg, C. D. (1981). Approaching supervision from a developmental perspective: The counselor complexity model. *Journal of Counseling Psychology*, *28*, 59–65.

Stoltenberg, C. D. (2008). Developmental approaches to supervision. In C. A. Falender & E. P. Shafranske, *A casebook for clinical supervision: A competency-based approach* (pp. 39–56). Washington, DC: American Psychological Association.

Stoltenberg, C. D., & Delworth, U. (1987). *Supervising counselors and therapists: A developmental approach*. San Francisco, CA: Jossey-Bass.

Stoltenberg, C. D., & McNeill, B. W. (1997). Clinical supervisor from a developmental perspective: Research and practice. In E. Watkins Jr. (Ed.), *Handbook psychotherapy supervision* (pp. 184–202). New York: Wiley.

Stoltenberg, C. D., & McNeill, B. (2009). *IDM supervision: An integrative developmental model for supervising counselors and therapists* (3rd ed.). New York, NY: Routledge.

Stoltenberg, C. D., McNeill, B., & Delworth, U. (1998). *IDM supervision: An integrated developmental model for supervising counselors and therapists*. San Francisco, CA: Jossey-Bass.

Storm, C. L. (1997). Live supervision revolutionizes the supervision process. In T. C. Todd & S. L. Storm (Eds.), *The complete systemic supervisor: Context, philosophy, and pragmatics* (pp. 283–287). Boston, MA: Allyn & Bacon.

Storm, C. L., & Heath, A. W. (1982). Strategic supervision: The danger lies in discovery. *Journal of Strategic and Systemic Therapies*, *1*, 71–72.

Storm, C. L., & Heath, A. W. (1991). Problem-focused supervision: Rationale, exemplification and limitations. *Journal of Family Psychotherapy*, *2*, 55–70.

Storm, C. L., & Todd, T. C. (1997a). *The complete systemic supervisor: Context, philosophy, and pragmatics*. Boston, MA: Allyn & Bacon.

Storm, C. L., & Todd, T. C. (1997b). *The reasonably complete systemic supervisor resource guide*. Boston, MA: Allyn & Bacon.

Stromberg, C. D., Haggarty, D. J., Leibenleft, R. F., McMilliam, M. H., Mishkin, B., Rubin, B. L., et al. (1988). *The psychologists' legal handbook*. Washington, DC: Council for the National Register of Health Service Providers in Psychology.

Studer, J. R. (2005). Supervising school counselors-in-training: A guide for field supervisors. *Professional School Counseling, 8*, 353–359.

Stycznski, L. E., & Greenberg, L. (2008). Supervision of couples and family therapy. In A. K. Hess, K. D., Hess, & T. H. Hess (Eds.), *Psychotherapy supervision: Theory, research, and practice* (2nd. ed., pp. 179–199). Hoboken, NJ: Wiley.

Sullivan, L. E., & Ogloff, J. R. P. (1998). Appropriate supervisor–graduate student relationships. *Ethics & Behavior, 8*, 229–248.

Sutter, E., McPherson, R. H., & Geeseman, R. (2002). Contracting for supervision. *Professional Psychology: Research and Practice, 33*, 495–498.

Taibbi, R. (1993). The way of the supervisor. *Networker, 17*, 50–55.

Taibbi, R. (1995). *Clinical supervision: A four-stage process of growth and discovery.* Milwaukee, WI: Families International.

Tanenbaum, R. L., & Berman, M. A. (1990). Ethical and legal issues in psychotherapy supervision. *Psychotherapy in Private Practice, 8*, 65–77.

Teitelbaum, S. H. (1990). Supertransference: The role of the supervisor's blind spots. *Psychoanalytic Psychology, 7*, 243–258.

Teitelbaum, S. H. (2001). The changing scene in supervision. In S. Gill (Ed.), *The supervisory alliance: Facilitating the psychotherapist's learning experience* (pp. 3–18). Northvale, NJ: Jason Aronson.

Thomas, F. N. (1996). Solution-focused supervision: The coaxing of expertise. In S. D. Miller, M. A. Hubble, & B. L. Duncan (Eds.), *Handbook of solution-focused therapy* (pp. 128–151). San Francisco, CA: Jossey-Bass.

Thomas, J. T. (1994, September). Mandated reports of ethical violations: What psychologists need to know. *Minnesota Psychologist, 43*, 5–8.

Thomas, J. T. (2000, Spring). Providing consultation for colleagues. *Georgia Psychologist, 54*, 21.

Thomas, J. T. (2001, January). Psychologists facing board complaints: Common experiences and responses. *Minnesota Psychologist, 1*, 5–8.

Thomas, J. T. (2002). *Navigating the complaint process: A guide for Minnesota psychologists.* Minneapolis, MN: Minnesota Women in Psychology.

Thomas, J. T. (2005). Licensing board complaints: Minimizing the impact on the psychologist's defense and clinical practice. *Professional Psychology: Research and Practice, 36*, 426–433.

Thomas, J. T. (2007). Informed consent through contracting for supervision: Minimizing risks, enhancing benefits. *Professional Psychology: Research and Practice, 38*, 221–231.

Thomas, V., & Striegel, P. (1994). Family-of-origin work for the family counselor. In C. H. Huber (Ed.), *Transitioning from individual to family counseling* (pp. 21–32). Alexandria, VA: American Counseling Association.

Todd, T. C. (1981). Paradoxical prescriptions: Applications of consistent paradox using a strategic team. *Journal of Strategic and Systemic Therapies, 1*, 28–44.

Todd, T. C. (1997). Purposive systemic supervision models. In T. C. Todd & C. L. Storm (Eds.), *The complete systemic supervisor: Context, philosophy and pragmatics* (pp. 173–194). Boston, MA: Allyn & Bacon.

Todd, T. C., & Storm, C. L. (1997). Thoughts on the evolution of MFT supervision. In T. C. Todd & C. L. Storm (Eds.), *The complete systemic supervisor: Context, philosophy and pragmatics* (pp. 1–16). Boston, MA: Allyn & Bacon.

Toldson, I. A., & Utsey, S. (2008). Race, sex, and gender considerations. In A. K. Hess, K. D. Hess, & T. H. Hess, *Psychotherapy supervision: Theory, research, and practice* (2nd ed., pp. 537–559). Hoboken, NJ: Wiley.

Tomm, K. (1987a). Interventive interviewing: Part I. Strategizing as a fourth guideline for the therapist. *Family Process, 26,* 3–13.

Tomm, K. (1987b). Interventive interviewing: Part II. Reflexive questioning as a means to enable self-healing. *Family Process, 26,* 167–183.

Tomm, K. (1988). Interventive interviewing: Part III. Intending to ask lineal, circular, strategic, or reflexive questions? *Family Process, 27,* 1–15.

Triantafillou, N. (1997). A solution-focused approach to mental health supervision. *Journal of Systemic Therapies, 16,* 305–328.

Tromski-Klingshirn, D. M., & Davis, T. E. (2007). Supervisees' perceptions of their clinical supervision: A study of the dual role of clinical and administrative supervisor. *Counselor Education & Supervision, 46,* 294–304.

Tuckman, B. W. (1965). Developmental sequence in small groups. *Psychological Bulletin, 63,* 384–399.

Tuckman, B. W., & Jensen, M. A. C. (1977). Stages of small-group development revisited. *Group and Organizational Studies, 2,* 419–427.

Tummala-Narra, P. (2004). Dynamics of race and culture in the supervisory encounter. *Psychoanalytic Psychology, 21,* 300–311.

Usher, S. F. (1993). *Introduction to psychodynamic psychotherapy technique.* Madison, WI: International Universities Press.

Van Horne, B. A. (2004). Psychology licensing board disciplinary actions: The realities. *Professional Psychology: Research and Practice, 35,* 170–178.

Varghese, G. T. (2006). Discussing the undiscussable: The limits of supervision. In J. H. Gold (Ed.), *Psychotherapy supervision and consultation in clinical practice* (pp. 59–71). Lanham, MD: Jason Aronson.

Vasquez, M. J. T. (1992). Psychologist as clinical supervisor: Promoting ethical practice. *Professional Psychology: Research and Practice, 23,* 196–202.

Walden, S. L. (2006) Inclusion of the client's voice in ethical practice. In B. Herlihy & G. Corey (Eds.), *Boundary issues in counseling: Multiple roles and responsibilities* (2nd ed.). Alexandria, VA: American Counseling Association.

Walker, M., & Jacobs, M. (2004). *Supervision: Questions and answers for counsellors and therapists.* London, England: Whurr Publishers.

Wallerstein, R. S. (1992). The context of the issue. In R. S. Wallerstein (Ed.), *The common ground of psychoanalysis.* Northvale, NJ: Jason Aronson.

Walzer, R. S., & Miltimore, S. (1993). Mandated supervision: Monitoring and therapy of disciplined health care professionals. *Journal of Legal Medicine, 14*, 565–596.

Ward, C. H. (1960). An electronic aide for teaching interviewing techniques. *Archives of General Psychiatry, 3*, 357–358.

Watkins, C. E., Jr. (1995). Psychotherapy supervisor development: On musings, models, and metaphor. *Journal of Psychotherapy Practice and Research, 4*, 150–158.

Watkins, C. E., Jr. (Ed.). (1997a). *Handbook of psychotherapy supervision.* New York, NY: Wiley.

Watkins, C. E., Jr. (1997b). Some concluding thoughts about psychotherapy supervision. In C. E. Watkins Jr. (Ed.), *Handbook of psychotherapy supervision* (pp. 44–62). New York, NY: Wiley.

Welch, B. L. (2001). Caution: State licensing board ahead. *Insight: Safeguarding Psychologists Against Liability Risks. 1*, 1–6.

Welch, B. L. (2003).Supervising with liability in mind. *Insight: Safeguarding Psychologists Against Liability Risks. 1*, 1–6.

Welfel, E. R. (2006). *Ethics in counseling and psychotherapy: Standards, research, and emerging issues* (3rd ed.). Pacific Grove, CA: Brooks/Cole.

Wendorf, D. J., Wendorf, R. J., & Bond, O. (1985). Growth behind the mirror: The family therapy consortiums' group process. *Journal of Marriage and Family Therapy, 11*, 245–255.

Wetchler, J. L. (1990). Solution-focused supervision. *Family Therapy, 17*, 129–138.

Wheeler, D., Avis, J. M., Miller, L. A., & Chaney, S. (1986). Rethinking family therapy education and supervision: A feminist model. *Journal of Psychotherapy and the Family, 14*, 53–71.

Whitaker, C., & Keith, D. (1981). Symbolic-experiential family therapy. In A. Gurman & D. Kniskern (Eds.), *Handbook of family therapy* (pp. 187–224). New York, NY: Brunner/Mazel.

White, M., & Russell, C. (1995). The essential elements of supervisory systems: A modified Delphi study. *Journal of Marital and Family Therapy, 21*, 33–53.

White, T. W. (2003). Managing dual relationships in correctional settings. *National Psychologist, 12*, 14–15.

Wiger, D. E. (2005). *The psychotherapy documentation primer* (2nd ed.). Hoboken, NJ: Wiley.

Williams, M. H. (2001). The question of psychologists' maltreatment by state licensing boards: Overcoming denial and seeking remedies. *Professional Psychology: Research and Practice, 32*, 341–344.

Woods, P. J., & Ellis, A. (1996). Supervision in rational emotive behavior therapy. *Journal of Rational-Emotive & Cognitive Behavior Therapy, 14*, 135–152.

Worthington, E. L., Jr. (1987). Changes in supervision as counselors and supervisors gain experience. *Professional Psychology: Research and Practice, 18*, 189–208.

Worthington, R. L., Tan, J. A., & Poulin, K. (2002). Ethically questionable behaviors among supervisees: An exploratory investigation. *Ethics & Behavior, 12,* 323–351.

Yalom, I. (1995). *The theory and practice of group psychotherapy* (4th ed.). New York, NY: Basic Books.

Yontef, G. (1997). Supervision from a Gestalt therapy perspective. In C. Watkins Jr. (Ed.), *Handbook of psychotherapy supervision* (pp. 44–62). New York, NY: Wiley.

Yorke, V. (2005). Bion's "vertex" as a supervisory object. In C. Driver & E. Martin (Eds.), *Supervision and the analytic attitude* (pp. 34–49). London, England: Whurr Publishers.

Younggren, J. N., & Gottlieb, M. C. (2004). Managing risk when contemplating multiple relationships. *Professional Psychology: Research and Practice, 35,* 255–260.

Zakrzewski, R. F. (2006). A national survey of American Psychological Association student affiliates' involvement and ethical training in psychology educator–student sexual relationships. *Professional Psychology: Research and Practice, 37,* 724–730.

Zaphiropoulos, M. L. (1984). Educational and clinical pitfalls in psychoanalytic supervision. In L. Caligor, P. M. Bromberg, & J. D. Meltzer (Eds.), *Clinical perspectives on the supervision of psychoanalysis and psychotherapy* (pp. 257–273). New York, NY: Plenum Press.

Zur, O. (2007). *Boundaries in psychotherapy: Ethical and clinical explorations.* Washington, DC: American Psychological Association.

INDEX

Graf, Max, 60
Group development, 181
Groups. *See* Consultation groups;
    Supervision groups
Group therapy, 174
"Guidelines for Providers of Psychological
    Services to Ethnic, Linguistic,
    and Culturally Diverse Popula-
    tions" (APA), 50
Guilt, 191
Gutheil, T. G., 134

Haas, L. J., 138–139
Haley, Jay, 51
Handelsman, M. M., 4
Harkness, D., 64
Harris, E. A., 9
Health care records, 222
Health Insurance Portability
    and Accountability Act
    (HIPAA), 222
High-risk situations, 159
Holloway, E. L., 75
Homework, 41
Hyman, M., 60
Hypnosis, 177

Illness, 143
Impairment, 143, 224
Impasses, 215
Inappropriate touch, 185
Individual differences, 78
Influence, 104–107
Informed consent, 141–161
    in ACA Ethics Code, 22
    in APA Ethics Code, 19
    applicability, 142–143
    in ASPPB supervision guidelines, 30
    for consultation, 160–161
    in consultation/supervision
        groups, 173
    within ethical standards/guidelines,
        148–152
    ethics codes on, 141–142
    and mitigation of problems, 145–148
    objectives, 143–145
    and self-disclosure, 53–55, 124
    with supervision contracts, 152–160
    for transition to psychotherapy, 129
Inman, A. G., 76

Insight, 53
Integrated/integrative model of
    supervision, 76–90
Internships, 8, 110, 131, 154, 156,
    183, 219
Interpersonal assessment, 78
Interruption, of supervision, 224
Interventions, 51–52, 55, 78, 80
Intimidation, 63
Invited consultant groups, 165
Isomorphic structures, 49

Jacobs, D. H., 60, 63
Jealousy, 167
Johnson, W. B., 96
Jungian supervision model, 37

Kadushin, A., 64, 104
Keith-Spiegel, P., 156
Klein, Melanie, 60
Knapp, S. C., 4
Knapp, S. J., 6
Koocher, G. P., 156

Ladany, N., 75, 76, 168
Lazarus, A. A., 96
Learning, 174–175, 188
Learning alliance, 62
Learning theory, 41
Legal issues, 160
Legal liability, 6, 9, 111, 159–160, 215
Legitimate power, 104, 105
Lent, R. W., 74
Letters of recommendation, 128
Level 1 supervisees, 79–83, 202
Level 2 supervisees, 83–88
Level 3 and 3i supervisees, 88–89
Licensing boards, 5, 9
    and ASPPB, 19, 29–30
    in mandated supervision, 184–185
    power of, 104
    and prelicensure supervision fees, 154
    and supervision guidelines, 29
Licensure, 9
    by ASPPB, 19
    and professional employment, 111
Liddle, H. A., 48
Liese, B. S., 44
Live supervision, 52–53, 55–56
Loyalty, 124
Luepker, E. T., 214

ABOUT THE AUTHOR

Janet T. Thomas, PsyD, is a licensed psychologist in Saint Paul, Minnesota. She earned a doctorate in counseling psychology from the University of St. Thomas, Saint Paul, Minnesota, and has been in independent practice since 1991. In addition to psychotherapy and assessment, her clinical work includes clinical consultation and supervision with psychologists and other mental health professionals as well as specialized work with those facing ethical dilemmas, licensing board complaints, and lawsuits. Professional experience includes work in an in-patient psychiatric hospital, a medical clinic, a rehabilitation unit, a community mental health agency, an assessment clinic, and college counseling centers.

Dr. Thomas began teaching psychology graduate students in 1990. She has served on the adjunct faculties of Saint Mary's University of Minnesota, Minneapolis; the University of St. Thomas (Minneapolis campus); and Argosy University, Saint Paul, Minnesota. She has taught professional ethics, counseling skills, practicum, supervision and consultation, and professional psychological writing.

Dr. Thomas has been the recipient of several awards for her work, including Outstanding Student Advisor and Outstanding Faculty Member at Saint Mary's University and the Minnesota Women in Psychology Founding

Mothers' Award for her contributions to that organization and its mission. Professional contributions include journal articles, book chapters, and presentations on topics related to ethics and supervision in Minnesota and nationwide. Dr. Thomas is a former chair of Minnesota Women Psychologists and of the Minnesota Psychological Association's Ethics Committee.